The Challengers

The Challengers

A series of plays for
Yorkshire Television

Written by
Edmund Ward

Designed by Vic Symonds
Executive Producer Peter Willes
Directed by Marc Miller
Director of Programmes Donald Baverstock

Elek London

Published in Great Britain in 1972 by
PAUL ELEK BOOKS LTD
54–58 Caledonian Road
London N1 9RN

ISBN 0 236 15457 5

MADE AND PRINTED IN GREAT BRITAIN BY
THE GARDEN CITY PRESS LIMITED
LETCHWORTH, HERTFORDSHIRE SG6 1JS

CONTENTS

LIST OF ILLUSTRATIONS

EDMUND WARD: Born Nottingham. First novel, 1957, was *Summer in Retreat* which won the Authors' Club Award. Other novels are *The Gravy Train* and *The Private Tightrope*. Feature journalism and fiction for *The New Yorker*, *The Queen*, *Punch*, etc. Began as television playwright in 1962 with *The Casualties*. Subsequently won two Writers' Guild awards for *The Planemakers* and *The Power Game*. Devised and wrote *The Main Chance* for Yorkshire Television which was given first prize—the only British entry to be awarded this distinction—in the drama section of the Hollywood Festival of World Television. Followed this with *Grady*, a trilogy of plays about an individualist militant and then *The Challengers*. Has also written four feature films and a West End play *Ring of Jackals*.

THE CHALLENGERS was transmitted by Yorkshire Television in January and February of 1972. The Production team was as follows:

Executive Producer:	PETER WILLES
Director:	MARC MILLER
Casting Director:	JACKY STOLLER
Designer:	VIC SYMONDS
Floor Managers:	DAVID REYNOLDS/GEOFF SMITH
Stage Manager:	PRUE SAENGER
PA:	CAROL WILLIAMS
Assistant Floor Manager:	KEITH W. RICHARDSON
Assistant Stage Manager:	KAY HARRINGTON
Lighting:	BOB GRAY/BRIAN HILTON
Cameras:	GERRY LORD/ARTHUR TIPPER
Sound:	GLYN EDWARDS/NORMAN BLIGHT
Vision Mixer:	CHRIS FOLEY
Technical Supervisor:	GARY WARD
Wardrobe:	BRENDA FOX
Makeup:	PHILIPPA HAIGH
Scenes:	BILL DONNELLY/FRED NEWALL/E. DE QUINTANO/ WILF BRADSHAW
Props:	DAVE McBURNIE
Production Buyer:	PETER GRAHAM
Film Cameraman:	BRIAN WILSON
Film Sound:	TERRY RICKETTS
Film Editor:	TIM RITSON

Foreword

by DONALD BAVERSTOCK, *Director of Programmes,*
Yorkshire Television

Television series are an unconscionable time in the making. As I remember, two years ago or more, we were not very elated at Yorkshire Television when we first heard that Edmund Ward, one of our most valued writers, wanted to spend time researching the possibility of a series dramatising British political life. He had already given us *Grady*, a series of three plays about trade unionists, but we knew only too well what an achievement his had been to make their ponderous motions convincingly dramatic to the viewing public.

I will confess that my first reaction on hearing of the idea of *The Challengers* was to say to my Head of Drama, Peter Willes, 'Why, oh why, does he want to go and swim against the tide yet again?' Many people experienced in television programming will agree that there are some subjects—politics, education, trade unionism, abstract art—which have to be treated very warily. They know that the audience will be inclined to start looking at them more with positive distrust than lively anticipation. This may be because such subjects always threaten to be obscure or 'wordy', or it may be because leading people in some of these fields appear so often on television that they become difficult to represent with credibility.

However, any company that specialises in producing major television series has to accept that the loyalties and the enthusiasms of writers with the rare talents of Edmund Ward will often insist on going their own way and will not be retained unless they are encouraged in the more difficult enterprises that they sometimes set themselves. We therefore agreed to invest in his long period of research before awaiting the first scripts. We knew that, with him, they would be producible. We knew that they would not fall below a certain level of interest, but we did assume that they would not be very acceptable. We were wrong. The six plays were very popular and critically well received. They attracted, according to our research, well over a third of the British public to stay with them and to watch them each Monday evening at 9.00 p.m. for the six consecutive weeks. If suspicions of the ambience of politics are instinctive in the public, then Edmund Ward overcame them very quickly in the first play.

There were several reasons, as I see it, for his success. He was brilliantly served by our casting department under Miss Muriel Cole. The two principals, Colin Blakely and Michael Gambon, epitomised in their idioms and their accents, their manners and even their looks, two kinds of politicians instantly recognisable to most of our viewers. Furthermore, Peter Willes, who took overall responsibility for the series from the start, appointed Marc Miller to direct all six, and Marc Miller is undoubtedly one of the best television directors now working in this country.

There is also the perspective of Edmund Ward. He builds his dramas around the fact that much of the political activity in Britain is not expressed in the simplified arguments between the principal parties, nor is it about the personality disputes of their leaders, whom we see on television so frequently. Instead he sees that the political clashes are more often a reflection of the sectional pressures, the economic groupings, and above all, the geographical interests which all MPs of any party have to be cognisant of in representing their different constituencies—the many activities which Mr Roy Mason illuminates from his own long experience in one of the end papers to this volume.

The British political system, as it has developed into the twentieth century, has grown up in a nation which (except for Ireland) has been united for a long time. There has been no revolution, no civil war, little religious rancour of any significance, few linguistic angers (except now in its western margins), no territorial change and hardly any violence in the streets for more than 300 years. This is historically remarkable if it is remembered that few countries in the world have been without a revolution or civil war or invasion or major territorial changes outside the last 100 years. The British political parties have developed within this context of long civil peace, and to some extent the parties function as necessary divisive forces within this unity—with their divisions hingeing for the most part on historical traditions and class loyalties.

In these plays, Edmund Ward includes scenes in the House of Commons, scenes of MPs dealing with their Whips and scenes which touch upon 'the standing of MPs', amongst their colleagues, the importance of which Sir Donald Kaberry rightly emphasises. There are scenes, too, in which we glimpse the other unique aspects of the Palace of Westminster as described by Mr Ian Aitken. But what Edmund Ward does above all is to show that behind these procedures and these traditional differences between the parties, there also lie the other politics of competing domestic interests, the process of achieving what in American history has been called 'the rule of the concurrent majority', without which sensible democratic politics cannot work. He shows that this process is like an iceberg where only a fraction of those immersed are parliamentarians. This is another of Edmund Ward's achievements in these plays. He dramatises, which means he brings fully to life, many of the types of people active on the British political scene, their attitudes, their motives and their methods, and important though they are, many of them are not MPs. He then shows how this whole gallery of characters participates in the running of the system we have at present. In so doing, he makes, as Mr Christopher Dunkley suggests, a major contribution to the art of political fiction or drama which, since Disraeli, has not been a prolific part of English writing.

Introduction

by EDMUND WARD

The two Members of Parliament who are 'The Challengers' represent the adjoining constituencies which make up a town called Andersley.

Andersley is roughly comparable in size to Derby, Norwich or Walsall—three of the dozen or so areas in this country with two constituencies in which one Member is Socialist and his neighbour Conservative.

Its population is about 150,000, its origins those of a small market town swamped early in the industrial revolution. Some history remains in a bottleneck section of the High Street and a narrow access road into the centre past the Abbey. A river loops across the northern edge of the town and the nineteenth century linked this to a canal system and a sprawl of railway.

To the east, the Notts, Derby and Yorkshire coalfield adds a fringe of slag-heaps and colliery winding wheels. On the alluvial plain have grown the other old industries—dyeworks, woollen mills, heavy engineering and specialist foundries existing on sub-contracts from the big wagon sheds of the railway maintenance yards.

Tacked on to the south of the town are two industrial estates, one of them pre-war, where biscuits, hosiery and light engineering take up some of the slack as older industries decline. This side of town is only moderately prosperous and unemployment figures are slightly higher than the national average.

To the west of Andersley is the wooded river escarpment of an old Pennine fault. Above this, the country rises, at first gently and then to the steep and bracken-covered Dale tops where buzzards wheel and watch the pall of the town twenty miles away. Between the buzzards and the biscuit factories is a wide crescent of good agricultural land, a rich swathe carefully farmed by careful men.

On this immediate side of the town boundaries and within the Parliamentary constituency of Andersley

West, the rural fringe is jealously preserved and the suburbs become villages, a rearguard bastion to the big houses on the escarpment proper.

Between rural and industrial, there are still some steps on the feudal ladder but these assume smaller importance as the descent is made from the moors and the rural suburbs to the council estates on the other side of town.

On that same steady slope, the recreations change and are becoming interchangeable. The yeoman farmers and minor county set patronise the pony clubs and point-to-points but the local football club at the bottom of the second division has the local baronet as its chairman. Farm bailiffs and their employers lay bets at the illegal coursing on the moors.

Attendance is dwindling at the rugby league ground, two cinemas have just closed, the bingo halls offer joints of meat as Friday prizes, the racing pigeons are still stacked in crates on the railway platform.

There is still a market day but this is more a benefit for publicans with extended licensing hours than a forum for fatstock, and the old sheep-pens are now an asphalt playground for children. A new technical college was opened two years ago but the eighty-year old grammar school still clings to its title and the name of the Victorian mogul who endowed it.

The population derives its character from the intransigence of heavy industry and relics of a pride in craft remain. The textile trade and later light industry gave rise to a tradition of working women and the independence this induces in them exists side by side with a respect for their men who earn money hard and sometimes dangerously.

Encroaching on this very quickly are the lessons being taught by the newer managerial classes who spread a blanket of influence across the town, but factories side by side can still operate on opposite policies of paternalism and critical-path analysis.

John Killane becomes Conservative MP for Andersley West in the first play. He was born in 1936, in a Bournemouth nursing home, the second son of an unambitious Anglican clergyman who botanised happily across a prosperous living in rural Hampshire, content to let a more mercenary brother-in-law collect the school-fee bills for all the family children.

Killane went to prep school, through a minor public school on a church scholarship, then to London University for a good degree in mathematics. He is fond of the place he went home to for holidays but has no strong local roots or ties. From university, he went to one of the big oil companies as a statistician, then moved to become assistant head of their European market research division following six months training in America.

In 1964, he joined an ex-colleague and the disgruntled principal of a mass-opinion survey and the three of them set up an independent market-research agency—financed by the mercenary uncle who was paid back within two years.

The agency became successful very quickly by reason of a combination of talents. Killane's contribution was the interpretation of results, the ability to take cold, hard figures and use knowledge and intuition to translate the figures into people. His mathematical skills became only an adjunct to this flair. Killane was earning about £10,000 a year.

With his ability for translating figures into people, the opportunity to use a statistician's skills to compare the systems of government of other countries with that of Britain, Killane's upbringing and a strong sense of history asserted themselves.

His leanings were Conservative, his first motives only the desire to use the skills of his profession to bring about more efficient government. Both political parties have panels of advisors from the selling, economic and academic professions—admen, designers, statisticians, specialist lecturers—who contribute time in support of their beliefs.

Killane joined and was then quickly running the *ad hoc* research panel. Then he wanted more than to give advice. He wanted to put his translation of figures into action. This was after two years on the advisory sidelines when he had made it his business to know a great deal about the mechanics of politics.

The selection committee was not entirely unanimous. In Killane's favour was evident sincerity, willingness to serve, a proven commercial record, youth, good looks, a brilliant mind. Against him was a certain irreverence, a sharp wit, an independence—financial and moral—and some lack of experience. Also against him was a messy divorce, kept quiet and with Killane blameless. The judge gave him sympathy and custody of the two children.

Killane was offered a candidacy in somewhere like Swindon, fought it well and lost. Even in the anonymous hubbub of a general election, his campaign made its mark for energy, professionalism, and sincerity. Killane is not a hustling seeker after power or privilege and it showed. He was sent up—without much optimism—to nurse Andersley West, then a Labour seat with majority of about 3,000.

He managed to prove that being a single man is not a disadvantage if that single man has enough energy and charm. The Conservative ladies are often the mainspring of the local associations—particularly in fundraising—and a candidate's wife is expected to take her share of the load. For Killane, the ladies worked a little harder.

The minor squirearchy respected his good manners, the rising meritocracy admired his technical skills. But he was still not one of them. He was from the South, had friends at Central Office, ran a business in London. They would have preferred a local man.

Another factor against him was the element of the solitary in his character. Outwardly approachable and charming, Killane is a difficult man to know. Some of this stems from his capacity for analysis, some of it from the divorce scars. And he is lonely in Andersley.

It would be better for Killane in Andersley if he were more of a hypocrite, affected a few local phrases, adopted some form of protective local colouring. He will not do this. But where no one can fault him is in his knowledge of local conditions, the result of week-ends of hard work. The knowledge, though, is still acquired, not intuitive or inbred, and Killane still has a lot to learn about local character—and knows it.

Then the Labour incumbent dies. Killane fights the by-election and wins it with a majority of about 2,000—against the odds and local betting. He is now forced to face his own motives for seeking office and whether the achievements are worth it. He will be up against the Labour Member for the other half of the town, a skilled, hard and experienced politician.

He will be expected to contribute to local issues now, not theorise about them. He will be expected to repay favours, real or imaginary.

Killane remains on the board of the agency he helped to found but on a much reduced salary. In round terms, the office of MP will cost him about £5,000 a year. And, without his special skills, the agency may tend to stagnate and partners may put pressure on Killane to use Parliamentary position to tout for business.

He will move in the new worlds of Westminster and Andersley, shed some prejudices, learn some lessons. Killane has been successful in translating figures into people. Now he must deal with the people themselves and be fully committed. He is dealing with a town now, not a research document, and a town where he is a comparative stranger with only his wits and his be-liefs to help him.

In opposition to Killane is Sam Brodie, Labour MP for Andersley East. He was born in 1925 in Andersley in one of the good terrace houses torn down to make way for the new Technical College. His father was a railway fitter and Brodie left school at fourteen to become an apprentice in the wagon sheds. Three years in the Army resulted in demobilisation as a REME sergeant with a decoration for genuine bravery and solid technical and administrative skills.

Brodie returned to the railway maintenance sheds,

qualified as a charge-hand, went to night-school, became foreman, then joined the managerial echelon as a shop manager and turned in his union card. This was the period when he also played three seasons as forward for the local Rugby League team.

From contact with the club committee—men of influence and money—came the early days of politics. Brodie became a local councillor in 1955 at the age of thirty. There was only one side to join—Labour. The reasons were vague at first, rooted in upbringing and an inherited belief. They became much clearer as he became more involved in taking decisions affecting the whole town instead of just a wagon shed. Brodie's urge to public service stems from a deep sense of belonging to the town where he was born and a concern for its people.

In the General Election of 1959, he was elected to Parliament, a completely natural choice, bringing authority and strength to representing his town, a man committed to serving local causes. The idealism of the early days—both at local and national level—was never tinged with self-deception. He knows the working classes well enough to respect them but not to fall into the liberal trap of painting them as angels.

Brodie was re-elected with increased majorities in 1964 and in 1966 but his majority dropped to its original level in the election of 1970. His seat is far from marginal but he cannot neglect it. From 1967 to 1970, he was a Parliamentary Secretary, the sort of junior minister post which put another £2,000 on his salary. His special interests in the House are industrial redevelopment, transport, and natural resources.

These interests form a simple pointer to Brodie's complexity. Industrial redevelopment reflects his sense of reality, the knowledge that a wage packet is the best proof of concern by a representative for his people. Natural resources reflect a deep love for the contours of the land and the area which bred him. The interests are backed by a wide knowledge of them.

Brodie moves easily across all sections of society, the

local accent modified now, the clothes chosen to suit himself and not any cloth-cap image. He has lived and worked in Andersley all his life, is well-known and well-respected.

One facet which some people forget is the taste for blood necessary to a Rugby League player as good as Brodie was, the decoration earned under fire, the sense of pride in his own achievement. Brodie, angry, puts away the rule-book and has never been beaten. The anger may not always be on his own behalf and has cropped up often enough for him to have enemies. Brodie is not an ambitious man in material terms but knows his own worth. He would have set out for the Crusades as a minor squire and returned with scars, a title and a couple of castles.

Brodie was married in 1952 to the daughter of a local bank manager. There are three children. Andrew and Thomas, sixteen and twelve years old, both at the local grammar school. There is a daughter, Elizabeth, seven, at a special school twenty miles away. She is not backward but she is not bright and represents a vulnerable chink in Brodie's armour.

Brodie and his family walk a financial tightrope and he would have been much better off in money terms if he had stayed in industry. During the period when he was a junior minister, Brodie bought a larger house and the mortgage is over-extending him.

In London, he stays for three or four nights a week in one of the back rooms of a small Kings Cross hotel and will often take the late train on Thursday night— using his MP's free travel pass—to save a hotel bill of £1.75 Brodie's income in 1971 was between £2,500 and £3,000 a year and normal income tax still had to be paid on this. And Brodie is luckier than some because the treasurer of the local Labour party is a very skilled accountant who handles the family finances cleverly and without charge.

And, with the financial pinch, other temptations began to loom larger. As an MP, Brodie could expect a pension calculated at £75 per year for each year served.

If he died, his widow would get half this rate. He may be lucky when his party assumes government again and be offered a post at more money.

Following from this, and with his prospects, it is difficult for Brodie to oppose his party masters even whilst in opposition. The prospect of office is the premium for his old age and his children's future.

There is, however, the common insurance against political uncertainty—the commercial directorship. Two or three of these at £1,000 a year would solve a lot of problems and Brodie is starting to weigh personal gain against the dogged ideals of public service which remind him that he must remain his own man.

He is still happy walking round Andersley or up on the hills above it or in the local crowd at a good Rugby League game. He misses the early days when he could afford to spend two evenings a week exercising a good singing voice in the local choral society. And, at least once a month in the season, he will take a day's fishing, just himself and the not-bright young daughter, and they will sit quietly together in their own world on a river bank.

Brodie at forty-six is a man in transition—personally, politically and emotionally—and must make his decisions against the constituency backcloth where his every move is apparent.

The Challengers is a series of plays about these two men, two Members of Parliament—one Labour, one Conservative. It does not deal only with their lives in the House of Commons, the grime in the wainscots of the corridors of power, the caucus rooms, the lobbies. It deals with constituency life, the shifts and balances and problems that an MP must face in the community which elected him, where he is answerable to the 35,000 people who cast votes and for whom he is a mixture of God, scapegoat, collective voice, wielder of influence and someone to open a jumble sale.

There are 630 Members in the House of Commons, the best club in the world, and some of them have spent most of their lives trying to get there. They represent all sorts and conditions of men and motives and within the precincts of the Palace of Westminster, they enjoy a unique privilege and exclusivity.

What happens when these men catch the train to their constituency? How much must they justify their week's work, their income, their beliefs? What sort of favours are they asked, what sort of problems are they expected to resolve? How much will they dislike each other and why? And the questions have to be answered, not within the proconsular confines of Parliament among their peers, but in the local High Street, the church-hall committee rooms.

Who are the people that surround them when the train stops 200 miles from Westminster, the components of a force which elected them? What is expected of a Member from his agent, the area officer of the party, the local chairman, a town councillor, a desperate woman in tears at the fortnightly surgery? The Member has dealt in words all week and now he must take to action—if he can.

How much tax do they pay, how and where do they live, what is the price they put on public service, why did they undertake this service in the first place, are the achievements worth the effort? And in the self-questioning of the small but brilliant spotlight of the constituency, they must always be aware of the difference between the public and the private face they wear.

What are the temptations and the pressures, how much weight is put on an indiscretion unnoticeable in London but now blatant under the microscope of a much smaller community?

What are the rewards—money, high office, prestige, an assuaged idealism? How much can early belief be weakened, initial principle compromised, how soon will the dictum that 'Politics is the art of the possible' become a motto to hang on the wall?

How much can one man's sense of history or love of country weigh in the balance of the future of its people? And how will he contend with the time-servers and place-seekers and saints along the way?

The Challengers is about two men who must find answers to these questions within the context of their own hostility to each other's principles, in the setting of the town they serve, rival lions in an arena where their families and friends and supporters are involved spectators.

Play One

THE TOMORROW BUSINESS

Cast

JOHN KILLANE	*Michael Gambon*
SAM BRODIE	*Colin Blakely*
CLIFF LAMBERT	*Richard Hampton*
ANNIE MACKINNON	*Joanna Van Gyseghem*
ALAN LOWERY	*Peter Pratt*
PETER CHAPMAN	*William Gaunt*
STUART WALKER	*Brian Spink*
ERNEST DEWHURST	*Bill Dean*
ELIZABETH BRODIE	*Margaret John*
HECKLER	*Ted Carroll*
JOE GARSFELD	*Alex Scott*
JAMES CURTIS	*Edward Harvey*

Non-speaking

Mrs Langley, John Killane's aunt; voluntary workers of both Labour and Conservative parties and audiences at political meetings; staff at polling station and election crowd; steward at Working Men's Club; elderly hotel waiter; counting officers at the by-election; the gaudy Sunday lunchtime customers at a Hampstead pub, the young and middle-aged would-be beautiful; uniformed policemen supervising the loading of the ballot boxes and the count; Mayor and civic dignitaries at the announcement; barman in Hampstead pub; prosperous publican.

Interiors

1. Mrs Langley's bedroom
2. Children's bedroom
3. Labour Committee Rooms
4. Conservative Committee Rooms
5. Killane's hotel room
6. Working Men's Club
7. Sam Brodie's living room
8. Hampstead pub
9. Labour and Conservative church halls—backdrop only
10. Curtis's office

Exteriors

1. Andersley street with Conservative sound truck and Labour Party headquarters
2. Polling station—voters arriving
3. Polling station—the election closing and then ballot boxes being loaded
4. Public room at Town Hall during vote-counting process
5. Town Hall steps at night with the party faithful gathered and the candidates arriving
6. View from Killane's window over Andersley at night
7. Town Hall steps during election result announcement

ACT ONE

Titles

Massed brass bands are playing. Sousa but harshly elegiac—'The Crusaders'.

The shadowed faces of two men face each other in profile as a swooping aerial view of a town unrolls. The viewpoint moves quickly from good farming country along a main road through the city centre into the river area of terraced streets.

As the terraced streets magnify, a school is seen at one end decked out briefly as a polling station.

From here the two profiles become full face, almost as if taken from election posters, and over them is a very quick montage of still photos—the flowered hats of the Conservative Ladies' Conference, a fire engine, police car, men pouring from a factory gate, a cattle market, children's playground, the triumphal procession with banners and bands at the Durham Miners' Gala. Heath, Wilson, Thorpe gesturing from behind microphones on other, separate occasions.

1

Interior. Bedroom. Night.

Corner set, signs of opulence—a quilted bed-head, rosewood bedside cabinet with pastel phone on it, a bud vase with a single bloom.

The telephone begins to ring. Because the subscriber is slightly hard of hearing, the GPO have amplified the volume of the receiver and the ringing noise is insistent and strident.

5

The woman is Mrs Langley, John Killane's aunt, pleasant-faced and robust. Normally placid, she wakes quickly and in terror. She is wearing a small unobtrusive hearing aid. She picks up the telephone, holds it a little way from her ear. It is obvious that this call is one of a series.

TELEPHONE VOICE: Nobody's going to vote for John Killane because he's not going to be there any more. And neither are you. And neither are his kids. Vote for John Killane and this is what will happen.

The voice stops and there is a rapid ticking noise as somebody holds a large alarm clock—the essential mechanism of an amateur time bomb—against the receiver at the other end.

Mrs. Langley throws the receiver down, not on its rest, and the ticking goes on.

2

Interior. Children's Bedroom. Night.

Furnished with expensive functionalism from Heal's and Habitat. It is not untidy and the toys seen around are a mixture of traditional and modern—a one-eared Teddy Bear sprawled across a pile of educational building bricks.

Killane's twin girls, one dark, one fair, are asleep in bunk beds and do not move as Mrs Langley stands by them for a moment, terror still on her face. They are about seven years old, happy, healthy and well-cared-for.

3

Exterior. An Andersley Street. Day.

Film sequence.

The scene opens immediately on sound with an amplified voice from a mobile public-address system.

KILLANE (*His voice amplified*): Vote for John Killane. If you want a new look and a better future for Andersley, this is the man to vote for. Vote for John Killane.

The address truck is a converted pick-up. Its sides have been built up with hardwood to form the shell of a mobile platform and it is plastered with posters showing Killane's face.

Killane is standing in the back of the truck talking into a microphone. There is a great deal of anger both in his face and in the delivery.

KILLANE (*His voice amplified*): Vote Conservative. Vote for John Killane.

The truck comes to a halt and seen very prominently is a massive banner stretched across the entrance to a Labour Working Men's Club.

The banner reads 'Labour Committee Rooms'. The poster outside is of a different face, that of Alan Lowery and reads 'Vote Labour, Vote for Lowery.'

Killane vaults over the edge of the truck, hands the microphone to the driver who is climbing from the driving side looking worried.

The driver is Peter Chapman, one of Killane's partners in his London business. He is about thirty-seven. His careless amiable charm covers a sharp analytical mind. He is an easily happy man; strictly non-political and slightly puzzled by his partner's addiction to politics but loyal enough to humour him.

John Killane is about thirty-five, partner in a successful market-research business which he helped to found.

He went into politics via his professional skills and his main asset is the ability to interpret research results, take cold hard figures and translate them into people. The selection committee approved Killane for his sincerity, a willingness to serve, youth, good looks, and a brilliant mind. Two of the committee were doubtful because of a certain irreverence in him and a strong streak of financial and moral independence.

CHAPMAN: You can't do anything. Not here.

Killane is standing close enough to one of the posters on the van for him to be immediately recognisable as the candidate.

KILLANE: Oh, yes, I can. I can pick up the nearest bloody telephone and stuff it down somebody's throat.

CHAPMAN: All that'll get you is a bill from the GPO.

KILLANE: It'll be worth it.

Chapman puts a restraining hand on his arm.

CHAPMAN: Look, I'm just your business partner. Unofficial driver, official tea boy. I said you were off the hinge even *wanting* to become an MP. (*Gestures at pick-up truck.*) Why don't we just turn this circus round and drive it back to London where we belong.

KILLANE: After the Election.

CHAPMAN: At least, don't go in there. I'm too old and nervous to give you a blood transfusion when you come out.

KILLANE: Take the circus back to our committee rooms. I'll see you there.

4

Interior. Labour Committee Rooms. Day.

For the period of the election it is quite common for

the local constituency headquarters—which should be a small office—to be moved to larger premises. It is illegal for those premises to be where intoxicating liquor is sold but an exception is made in the case of a permanent political club having a political test of membership.

The room, therefore, shows signs of conversion from its original function. It is on the ground floor of the club and is used as the singing-room part of the premises. An upright piano is in one corner but the brewer's signs have been taken from the walls. There are, however, a few of the small round tables and arm-chairs remaining. Trestle tables, desk and telephones have been moved in. These are loaded with election literature and there are now charts taped to the walls. These charts are quite large—designed and issued from party HQ in London—and serve as a programme of meetings, a record of districts to be canvassed etc. There are also some portraits on the walls. One is of a miner's lodge prior to the General Strike, one of Nye Bevan and more recent ones of Harold Wilson and George Brown.

The room has a busy, if impromptu atmosphere. There are, for instance, two girls at the table, folding election addresses into envelopes and a youth is busy loading these into a mailbag. A girl stands near one of the charts making a check-list into a notebook.

The main focus of attention, however, is on three men seated round the desk at one end of the room.

The man obviously running the discussion is Sam Brodie, the Labour MP for the adjoining constituency. Andersley is a two-constituency town—like Derby, Norwich or Walsall—and the seat in dispute is a firm Labour stronghold.

Brodie is about forty-six. Born in Andersley, son of a railway fitter, ex-foreman and then shop manager for the local wagon sheds. He became a local councillor in 1955; a big solid man, ex-Rugby League forward. He was elected to Parliament in 1959 and was good enough to be a junior minister from 1967–70. He moves easily across all sections of society, the local accent modified a little now, the clothes and manners chosen to suit himself and not any cloth-cap image.

The man sitting at the desk is the Labour agent for Andersley. This is Cliff Lambert. He is about thirty-three, acid-tongued and square-built, born in Birmingham of Welsh parents, a gifted speaker, totally committed to the cause and a tireless tearaway on its behalf.

The third man, wearing the candidate's rosette, is Alan Lowery. He is about forty, a somewhat humourless man—the one fault in an otherwise attractive personality—who teaches history at the local grammar school. There is a thoughtful quietness about him which is quite impressive contrasted with Lambert's volatility and Brodie's sense of strength.

LOWERY: There are too many meetings with the little old ladies waiting for the Bingo to start. Half the time they don't know what I'm on about.

LAMBERT: That's a bit your own fault, boyo. Stick to the price of school meals and stay off arms to South Africa.

BRODIE: Not all the time. (*Grins at Lowery.*) Say what you've got to say. The old ladies may have come to play Bingo but they'll still vote for you.

LOWERY: I'd rather they voted for the things I believe in.

LAMBERT: That, too. And don't worry about being nervous. I've been agent for twenty candidates and they've all been nervous. Look, this has been a Labour seat for twenty years. We'll get in on a cakewalk and the Grocer'll jump off his yacht.

At that moment Killane comes into the room. He is a little more in control now and the anger is icy.

10

KILLANE (*Directly to Lowery*): I want to talk to you. Privately. *Now.*

LAMBERT: And '*please*'. Where are your Conservative manners?

KILLANE (*Ignoring Lambert*): *Now.*

Brodie moves in, takes charge, rises, turns to speak to the voluntary workers in the room.

BRODIE: Give us a minute, will you, friends? Sorry to disturb you.

The voluntary workers file out and Brodie closes the door behind them. Killane has not really waited for the room to clear.

KILLANE: I want your telephone cranks pulled off. I don't want my house telephoned four times a night. I don't want threats to my children. I don't want lunatics promising time-bombs.

LOWERY: You think we're doing that?

KILLANE: Somebody is. And they're on your side. So put the word about.

LAMBERT: You must be bloody hard-up for votes.

BRODIE: Have you reported it?

KILLANE: To the police and the exchange supervisor. Now somebody's got the unlisted number.

LAMBERT: Oh, they would. And the next thing Mr Killane does is send a photo of the kids and the old Auntie to the newspapers. 'Threats on Tory Candidate's life.' Good for the pacifist vote.

Killane spins in anger, snatches up the telephone receiver, thrusts it at Lambert.

KILLANE (*Snarling*): Here. Go on, check it. Ring the police, ring the exchange.

LOWERY (*To Lambert*): I think you've said enough,

11

CLIFF. (*To Killane*) And I don't think losing your temper will help. I'd just like to tell you that this party and this organisation know nothing about any telephone calls—threatening or otherwise.

BRODIE: And just in case, I'll put the word about.

LAMBERT (*Incredulous*): You don't believe him? You can't. It's medieval.

BRODIE (*Hard*): When they put me in again for the other half of Andersley, it was 1970. I'd been an MP for eleven years, a junior minister for three. Then I got two letters a week for six months. (*To Lambert*) You saw them.

LAMBERT: Some bloody Tory maniac.

BRODIE (*To Killane*): I've got a daughter. She's not very bright. Not backward, just not bright. In a special school. The letters said: 'You don't belong in Parliament, Brodie. You belong in the same nut-house as your loony kid.' I'll put the word about.

Brodie's delivery is laconic, but some of the remembered pain shows through.

KILLAINE: Fair enough.

5

Interior. Conservative Association Committee Rooms. Day.

This is a more spacious room on the first floor of the Conservative Club. Its official use is that of a billiard room and the two billiard tables, one large and one small, have been carefully covered with hardboard and now hold similar piles of literature to those seen in the Labour Party headquarters. There is still the billiard marker board and racks of cues on the wall. The room has not been altered very much since it is still put to its original function on Fridays and Saturdays when voluntary helpers unload the literature and take the charts from the walls.

The charts are roughly the same but the posters and slogans have changed and the only portraits are of Sir Winston Churchill and the Queen.

Mandatory on the wall is a 'Summary of Election Offences'—obtained from Conservative Central Office.

NOTE: Strictly speaking, both the agent and the Candidate should have a private office but for set purposes a corner desk will again suffice.

Again mandatory and stemming from the agent's legal position is the need for both Annie Mackinnon and Cliff Lambert to be continually approached to sign authorisations for voluntary workers responsible for meetings, transport, clerical organisation, etc. [See the authoritative High Court judgement on the principle of agency, stated by Mr Justice Willes (Blackburn Election Petition, 1869).]

Peter Chapman is sitting on the edge of the billiard table drinking tea from a large blue and white beaker.

CHAPMAN: I had a great idea for this election. I was going to get a big flock of budgerigars, teach them all to shout 'Vote for Killane', and turn 'em loose.

A girl looks up from the desk. This is Annie Mackinnon.

ANNIE: Not while I'm his agent. You'll lose the RSPCA vote.

Annie Mackinnon is about twenty-nine. A Scots girl brought up in Manchester who has been a welfare officer and is now a professional political agent. There is nothing of the Florence Nightingale in her but traces of a youthful idealism remain. She enjoys the social life of a Conservative agent but there is an occasional twinge of guilt about it.

13

A man walks into the room carrying a bundle of folded election throw-aways for distribution at meetings. He is looking very cheerful. This is Stuart Walker, who is Conservative Area Officer of the fifty-odd constituencies in the region. At by-elections, Walker acts in an advisory capacity to the local agent—although the local agent is legally responsible for running the election. Walker is about forty-three, professional, laconic, relaxed, known everywhere. He has forgotten more about politics than most people have seen.

WALKER: God bless local printers. This is a lovely clean job.

CHAPMAN (*Sadly*): That was another idea I had. Pornographic campaign posters.

ANNIE (*Trace of exasperation*): If politics depended on voluntary workers like you, we'd deserve a dictatorship.

CHAPMAN: I'm not a voluntary worker, love. I don't know one end of a democrat from another. I'm just here to remind John he also owns a successful market-research business. And drink your tea and get in the way. (*Worried in spite of himself.*) He should be back by now.

WALKER: Where is he?

CHAPMAN: Organising a punch-up with the Opposition.

WALKER (*Quickly*): Telephone calls? Again?

CHAPMAN: He was very angry.

WALKER: He's a candidate. He can't afford to be angry. I told him to let me fix it.

CHAPMAN: They're *his* kids.

ANNIE: I wouldn't like to get the wrong side of him on that. (*To Chapman*) Peter, I haven't had any bills for your petrol for about a week.

14

CHAPMAN: Put it down to goodwill. My contribution to the cause.

ANNIE: Peter, I've told you a dozen times we have to account for every penny. We're allowed about £1,300 and that's all. By law. Representation of the People Act.

CHAPMAN: But I haven't got the bills.

WALKER: You'd better ring the garage and get them. Now, please. It's serious.

Chapman shrugs, puts down his beaker of tea and moves to the telephone.

6

Interior. Labour Party Committee Rooms. Day.

The voluntary workers are back in the room and Brodie, Lambert and Lowery are around the desk.

Lambert is speaking briskly, with authority.

LAMBERT: We've got four days to go. The postal vote's wrapped up—invalids, blind people, merchant seamen, twice as many as last year. I've got two dozen canvassers out knocking on doors. I've got questioners planted at every one of their meetings. What I think we should do now is cram in as many factory gates as we can. Keep it loud, keep it simple—'You're not slave labour, so vote like it'. Hammer the Industrial Relations Bill. I know we're in but I want a damn great majority to prove it.

BRODIE (*Quietly*): Why not ring round the shop stewards? Word of mouth. Aim at organised meetings.

LAMBERT: It worked for you, Sam, but this part of town's different. (*An edge to the flippancy.*) Besides, you're not telling me how to do my job, are you?

15

BRODIE: If I had to, I would.

The voice is quiet but when the telephone rings Lambert is glad to pick it up.

LAMBERT (*Into telephone*): Labour Party. Alan Lowery's Committee Rooms. (*The voice changes into cordiality*) Hello, Ernest. Yes, he's here. Yes, I'll tell him. Both of them? (*He laughs.*) Any time *you* talk to me about mutual advantages, I make sure my wallet's still there. Yes, I'll see to it.

Lambert puts the phone down, looks up with some surprise at Lowery and Brodie.

LAMBERT: Mr Ernest Dewhurst, Chairman of the Labour majority of our respected town council would like to see both of you—if convenient—at about seven tonight.

BRODIE: About seven? He must be thirsty.

LOWERY: I was going to go canvassing.

BRODIE: Not when Ernest wants to see you. (*Turns to leave, talks to Lambert.*) Don't forget about Killane's telephone.

Brodie leaves and Lambert leans back in his seat.

LAMBERT: That's what being a member for thirteen years does to you. The objective eye. The fair-minded approach. The clean fight. There's no such thing as a clean fight. Not if you want to win badly enough. Killane knows it. That's why I don't believe him about his telephone calls.

LOWERY: I'm not sure. It's possible. And politics is the art of the possible.

LAMBERT: Oh, no, it isn't, Mr Lowery. Politics is walking till the soles of your shoes drop off. And talking till your voice dries up. And going to bed every night thinking: 'This was a day I believed in.'

LOWERY: I agree with all that.

LAMBERT: I hope so. Because I don't think Killane does. That's another reason we'll beat him.

7

Interior. Conservative Association Committee Rooms. Day.

Walker is doing his best to reprimand Killane gently.

WALKER: I wish you'd left it to me, John.

Killane is standing near the wall chart showing the routes of the canvassing teams.

KILLANE: But I didn't. And you're probably right.

WALKER: I know I'm right. Cliff Lambert has a word with his chief reporter crony and the headline reads: 'Tories try smear campaign.'

KILLANE: Till Brodie stopped him, that's what Lambert thought *I* was after. (*Becomes intent on the chart where streets have been ticked off, turns to Annie Mackinnon.*) Annie, can you come and look at this?

Annie comes across with a pile of canvass cards in her hand.

ANNIE: Canvassing is up-to-date. We've got four teams out now.

KILLANE: What about the random canvass I asked for?

WALKER (*Interrupting smoothly*): I'm afraid that's my doing, John. Annie told me you wanted to take six two-men teams and use them on specific addresses. I told her it wasn't on. There isn't time. They've all been allocated districts.

ANNIE: The street system we've got is a good one. It always worked before. You get at more people.

17

KILLANE: And a bigger percentage of doubtfuls. (*To Walker*) Stuart, you're area organiser. This is only one of the fifty-odd constituencies you run. And you're here as an adviser—without your big stick. Annie's the legally appointed election agent. Responsible for its continuity, its operation and its finances. And responsible to me. Tomorrow morning, I want a random canvass carried out on the individual houses I've listed. Working from this chart.

He jabs a finger at a supplementary strip of paper taped at the side of the orthodox wall chart. This strip is blue and contains a six-column list of computer typing.

WALKER: I'd still advise against it, John. I've steered about 200 elections. I know what I'm up to.

KILLANE: And I ran a market research firm up from a second-hand desk and a borrowed typewriter to a business grossing a hundred thousand a year. I did it on lists of figures and I made a lot of money for a lot of people.

As he talks, he goes to the desk and takes out two research reports. These are thick spiral bound volumes in pliofilm covers, quarto size. He puts these carefully on the billiard table and leans across to talk quietly and firmly to Walker.

KILLANE: ALCO did a car ownership and mortgage attitude survey in Andersley and I've put in two weeks of sweat stripping facts out of it. That's where the list on the wall came from. I want somebody to knock on every door on that list.

ANNIE: That's nearly 3,000 people.

KILLANE: And nearly 3,000 votes.

WALKER: We can't afford it and there isn't time.

KILLANE: We've got to afford it and we'll make time. And if you won't turn the teams loose, Peter and I'll do it. I'll cancel every meeting and every speech I've got.

WALKER (*Formally*): We must accept your instructions. I should say that I may need to make a report on it.

KILLANE: Fine. Make your report but set that canvass up before you do.

Killane picks up the thick set of volumes and walks out.

Walker grins, lights a cigarette, sits on the billiard table.

WALKER: Watch, listen and learn, Annie. Every candidate has his own secret for success. Especially at this stage in the game. It's their version of the Treble Chance. They know exactly what doors to knock on to pull off that magic ten per cent swing. I had an old boy once who counted on the Methodist vote. And there was another one, bit of an athlete. He thought we'd win if we talked to everybody who took cycling seriously.

ANNIE: I think this is a bit different. As he said, translating figures into people is John's business.

WALKER: So let's make a start on his dream-world canvass. (*Crosses to chart.*) He isn't going to get in, you know. It's a fact of life. We're in Government and they're in Opposition. And the Opposition *always* win by-elections in seats like this. With an increased majority. Nobody bothers too much. It's a legitimate squawk about policies going through.

The delivery is casual, factual, unworried.

ANNIE (*Grinning*): If I'm as cynical as you are after twenty years as an agent, I'd better go back to welfare work now.

8

Interior. Hotel room. Day.

This is a big room in the best hotel in Andersley but both building and room will never feature in the tourist advertisements of the British Travel and Holidays Association.

The wallpaper is dark and durable, the bedstead is brass, the mattress is now moulded to trampoline shape. The carpet is dark floral Victorian, the wardrobe is megalithic mahogany and, as always in rooms like this, the first thing the occupant sees as he opens his eyes in the morning is a gigantic portrait of 'The stag at bay' placed there as a reminder of what might happen to him if he does not pay his bill.

Killane has made no attempt to brighten up the room where he has spent the last month. Books, magazines, files, newspapers are stacked tidily around. There is, however, a drinks tray on the dressing table.

Chapman, with a clipboard on his knee, is sitting on one of the uncomfortable chairs and Killane is walking up and down the room.

A very old porter in a white jacket is picking up a tea tray and Killane opens the door for him.

CHAPMAN (*Scribbling figures*): They can do a random canvass in the time. If they put all the teams on. I can do some of the driving.

KILLANE: Good. Thanks, Peter.

Chapman tosses the clipboard on the bed.

CHAPMAN: I could do with a drink.

KILLANE: Me too. I'll ring down for some ice.

CHAPMAN: Oh, no, you won't. You'll drink it tepid. It takes that old boy ten minutes to climb two flights of stairs. Every time he walks through that door, it looks like his last trip.

As he talks he has crossed to the drinks tray and poured—whisky for himself, gin for Killane. He adds nothing to his own whisky and just a splash of tonic to Killane's gin.

KILLANE (*Raising glass*): Roll on next Tuesday.

CHAPMAN (*With feeling*): Amen to that. I'm going to write a book about it. 'I was a Fugitive from a Ballot Box.'

KILLANE (*Grinning*): You're a socially irresponsible whisky-swilling drop-out and I think if you hadn't been up here I'd have turned into a drop-out myself.

CHAPMAN: There's still time. Look, John, why don't we just take off? Leave a note on the door: 'Come back, Harold, all is forgiven.' What the hell do you want to go into Parliament for anyway?

KILLANE: It would take a while to explain that. And perhaps I don't even know.

CHAPMAN: I've known you fifteen years. You and me and old Four-eyes who's running the shop in London. We slogged our guts out. We've got a good research agency and we're all taking about ten grand a year plus out of it.

KILLANE: *I* won't be soon. Not if I'm elected.

CHAPMAN: That's what I mean. You'll get a two thou. consultancy and the petty cash they pay you for being an MP. What for? And for years. Even John the Baptist could look forward to a square meal after forty days in the wilderness.

KILLANE: You remember when we started the business? The questionnaires, the attitude surveys. Asking people everything. From what colour socks they wore to did they believe in God. And when they'd finished answering the questions, we came up with research documents. The right market for the right product. What I couldn't get into the documents were the faces

21

and the gossip after the questions. And it bothered me. The quiet patient people.

CHAPMAN: I must have drawn *your* share of loud-mouths. Don't get romantic. Not with me.

KILLANE: I had my share. The bigots and the stupid. But mostly the patience and the reasonableness. A sense of order. A sense of endurance. Especially here. In Andersley. The rough jobs, the slog. It made all the questionnaires a bit pointless. The people were more important. What do they really want and who's going to get it for them?

CHAPMAN: Why you?

KILLANE: I don't know. All I know is a bit about people and the fact that this is a good town in a good country.

CHAPMAN (*Mock rueful*): Oh, dear. If I knew the words, I'd sing the Conservative version of the Red Flag.

KILLANE (*Grinning*): Not after one drink, old son. Not you.

At that moment, the telephone rings and Chapman is across to it quickly. It may be another report of threatening calls and he would prefer to act as buffer.

CHAPMAN (*Into telephone*): Yes? Oh, it's you, Annie. No, love, there was just a chance it might have been some other freak. Yes, I'll tell him. Fine. Onward and upward.

Chapman puts the telephone down and turns to Killane.

CHAPMAN: Annie says that Councillor Ernest Dewhurst would like to see you in the Working Men's Club at seven o'clock.

KILLANE: I've got a meeting then.

CHAPMAN: Annie says she's moved it. She says Dewhurst is probably more important.

KILLANE: Well, that's what an agent's for.

CHAPMAN: I think I'll take the sound truck and go and shout the odds some more. 'Vote for Killane.' 'The people's friend.' God knows why.

During this speech Killane has crossed to the veined wash basin and started to clean his teeth. He spits out toothpaste, looks at his teeth in the mirror as Chapman goes out.

CHAPMAN: You'll never learn to smile like Sir Alec. He's got twenty years start on you.

9

Interior. Working Men's Club. Night.

This need only be a corner set but no bar is needed since there is steward service. The club is fairly prosperous and the table seen is of good quality with comfortable chairs. On the wall near it is a picture of the local Rugby League team and a notice board advertising raffles, outings, darts and snooker fixtures.

Sam Brodie is sitting at the table and there are two pints of beer in front of him.

Ernest Dewhurst comes up to the table, nods at Sam, sits down, takes a quiet and satisfying drink before speaking. There is no lip-smacking or simulated beer-commercial glee.

Ernest Dewhurst is about fifty-five, an alert, and intelligent man with a full share of human failings and virtues. He is a toolmaker by trade and an old-style local politician by inclination, shrewd, and experienced after a lifetime of unpaid public service. He is chairman of all the important committees and virtually the

23

*boss of the ruling Labour Council. He is untouched
by public opinion, capable of being a dictator. He has
very little interest in national issues but is deeply and
genuinely proud of his own town of Andersley.*

DEWHURST: You're on time, Sam. As usual.

BRODIE (*Faintly mocking*): It's not every day you
get a royal command from Councillor Dewhurst.

DEWHURST (*Mocking back*): Oh, I'm just one of the
little fishes. Swimming along in my own little pool.

BRODIE: Pulling the town council behind you.

DEWHURST: I've heard people say that.

BRODIE: You're a bloody old villain and I'm glad
you're on our side.

DEWHURST: That's more like you. This election, Sam.
Will we get in again?

BRODIE: Easily. We're pretty safe.

DEWHURST: So they say. We've had Callaghan and
Stewart. Anybody else honouring us with their
presence?

BRODIE: Harold said he'd try.

DEWHURST: Chance.

BRODIE (*Hard, loyal*): He's busy.

DEWHURST: And this Lowery, this school-teacher chap
we've got. Will he be any bottle as a Labour MP?

BRODIE: I think so. He's confident enough and the
subjects he knows, he knows well.

DEWHURST: That's what bothers me a bit. He's got
more theories than the grammar school library. But
I've never seen a theory build a council house.

BRODIE: I've seen theories provide the money to
build them.

24

DEWHURST: *And* take it away. What about this London chap? This Killane.

BRODIE: Early to tell. He'll need watching. Then again he might be just another carpet-bagger. Live in London, trot up here twice a month. Be an MP because it's good for business and the bars are open all day.

DEWHURST (*Persisting slightly*): Good businessman though?

BRODIE: Successful, anyway.

Dewhurst nods, satisfied. Takes another drink of beer as Killane comes up to the table.

BRODIE: Mr Killane, Councillor Dewhurst.

DEWHURST: We've met. Sit down, lad.

The steward, without being asked, puts a pint of beer in front of Killane who looks at it with some amusement.

KILLANE: I've got a meeting at eight o'clock.

DEWHURST: Peppermints. Get some of these down you. (*Reaches into waistcoat pocket, takes out a tube of peppermints, gives them to Killane.*)

KILLANE (*Smiling*): I see what they mean about you and practical politics.

DEWHURST: Never offend the temperance vote, lad. They're entitled to their vices, just like anybody else.

At that moment Alan Lowery comes up. Another pint of beer appears.

LOWERY: I don't drink, thanks.

Dewhurst reaches across, pulls the pint towards him, makes no comment.

LOWERY: And this isn't the most convenient time, Councillor. There *is* an election on and we've both got lots to do.

25

DEWHURST: I know all about that. (*Touch of sharpness*.) But if an MP like Sam Brodie who's been an Andersley member for thirteen years can find the time, I should think a candidate could. Anyway I'll get on with it and you can go back to playing gladiators with this London chap.

KILLANE: I think it's a little more than that.

DEWHURST: It might be for you. One of you gets elected, serves his term, lives, dies. This town goes on. This is where the nuts and bolts are. (*To Lowery*) And don't worry, Mr Lowery, I've got fifty party workers walking streets for you while we're sitting here.

BRODIE: Come on, Ernest. Let's be knowing what it's about. Then these two can get on and I'll listen to your views on the local universe.

DEWHURST: Simple. Jobs. Eight-per-cent unemployment in this town. Most of it skilled. That makes too many people on the dole for my liking. So what are you lot going to do about it?

LOWERY: I think you'll see from my election address that I regard the attraction of new industry to this area as a top priority and if and when I get to Westminster . . .

DEWHURST: Not the speeches, lad, the action.

BRODIE: Give him a chance, Ernest. When you get down to Westminster, you're one out of 630. I've pestered enough Ministers. I know.

DEWHURST: How about you, Mr Killane?

KILLANE: MPs get long holidays. Use them. Don't pester Ministers. Pester the big combines. I think I know what Andersley's got to offer. It's just a question of getting out and selling it to the people with a cheque book on their desks.

DEWHURST: And I know that's what Sam thinks.

So here's where you start. There's some Swiss American firm looking for towns to shortlist. A chap called Garsfeld's running it. He's looking for a site for a new factory estate. Organised and built and leased as a package. A guarantee of five thousand jobs. Wants to know what sort of concessions we can offer.

LOWERY: We'll need to know a lot more about it.

DEWHURST: Not when he's offering 5,000 jobs, we won't.

BRODIE: How did you find out, Ernest?

DEWHURST: A friend of a friend sort of heard it at a conference.

BRODIE: One of your union cronies.

DEWHURST (*Firmly*): Not a crony. I wouldn't give him kennel-room. We just do each other favours.

Killane grins.

KILLANE: Don't expect any favours from Garsfeld.

BRODIE: You know the set-up?

KILLANE: Bits about it. Very tough, very professional. Basically Swiss. American management. Invests around 8 million pounds. That's every year. International money.

LOWERY: Couldn't this have waited until after the election? It's only next Tuesday.

DEWHURST: That's the day he flies back to America. So they tell me. Up to you, gentlemen. Get on with your election and may the best man win—providing he's Labour.

KILLANE: Then why include me at all?

DEWHURST: Insurance. I'm a politician and there are two things a politician needs. Insurance and peppermints.

10

Interior. Bedroom. Night.

Mrs Langley is quietly sleeping as the telephone begins to ring again.

She wakes up terrified, listens to the telephone, then picks it up, holds it away from her ear.

TELEPHONE VOICE: Vote for Killane. If he's still there on Tuesday.

Mrs Langley pushes the telephone away as an alarm clock is heard ticking again.

END OF ACT ONE

ACT TWO

11

Interior. Killane's hotel room. Night.

Killane is standing with the telephone to his ear.

Peter Chapman is at the dressing table pouring drinks for himself and Annie Mackinnon who is sitting in the hard chair.

The small table has been pulled up to this and spread across it is the blue list seen on the wall at the committee rooms. She is checking a pile of canvass cards against this list.

KILLANE (*Into telephone*): Thank you, Inspector. I appreciate it. No, it shouldn't be for long. Three days. The election's on Tuesday. Thank you again.

He put the telephone down and turns towards Chapman who is all innocence.

KILLANE: Did you do that? Ask for a police guard?

CHAPMAN: Of course. Why not? Give the fuzz a crack at some overtime. They'll love it. Your housekeeper out there with tea and home-made cake every ten minutes.

KILLANE: It sounded as if you'd been pulling every string there was.

CHAPMAN: All right, maybe I overdid the prospective MP bit. Isn't that what it's for?

There is a tap on the door and Stuart Walker comes into the room.

KILLANE: Hello, Stuart. How's it going?

29

WALKER: Halfway through the list. We should clear the rest on Monday.

CHAPMAN: Why not tomorrow?

WALKER: Sunday. Anything you do on Sundays you do quietly and that doesn't include heavy canvassing. John can go to church if he likes and sing loud enough for everybody to notice it.

CHAPMAN: I still don't understand it. We could have whizzed a team up from London and wrapped up the whole of this random canvass in a day.

ANNIE (*Looking up*): Which would have cost £300 and the budget won't stand it.

CHAPMAN: You know, I think that's what really baffles me. Any self-respecting, medium-size catfood firm takes a pilot area and spends about three thousand quid just to make sure the customers can read the name on the label—never mind buy the product. And here we are pinned down to a lousy thirteen hundred pounds to elect a Member of Parliament.

ANNIE: That's the way it works. And I still want those petrol bills from you.

CHAPMAN: Yes, ma'am. (*Shrugs, baffled, says softly*) Fred Karno, where are you? I need help.

WALKER (*To Killane*): If you could, John, I'd like you to stay fairly near the telephone tomorrow. It's starting to warm up in the national press and they'll be down here on Monday. Press Conference about twelve. All right?

CHAPMAN (*Hopefully*): Drinks afterwards?

ANNIE: If they pay for their own.

WALKER (*Handing Killane a memo*): Here are three of the Lobby boys who want a word anyway. Ian Aitken, Wilf Sendall and Harry Boyne. *Guardian*,

Express, Telegraph. They've left home numbers as well.

The telephone rings and Walker crosses to answer it.

WALKER (*Into telephone*): John Killane's office. Yes, Who's speaking please? (*Turns to Killane.*) Mr Anstey.

CHAPMAN: What's he doing running around on a Saturday night? He's our accountant. He's supposed to be in bed.

Killane has crossed to take the receiver.

KILLANE (*Into telephone*): Hello, George. *Who* rang? Yes, I know all about his informal chats. Look, George, I'm not elected yet and it's about ten to one against. If Garsfeld wants to see an official representative of Andersley, he's got to talk to Brodie or Councillor Dewhurst. All right, give me the number. I'll think about it.

Killane puts the telephone down, speaks directly to Annie Mackinnon.

KILLANE: That was a message from Joe Garsfeld. He's consultant for the combine that might want to build a factory estate here. He wants to see me in London tomorrow. Lunchtime.

ANNE: No harm in that. As far as I can see.

She looks at Walker for confirmation, who nods.

KILLANE: Ask Brodie to come along?

WALKER: No. Why give it away?

ANNIE: I don't agree. If John gets in, this is something he and Brodie might have to work together on.

KILLANE: So we may as well start now. I'll talk to Garsfeld. Then I'll ring Brodie.

He sits on the bed near to the telephone, rubs his eyes. The campaign has been strenuous and some of the strain is starting to show. Then he picks up the telephone.

12

Interior. Sam Brodie's living room. Night.

This is a big, comfortable room but the furniture has seen a lot of hard use and is on the verge of being shabby. One corner of the room is occupied by a large old desk with reference books on the shelf behind it. The room is big enough for this office area to have become an integral part of the scene and this is where Brodie does a lot of his work.

The living area away from it also shows signs of Brodie's occupation with newspapers and books in a pile near one of the armchairs. There are good prints and not plaster ducks on the wall and most of the prints have a local flavour.

At the side of Sam's desk is a large-scale ordnance map of the area and over the years this has been inked and written on.

There is a TV set but it is an old model. The room is clean and cheerful, with everything polished, but it should be evident that it has been a long time since any ornaments, upholstery, etc have been replaced or added to.

Sam Brodie is sitting in the armchair leaning sideways to shuffle through the pile of papers and magazines. He is in casual clothes but these are the casual clothes of an assistant bank manager—elderly pullover over well-worn slacks. He does not wear carpet slippers, now or ever.

Brodie's wife Elizabeth is sitting on the sofa. There is a sewing basket next to her and she is working quickly and carefully through a pile of boys' shirts and jeans, sewing on buttons or mending small tears.

Elizabeth Brodie is about forty-two, still pretty in a serene and quiet way. The serenity is deceptive because of worries about money and the youngest child. Over the years Brodie has moved on, up and away from her. She has tried dutifully to read the books, to comprehend the issues but will not pretend to comprehension where there is none. This quality of naturalness is a greater asset to Brodie among his supporters than he recognises. There is tolerance for her husband's dream of the cause and a massive support for him but never at the expense of practicality and it is Elizabeth who manages the tightly-strained finances of the family.

ELIZABETH: If your two sons grow any faster, we'll have to open a clothes shop.

BRODIE: The way this town's going, we'd be the only customers. There's going to be a lot of patches on a lot of kids' trousers.

ELIZABETH: We'll be in good company then. They'll need new outfits soon, Sam.

BRODIE: Wait till next term. (*Grins.*) Might do the grammar school good to see a couple of real ragamuffins. Remind 'em what it's like at a few of the other schools in this town.

ELIZABETH: They still look a bit scruffy though. Especially at the side of my sister's two.

BRODIE: That doesn't bother me. They're a damn sight brighter and a damn sight better-mannered.

ELIZABETH: You should see them during the week sometimes when you're not here.

BRODIE: And besides, your sister's husband makes more money than I do.

33

ELIZABETH: Because he walked right into the job you left when you went into Parliament.

BRODIE: Big tycoon stuff. Manager down at the wagon sheds.

ELIZABETH: He still makes a better living than you do.

BRODIE: Depends what you mean by better.

The telephone rings and Brodie heaves himself up to answer it. There is no hurry in his movements. The telephone rings often.

ELIZABETH: If that's the Labour Women's Section, tell Mrs Harris I'll be round at ten o'clock sharp on Monday.

BRODIE: If that's Mrs Harris, you can talk to her. I don't fancy half an hour of operations and juvenile delinquency.

Elizabeth laughs, watches her husband pick up the telephone as she has watched him hundreds of times. There is a deep and quiet fondness between these two.

BRODIE (*Into telephone*): 7456. Sam Brodie. Who? Yes, hello, Mr Killane. No, you're not disturbing me. It's just that Tory candidates don't ring this number very often. Me? Of course I'd like to meet Garsfeld. But why do you need an official representative if this chat's informal? No, I'm not suspicious. I believe there's such a thing as public spirit, I just don't see much of it. Especially from your lot. All right, I'll be there.

He puts the phone down, turns to Elizabeth.

BRODIE: 'Beware the Greeks when they come bearing gifts.' I wonder if Killane's got any Greek blood?

ELIZABETH: Prince Philip has.

BRODIE (*Fondly*): You daft ha'porth, I didn't mean that. I've got to catch the 8.40 tomorrow. Is my bag packed?

ELIZABETH: You ask that once a week, and every time you get the same answer. Yes, it is.

BRODIE: And can I have some money?

ELIZABETH: In the jug. (*Ruefully*.) I'd got beef for tomorrow as well.

Brodie walks past her, touches her face.

BRODIE: We'll get up early and have it for breakfast.

He goes to the mantelpiece, counts out five or six pound notes from a small pottery jug.

13

Interior. Hampstead pub. Day.

This is a pub something like The Bird In Hand *or* The Crown *which retains a deliberately traditional pub interior—nicotine-stained lincrusta, polished wooden beer-handles, etc—but also stocks a wide variety of exotic drinks. The main decoration is provided by the patrons, especially at Sunday lunchtime with the bright, intellectual birds of passage flaunting their plumage—suede shirts, feather boas, ponchos, hot pants, some of them on ladies and gentlemen ten years too old for the gear.*

The conversation is incessant, sometimes high-pitched, counterpointed with the odd acid neutral lisp. The thick Sunday papers are in evidence, often being plagiarised in conversation and borrowed quotes from the New Statesman *also hang heavy on the air.*

Killane is sitting at a small table away from the bar reading the News of the World—*as a small gesture of independence but also a token of his curiosity. He reads every paper, not just the fashionable ones. He is wearing a high-necked cashmere pullover over a dark linen shirt, cavalry twill trousers, suede boots.*

Sam Brodie comes into the pub and in his dark blue suit looks out of place.

Through this scene, the birds of passage will come and go and Brodie will watch them as Killane watches him—an illustration of the two worlds they move in.

BRODIE (*To Killane*): Sorry I'm late.

He sits down and Killane pushes across the pint of beer he has already ordered for him.

KILLANE: Don't worry, Garsfeld's not here yet.

BRODIE (*Looking round*): They've got a lot to say for themselves in here.

KILLANE: Mostly art and politics.

BRODIE: Funny sort of politics.

KILLANE: You shouldn't say that. Most of them vote Labour. The Hampstead intellectual brigade.

BRODIE. What are you doing here then?

KILLANE: Listening. Nobody ever learns anything by talking.

BRODIE (*Grinning*): That makes a change.

KILLANE: I'd better explain why we're meeting here. Garsfeld loves the typical English pub. He thinks it's a better invention than the space module.

Brodie settles back, begins to relax, enjoy himself. He too, is a curious man.

BRODIE: And this is typical? I should be used to it by now. This is London. And London isn't England. But nor is Andersley. Two worlds. They both exist but finding your way round the pair of them can be difficult sometimes. What about this Garsfeld chap?

KILLANE: Deceptive. Big and breezy. And if thumbscrews ever come back into commerce, he'll be the first to use them. Here he is now.

Garsfeld is seen pushing his way through. He is carrying a full pint of beer with practised ease and shouts towards Killane.

GARSFELD: Hi, Johnny. Looked for you round the other side.

Joe Garsfeld is a man of about forty-five, barrel-built and amiable. His credentials are Harvard business school, Wall Street, and two years as a G2 Major. He speaks four languages fluently but reads balance sheets much faster than he reads words. The label on his business card reads 'Investment Consultant' and his terms for any given job are fee plus percentage of profit. The furniture in his Bruton Street drawing room office is worth perhaps £15,000 and is appreciating at the rate of 10 per cent per year, which is why he bought it in the first place. Garsfeld loves the making of money and the knife-fighting—is indifferent to the Hugh Heffner trappings it can bring.

Killane does not rise but waits for Garsfeld to sit down. To do this Garsfeld has to move Brodie's somewhat scruffy hold-all.

GARSFELD: Who the hell does this belong to? Some brush salesman?

BRODIE: No. It's mine.

KILLANE (*Smoothly*): Mr Garsfeld, may I introduce Mr Sam Brodie, the Member of Parliament for Andersley East.

Garsfeld reaches across to shake hands firmly.

GARSFELD: Glad to know you, Mr Brodie. I've never been to Andersley.

KILLANE: You should remedy that.

GARSFELD: Why? Looks like Andersley's coming to me.

BRODIE (*Quietly*): All we're doing at the moment is having a quiet Sunday drink in a typical English pub.

37

GARSFELD: So, Johnny Killane, politician. What's it feel like?

KILLANE: I'm still finding out.

GARSFELD: Your friend doesn't look much like an MP.

KILLANE: He's not my friend but he's one of the men you have to talk to. If you're really interested in Andersley.

GARSFELD: Oh, I'm interested. We've worked out a system of factory projects. We put up a complex of buildings. The sort of thing you call an estate. We guarantee occupiers and industry and all we want in return is a little co-operation.

KILLANE: Plus a reasonable profit on the construction. And a continuing profit on leasehold values.

GARSFELD: That's right. But the co-operation comes first. What sort of labour pool do you have up there?

BRODIE: There's about eight-per-cent unemployment at the moment.

GARSFELD: Good. That's always good.

BRODIE: Not for them, it isn't.

GARSFELD: What sort of labour?

BRODIE: Skilled. Mostly heavy engineering. Some miners on the market because pits are closing. It's a part of the country where they work, Mr Garsfeld. If a man says he's a tradesman, he *is* a tradesman.

GARSFELD: Any union problems?

BRODIE: No more than usual.

GARSFELD: And that's too damn many.

BRODIE: Like management problems.

GARSFELD: What about the Town Hall?

KILLANE: Labour-controlled. Has been for years. You'd have to talk to Ernest Dewhurst about that. He's willing to talk.

GARSFELD: This may seem a shade direct to you, Mr Brodie, but I don't want some town-hall office-boy hanging me up in red tape.

BRODIE: Nor does Ernest Dewhurst.

GARSFELD: What about you two?

KILLANE: Hold it. Mr Brodie is the only official representative here. I might be after next Tuesday but it's still a big 'if'.

BRODIE: You'll probably be talking to somebody called Alan Lowery . . .

GARSFELD (*To Killane*): I see what you meant when you said he was no friend of yours. The proposition is this. We've got about six million to invest and we know deals like this can work. We've done it in Holland, Germany, Belgium. We get co-operation, you get 5,000 jobs. That's what it adds up to.

KILLANE (*Quietly*): Who's the 'we' behind the money. Joe?

GARSFELD: You'll get the credentials. Besides, I'm buying, not selling. So that question was out of order.

KILLANE: Not to me, it wasn't.

BRODIE: Nor me.

Garsfeld beams.

GARSFELD: Gentlemen, it's going to be a pleasure doing business with you. If we do business. (*He rises.*) See you Thursday, Johnny.

KILLANE: If I'm elected.

GARSFELD: So then I'll see the other guy. If he can fix it. Nice to have met you, Mr Brodie.

39

Garsfeld gets up, pushes his way through the crowd.

BRODIE: What's that about Thursday? I thought he was flying back to the States tomorrow and wouldn't be available for six weeks.

KILLANE: I talked to him.

BRODIE: Bit tricky, aren't you?

KILLANE: Tricky enough.

Killane adds the usual very small dash of tonic to his gin, picks it up, sips it, watches Brodie.

14

Interior. Conservative Committee Rooms. Night.

The rooms are now full of a quiet calculated activity. All the telephones are in use and the voluntary helpers keep coming and going. They are carrying pamphlets and stickers, organising transport for the next day's election. The eve-of-poll machinery is in top gear. Annie Mackinnon is talking quietly but confidently to a rather harassed young man.

ANNIE: If you're going to take the minibus when they vote tomorrow, concentrate on the old people. Take somebody with you and try not to arrive at the same time as the meals on wheels. And late afternoon's best, before the telly starts and, whatever you do, don't rush them. Give them time for a chat. Make it an event. Understand?

The man nods and moves away quickly.

Walker comes across to her with the big marked electoral register in his hands.

WALKER: How up-to-date is this marked register?

ANNIE: Last year. We did a special canvass. Blue ticks for supporters, red ticks for the no-hopes.

WALKER: There's still a lot of space in it.

ANNIE: They're the ones we were trying to cover. Until John swung his special canvass on us.

WALKER: And where the hell is John? It's polling day tomorrow. He's got his last speech in an hour. He disappeared all day yesterday. Absentee landlords are one thing. Absentee candidates are in the wrong business.

During the last speech, a beaming Peter Chapman has come into the room. He is very slightly drunk but this is only apparent in a euphoric attitude. There is no slurring or swaying.

ANNIE (*With some urgency*): Peter, did you manage to cover Balaclava Street?

CHAPMAN: It covered me. There was a golden wedding jug-up at the third house I called at. They had two barrels of ale in the kitchen and half the street wandering through with their own glasses. So I just stayed there shouting 'Vote for Killane' and 'Tell your friends'.

ANNIE (*Trace of irritation*): And you think that'll do any good?

CHAPMAN: Oh, yes. When I left they were singing 'George Brown's Body'.

WALKER: Oh, no.

CHAPMAN: And I've promised a dozen tickets for the Black and White Minstrel Show. (*Holds his hand up towards an aggrieved Annie.*) At my own expense, love, and in return for the ale.

WALKER: Where's John? Do you know?

CHAPMAN: Oh, yes, Walking the streets, tapping on the doors, looking at the faces, listening to the chat.

WALKER: He's got his last meeting in half an hour. He should be here.

CHAPMAN: He'll be here. He'll finish listening then he'll start talking. He'll be all right.

15

Interior. Church hall. Night.

This need only be an improvised platform with a backdrop hung with banners—'Vote Tory—Vote for Killane'—and election posters with Killane's face.

Party stalwarts—as seen round the committee rooms— form the front row of the audience and three of them are on the platform together with Stuart Walker.

There is a table on the platform and Killane is standing against it—not behind it—and he has notes. Both hands are in his pockets, not negligently, but as a measure of control to stop his gesturing and his shoulders are very slightly hunched—in emphasis of determination and belief.

In the audience is one of the hecklers planted by Cliff Lambert. This man is a party stalwart of the other persuasion and should have been seen prominently at Labour Party Headquarters. He is about fifty, quite neatly dressed and with a shop steward's lack of self-consciousness in public debate.

HECKLER: We've heard all this guff before. I want to know about policy.

KILLANE: And I've just told you. Conservative policy was set out in the manifesto before the General Election. And it's been followed. If I didn't believe in that policy, I wouldn't be here.

HECKLER: Bloody hot air.

KILLANE: Not hot air, friend. Facts. The printed word. One of the stewards'll give you a copy of the manifesto on the way out. Read it for yourself.

HECKLER: What about the broken promises?

KILLANE: The Labour Party's? If I start on them, I'll be here all night. Ours? Just look at the record, please. Check the policy with the achievement. That's all I ask.

HECKLER: Not the way it works here. And what does somebody like you know about Andersley?

KILLANE: Fair question. All of you know a lot about Andersley because you were born here. I wasn't.

HECKLER: Some clergyman's son from Dorset.

KILLANE: That's what it says in the election leaflet. Shall I answer the question?

HECKLER: If you can.

KILLANE: What I know about Andersley, I've had to learn. The hard way. Which pits have closed, where the wagon sheds are, why the road past the Abbey needs widening, what stopped the finance on the Weldon housing estate, why part of the infirmary's been condemned, why Barrington Street market was closed. I know something about Andersley because I've worked at it.

HECKLER: Then what are you going to do about the eight-per-cent unemployment in this town?

KILLANE: You've had two Labour MPs for twenty years. What did they do to stop it happening? (*Pauses, the party point made, the personal viewpoint asserting itself*). Can I say one thing? If you're unemployed, a dole packet's just as skinny whether you vote Conservative or Labour. So let's drop the politics. A job's a job and there aren't enough of them in Andersley. If I'm elected, I think I can do as much as anybody to bring jobs here. It'll start in London. I know London. It'll start in commerce and industry and finance. I know those. No promises at all. Except one.

43

That I'll *try*. I'll use everything I know. I don't want any constituency in this country—but especially mine —with full Labour Exchanges and empty factories. That I can promise you. I'll try.

The sincerity is impressive and the hall is silent for a moment. Stuart Walker glances at his fellow platform members.

16

Interior. Labour Committee Rooms. Night.

Lowery, Lambert and Brodie have just entered the room. Lowery is taking off his coat and putting a briefcase on the desk. There are voluntary workers still present, the tempo is still fast and at the end of the scene, a girl will bring a tray of tea across to the three men.

LOWERY: They reckon Killane was very good tonight.

LAMBERT: Eve-of-poll speech. Last chance to make an impression. You were just as good.

BRODIE (*Gently*): Except the subject.

LOWERY: I know, Sam. I should have listened.

BRODIE: You fight by-elections on bread-and-butter issues. Housing, employment, education. Forget the rest. Mrs Bircumshaw in Railway Terrace isn't interested in prison reform or tariff rationalisation.

LAMBERT: And there might have been a bit too much about the morality of foreign affairs.

LOWERY: Look, I teach history and social sciences. I know about them. I believe in them. And the political applications. I believe it's important. In the wide context. Not just Andersley and its parish pump. (*Ruefully*). They weren't really interested. And I wasn't putting it across. That's the trouble with being a schoolteacher, I suppose. You always sound as if you're standing in front of a blackboard.

BRODIE: Don't worry about that. This Party's got enough performers. Political songs at the piano every time you turn on a television chat show.

LAMBERT: We've had this seat twenty years. We're not losing it now.

LOWERY: I hope not. I know what I want to do. I think I can do it.

BRODIE: We'll know tomorrow. I think you're as good as there.

The tea has arrived and been poured. Lambert has signed some authorisations. Lowery begins to check a list of polling stations where he will follow a route of cheer-up visits during tomorrow's election.

17

Exterior. Polling Station. Day.

Film sequence.

This is the school seen in the opening titles.

Party workers of both persuasions wearing rosettes are stopping voters on their way out and asking for the cards sent through the post so that some rough idea on the course of polling can be obtained and firm supporters enumerated. A further use to this is the door-knocking late at night to round up voters who have not been to the ballot.

A car bearing 'Vote for Killane' stickers disgorges supporters and almost immediately a van with 'Vote For Lowery' stickers pulls up behind it.

18

Interior Conservative Committee Rooms. Day.

There is the same feeling of the machine in top gear seen previously, a controlled excitement. Everyone is wearing rosettes.

Annie Mackinnon is talking into the telephone.

ANNIE (*Into telephone*): Yes, Stuart, all the transport teams are out and I've got as many people as I can still canvassing. No, John's not here. He's out with the sound truck. I couldn't stop him. Factories and polling stations, I think. Yes, I'll keep in touch.

The end of this conversation is interrupted by Peter Chapman who is rummaging in the desk drawers.

CHAPMAN: Where the hell are those research reports?

ANNIE (*Still into telephone*): Yes, I'll tell John.

CHAPMAN (*As Annie puts the telephone down*): Annie, have you seen the ALCO attitude surveys?

ANNIE : Those what?

CHAPMAN: The research reports.

ANNIE: Yes. One of the canvassers borrowed them. His brother runs a couple of businesses and he thought some of the stuff in there would be useful.

CHAPMAN: You're damn right it would. He'd better bring them back.

ANNIE (*Not really very worried*): Oh, I'm sure he will. Look, Peter, can you go over to Allen Road School and find out how it's going there?

CHAPMAN: If you say so. But see about those reports, Annie, it's important.

The telephone rings and Annie picks it up.

ANNIE (*Into telephone*): John Killane's Committee Rooms. Yes, just a moment. Peter, it's for you.

46

Chapman takes the telephone and listens.

CHAPMAN (*Into telephone*): Yes? Oh, hello, Inspector. How many? That's not funny. No, you did right to tell me. Yes, I know. He's got enough on his plate at the moment. Thank you.

Chapman depresses the receiver, raises it and dials quickly talking to Annie as he does so.

CHAPMAN: That was the police in London. They play dirty up here, don't they? If I needed to frighten two old women and two kids to get into Parliament, I think I'd shoot myself first (*Speaks into telephone.*) George. This is Peter. I've just had the police on. There have been eight intercepted calls. Now they've started on special-delivery letters, would you believe? Get over to John's house now. Just get there and stay there. (*He puts the phone down, moves to the door, his face showing disgust.*) And away we go to the Allen Road Primary School to see the democratic process in its full purity.

19

Interior. Labour Committee Rooms. Day.

There is the same air of controlled activity here but a good deal more confidence. Brodie is reassuring a tired Lowery as he and Lambert sit round the table drinking tea and going through a pile of newspapers.

BRODIE: The Press reports are pretty good. About even between you and Killane.

LAMBERT: I notice none of them came up with the dirt on Killane's divorce.

BRODIE: Most of them know it, anyway. His wife was a drunk who kept disappearing and he stood it for four years. Otherwise no judge would have given him custody of two children. I wonder why he didn't bring them up here. Little girls, twins. Should have been good for a few votes.

LOWERY: Prefers to fight his own battles. I'm just as glad about that, too.

LAMBERT: Alan, you're a nice man but politics isn't a nice business. You know what the last Tory candidate said to me? 'You're not a gentleman.' And I'm bloody glad I'm not. This business is too important for gentlemen. My father walked 150 miles from Wales and got a job labouring in Birmingham. He left the valleys in time but I've got a lot of uncles who didn't. And I go there once a year and I look at them and I listen to them and I want to take my hands to every true-blue bloody coal owner and his true-blue bloody descendants.

BRODIE: Times have changed a bit, Cliff.

LAMBERT: Oh, we've tried to change 'em, Sam. And the fat bellies who run this country now want us to think times have changed. I don't think they have. Not as much as they should. Not as much as I want them to change. Why else would I be working a seventy-hour week for a lousy £1,000 a year.

BRODIE (*Drily*): The Labour Party's always had its share of evangelists.

LAMBERT: You used to be one. I remember when you played politics like you used to play Rugby League. Put your head down and go. And leave blood after you. If Killane gets in, you're going to have to do it again.

BRODIE: If. Then I will.

20

Exterior. Polling Station. Night.

Film sequence.

The last voters are leaving the school and a voting officer comes out after them. He looks at his watch, picks up the wooden signpost marked 'Polling Station', takes it inside, closes the doors behind him.

21

Interior. Killane's hotel room. Night.

Stuart Walker and Annie Mackinnon are checking off a marked register against the piles of cards delivered by the voluntary workers from the Polling Stations.

Peter Chapman is fast asleep on the bed and Killane is staring out of the window.

ANNIE (*Quietly to Walker*): Doesn't look very good at the moment. If anything, we're about a thousand down on last time.

WALKER: What we expected. Early to tell. I can't work it out though. There's no pattern.

Killane turns from the window.

KILLANE: There's not likely to be. That's what a random canvass is about. Do it your way, street by street, and you're bound to get a grid. Do it your way plus mine and you'll get a grid plus variables.

WALKER: You sound very confident, John.

KILLANE: Not about the election. Only about the figures. I may not be much of a candidate but figures and probabilities and attitudes are where I live.

49

He looks at Annie Mackinnon, sees the fatigue, the pessimism, goes across to put an arm round her.

KILLANE: And whatever happens there'll be champagne and expensive perfume in buckets and the plushest, longest dinner I can find. Win or lose.

WALKER: If you think I'm wearing perfume at my time of life, you're mistaken. I'll wake Peter up and he can get us a drink now.

CHAPMAN (*Eyes closed, still on the bed*): I'm wide awake. Somebody said drink.

22

Exterior. Polling Station. Night.

Film sequence.

Four men carrying sealed ballot boxes are leaving the school. With them are two uniformed policemen and there is a police car behind the van into which the ballot boxes are being loaded.

23

Interior. Sam Brodie's living room. Night.

Two of the Labour Party stalwarts seen at Lowery's eve-of-poll speech are sitting on the sofa.

Lambert is at Brodie's desk with an electoral register and a pile of party tellers' cards in front of him. Brodie is sitting on the edge of the desk but Lowery is pacing up and down. Elizabeth Brodie has just brought in a tray of tea which she puts on a small table.

LAMBERT: It looks like a big turnout. So we're home and dried. Better practise your vote of thanks to the Returning Officer.

LOWERY: It's practised.

BRODIE: There shouldn't be long to wait now. Then when it happens, you still can't believe it.

LAMBERT: I've seen the successful ones burst into tears. Just like little kids. Mostly Tories though—to be fair.

LOWERY: Different life, different world. It's a bit frightening.

BRODIE: No bed of roses though. Ask her.

This is a reference to Elizabeth who has come up to give a cup of tea to Lowery.

Elizabeth straightens Brodie's tie, runs a finger round his chin.

ELIZABETH: That wasn't much of a shave you had this morning. Ask me what?

BRODIE: The life and times of a Member of Parliament.

ELIZABETH: All of it?

LOWERY: I'd like to know.

ELIZABETH: Start with money. He earns £3,250 a year. And pays tax on it. Leaves us about £2,500. Then he gets £500 a year for a secretary. Secretary. Ha. Last week I typed sixty letters. He spends four or five days a week in London and it costs him ten pounds for a room in lodgings as big as our broom-cupboard. Then there's the money he needs to eat and walk about and buy other people cups of tea with. He gets free telephone and postage—if it's to the constituency. A lot of it isn't. Same with travelling. Free pass from here to London and that's it. What he doesn't get allowed costs us about another £400 a year. We end up with about £1,500. Most Thursdays he comes home sitting up on the late train to save a forty-five shilling boarding-house bill. He does his job well—too well—

and by the time he's finished paying out he's keeping me and three children on what he could earn as a labourer.

NOTE: This was just prior to the recent increase in salaries received by MPs. It is worth noting that in 1964 British MPs were the second-lowest paid in the world. Below them was Pakistan.

BRODIE: All right, Elizabeth. I'm not a work-house case yet.

ELIZABETH: You asked me, love. So I told him. I just hope Mrs Lowery's a good manager.

Sam moves near to Elizabeth, shrugs slightly, puts her arm in his, stands very close to her. He turns and smiles down at her. After a moment, she smiles back, the bitterness fading.

24

Interior. Town Hall. Night.

Film sequence.

There is a long row of tables and the Returning Officer's staff is counting votes. Empty ballot boxes are mounting up in a pile and the Returning Officer walks up and down the row. There are uniformed policemen at the end of the tables and since each candidate is entitled to a counting agent—who may be his election agent—one representative of the people seen on the platform at both Conservative and Labour eve of poll speeches is present.

Annie Mackinnon comes into the room followed by Cliff Lambert. They each go to their respective counting agents.

The Returning Officer, James Henry Curtis, a tall man of about sixty, donnish, quite distinguished, dark-

suited, exuding high-minded bureaucracy, comes across to Annie Mackinnon.

CURTIS: About another twenty minutes, Miss Mackinnon. If you'd like to telephone your candidate.

ANNIE: Thank you very much.

CURTIS: Don't thank me. I'm getting a little old to be Returning Officer and I'd like to get to bed early, too.

He smiles at her, goes across to give the same information to Cliff Lambert.

25

Exterior. Town Hall. Night.

Film sequence.

The party faithful are gathered round the steps bearing their partisan banners, wearing their partisan rosettes. They are the faces seen in the front rows during the speeches. They are the people seen hurrying across the committee rooms, the voluntary workers. There are also the curious, attracted by the spectacle and lingering after the pubs chuck out.

Lowery comes through the group, shakes hands with two or three people, accepts pats on the shoulder. There is a massive confidence that victory is his. Lowery hurries up the steps and into the Town Hall.

26

Interior. Killane's hotel room. Night.

Film sequence.

Killane is leaning against the window looking out at night over the town.

27

Exterior. Andersley. Night.

Film sequence.

This is night over the town. The street lamps, and the roofscape, the hard and sometimes ugly edges of the buildings, the river gleam, the slopes to the escarpment and the farming country.

28

Interior. Killane's hotel room. Night.

Stuart Walker comes into the room.

WALKER: We'd better get down there, John. (*Pessimism overcoming him.*) Never mind. There'll be another day.

Killane nods and turns.

29

Exterior. Town Hall steps. Night.

Film sequence.

The Returning Officer and his assistant come out on to the steps. They form part of an entourage consisting of Brodie, Lowery, Lambert, Killane, Annie Mackinnon, Walker. There will also be civic dignitaries including the Aldermen and Mayor in robes. If possible, a TV set-up filming the proceedings. There will certainly be Press photographers elbowing and shoving and treading on as many innocent bystanders as possible and blinding the incautious with flashbulbs.

RETURNING OFFICER : I, James Henry Curtis, as Returning Officer for Andersley West, announce the results of the by-election, which has taken place on the 23rd November in this year of Our Lord 1971. Alan Herbert Lowery, Labour, 23,117 votes.

He is interrupted by a great burst of cheering. This is a higher figure than the last election.

RETURNING OFFICER : John Killane, Conservative and Unionist, 23,984 votes. Mr John Killane is duly elected Member of Parliament for Andersley West.

There is a hubbub of glee from the Conservatives almost drowned by shouts of 'recount'.

On the Town Hall steps Brodie is grim-faced and Lowery puts his hands over his eyes.

Killane turns to Annie Mackinnon.

KILLANE : The random canvass. The variables on the grid. Nothing beats figures.

Annie is near to tears and Stuart Walker is shaking Killane's hand enthusiastically. Then Walker embraces Annie, beaming, happy, almost jumping up and down.

NOTE : The reactions of both protagonists are for dramatic effect. They will probably have been told the result—formally or informally—before their appearance.

During the hubbub, a man has pushed through the crowd and on to the Town Hall steps. He is carrying the two thick research reports seen previously, whose disappearance has worried Chapman. He talks quickly and urgently and Lambert is seen nodding as he takes the reports and goes inside the Town Hall. No dialogue is audible because of the crowd noise.

Brodie, who has been listening, follows.

30

Interior. Conservative Committee Rooms. Night.

The party workers are happy and deserve to be. There is an excited jabber in the background consisting of phrases like—'I told you we could do it', 'Isn't it marvellous'. 'After twenty years we've thrown the bastards out', *and* 'I wasn't really optimistic', 'Harry made a damn good job of the transport', 'For once we got some decent publicity'. *This need only be background since the attention is focussed on Chapman and Killane who are both sitting on the desk.*

CHAPMAN: I feel like somebody's father-in-law. I've lost a bloody good business partner and gained an MP.

KILLANE: Cheer up, Peter. I'll still be there.

CHAPMAN: On Friday afternoons. I still think you're off the hinge.

They are interrupted by the entry of Lowery and Lambert and Killane turns in some surprise. Lambert is carrying the two thick research documents.

LAMBERT: I'd like to keep this quiet and private, Mr Killane. Have you seen these before? (*He taps the documents under his arm.*)

KILLANE: Yes.

CHAPMAN: Watch it, John.

LAMBERT: Too late. (*To Killane*) Did you make use of these during the election?

KILLANE: Yes, I did.

LAMBERT: How much would you say this research cost to get together?

KILLANE: I can tell you exactly. £11,500.

LAMBERT: And if you spend more than £1,300 on an election, you're guilty of either corrupt or illegal practice and that's what I'm going to charge you with.

You've been an MP for ten minutes, boy. And now you're dead.

During this conversation Stuart Walker and Annie Mackinnon have come up to join the group. On their faces is shock and horror as Lambert and Lowery turn to leave.

Killane's face is impassive.

END OF ACT TWO

ACT THREE

31

Interior. Killane's hotel room. Night.

Killane, Chapman, Walker and Annie Mackinnon have left the committee room celebrations.

Annie Mackinnon is opening telegrams.

CHAPMAN: Nice early result, anyway. We should make most of the late editions.

WALKER: Which could be the worst thing ever if Lambert's right.

KILLANE (*Directly to Walker*): Do you think he's right?

WALKER: I know two things. The rules and how badly you wanted to get in.

The telephone rings and Chapman answers it.

CHAPMAN (*Into telephone*): Yes? No, I'm sorry. Mr Killane can't speak to you at the moment. Illegal practice? Sorry, no comment.

Chapman puts the phone down quickly. Then he changes his mind, takes the receiver from the rest, leaves the phone off the hook.

WALKER: Lambert isn't wasting any time.

KILLANE: He might be.

WALKER: If he's right, you're out. Three weeks of sweat and hope for nothing.

KILLANE: How did we get in?

WALKER: Fine. I admit it. Your system of random

canvass. But using a lot of money for the research. More than we're allowed.

KILLANE: As a candidate I'm entitled to work and that's what I did. At my trade. I took the figures and used them. Not politics, mathematics.

ANNIE: There's a telegram here marked 'urgent'. Will you get in touch with the Legal Department, Central Office, first thing in the morning.

Killane takes the telegram form from her gently, screws it up, throws it in the rough direction of the waste-paper basket.

ANNIE: Aren't you going to do anything?

Walker shakes his head baffled as Killane pulls loose his tie.

KILLANE: Yes. Get some sleep.

32

Interior. The Returning Officer's room. Day.

This should be a small office of the Town Hall, possibly a corner set with a rather old-fashioned desk, in-tray, filing cabinet, rows of books and files.

Curtis is behind the desk, leaning forward, looking very serious.

Brodie, Lambert and Lowery are grouped in front of him and prominent on the desk are the two research volumes.

CURTIS: You realise, Mr Lambert, that this is a very serious allegation indeed.

LAMBERT: I do.

CURTIS: And that any election petition must be presented to the Master of the Queen's Bench accompanied by security for costs of one thousand pounds?

LAMBERT: Yes. I've taken advice.

CURTIS: I hope so. For your sake. And you say that Mr Killane admitted the cost of this research was £11,500?

LAMBERT: In front of both Mr Brodie and Mr Lowery.

At that moment Killane is shown into the room, nods to the group of men in front of the desk, and waits.

CURTIS: Mr Killane, it is alleged that the amount spent by you on the recent by-election is considerably in excess of the £1,300 allowed in this borough under the Representation of the People Act. If proven, this allegation means that the election is negated and that Mr Lowery will become Member of Parliament for Andersley West in your place.

KILLANE: If proven.

LAMBERT: Look at that pile of research, Killane. Everybody knows the money a job like that costs.

KILLANE: I told you how much it cost. The research, that is. The documents are another thing.

CURTIS: This is extremely serious, Mr Killane. Please be specific.

KILLANE: The research was commissioned by a private firm and then made available for publication. Copies can be obtained from the firm itself, two universities, and the Institute of Marketing. At a cost of 35 guineas. (*He takes a piece of paper from his pocket.*) Here is a copy of an invoice for 35 guineas, which will be duly entered in my election expenses. Any candidate or his agent anywhere could have paid the same amount of money for the same set of figures. (*Trace of arrogance now.*) Whether they could have used them or not is something else.

CURTIS: I shall have to check this invoice. If what you say is correct, that would seem to be the end of the matter.

LOWERY: It'll be correct all right. (*To Killane.*) What bothers me is why you didn't say so last night.

BRODIE: I'm with Lowery. (*To Killane*) Bit dirty, Mr Killane.

KILLANE: Yes. Deliberately and personally. Next time, Lambert won't be so quick to tell me that telephone calls threatening my children are a propaganda stunt. And next time the newspaper people he spent half the night telephoning won't trust him quite so much. (*Courteously to the Returning Officer.*) Thank you, Mr Curtis. I'm sorry you've been troubled.

He turns quickly and leaves.

LAMBERT (*Slight smile, rueful*): I walked into that one. But now we know and I won't walk into any more.

BRODIE: Nor me.

LAMBERT: That's good. That's more like it.

The last sentences have a quiet ferocity about them. If Killane wants a personal feud, Lambert and Brodie are more than willing to accommodate him.

33

Interior. Conservative Committee Rooms. Day.

The room is beginning to return to normal. The charts remain on the walls but the billiard table has been cleared and has reverted to its normal function.

Chapman is wandering around with a cue in his hand taking desultory shots.

The desk remains in the corner and Walker and Annie Mackinnon are sitting at this.

CHAPMAN (*The Minnesota Fats Line from 'The Hustler'*): 'Shoot pool, Fast Eddie, shoot pool.'

ANNIE: Don't tell me you have time to go to the pictures.

CHAPMAN: Every Thursday. I put it down in the diary as a creative meeting. With bosoms.

Walker is sitting relaxed on the edge of the desk.

WALKER: It's just beginning to sink in. We did it. All the late nights, all the people giving up spare time. And now it's worth it. Annie, when the association re-forms, it might be a good idea to get on with a membership drive.

ANNIE (*Looking up*): I'm making up district lists now. Let's cash in while everybody's happy and enthusiastic.

CHAPMAN: God, you're a cold-blooded pair. What about the cause and the glory?

ANNIE: That comes later. Bigger membership first.

CHAPMAN: And there's poor old John going round shaking hands and beaming at the party faithful. The Transport Director, the Meetings Director, the insomniacs who ran the District Committee Rooms. At least his gratitude's genuine.

WALKER: So's ours. But the gratitude's useless unless you keep the machine ticking over.

Interior. Hampstead pub. Day.

It is a week-day two days later and the pub is much quieter, the Sunday songsters fled.

Garsfeld and Killane are sitting with Ernest Dewhurst and Sam Brodie.

Garsfeld, despite the surroundings, is extremely businesslike.

GARSFELD: I realise that this is a somewhat unorthodox place to meet, gentlemen, but at this stage I have a short-list of four towns and I'd like to keep discussions informal.

DEWHURST: That's all right, Mr Garsfeld. I've spent thirty years doing business across the table at the Working Men's Club.

Garsfeld has taken three slim folders from his briefcase and gives one to each of the three men.

GARSFELD: This is a rough breakdown of the project. Land, communications, building and utilities. On the last page you'll see the project time. We have to turn money round. That way we show a profit. Politicians understand the hurry. Bureaucrats don't.

BRODIE: We got the point last time, Mr Garsfeld. You expect us to push this through the Ministries and you want Ernest to keep the local council in line.

DEWHURST: We've done some of that before. Of course, I don't know much about the big stuff at the House of Commons.

BRODIE (*Smiling*): Not much, you don't.

KILLANE: And I'm the new boy.

DEWHURST (*With glee*): That's good. So Sam'll get most of the credit and next time we'll have an MP from the proper party.

GARSFELD: That sounds like a private fight. All the information I can give you at the moment is in the folders there. Meet our conditions—or at least do better than the other three towns on the list—and in eight months you'll have a factory estate and 5,000 jobs.

DEWHURST: A game of monopoly with real people.

GARSFELD (*Liking the phrase, smiling*): That's about it. Thank you for your time.

He rises and leaves.

The move leaves Killane isolated and as all the men begin to study the folders given to them by Garsfeld, Brodie and Dewhurst form a separate unit, their heads together over a shared folder.

Killane watches them, very much aware of being the outsider.

35

Interior. Conservative Committee Rooms. Day.

The room has now been fully cleared except for the desk and looks clean and polished and comfortable.

Lambert is standing near the desk looking round the room, sardonically impressed. Walker and Annie Mackinnon are at the desk.

LAMBERT: Long time since I've been in here. Very nice. Vote Tory in comfort. I wish we'd got your sort of affluent subscribers.

ANNIE: You've got the trade union levy instead. The cheques are just as big and the income's a lot more regular. What can we do for you?

LAMBERT: Give your Mr Killane a message. One of my quote newspaper friends has sorted out his mysterious phone calls for him.

WALKER: And you've come to apologise?

LAMBERT: Not me. Not ever. Apologies are the sort of luxury I manage to do without. Results are better.

ANNIE: What about the phone calls?

LAMBERT: A man called Whittaker. Used to live in the big cottage near the Grange. He was dispossessed under a compulsory purchase order.

WALKER: Then he's telephoning the wrong man.

LAMBERT: He doesn't think so. It was under the last Tory government. One of their road schemes. He kept going to London but nobody would see him. Then out.

WALKER: So now we'll have a word with the police.

LAMBERT: No need for that. You don't need the police.

WALKER: I think I might have to insist on it.

LAMBERT: No. You might need police where you come from, Mr Walker, but this is Andersley. Most of the time we run our own business. Whittaker's got enough trouble.

He looks at Annie—who nods. Walker shrugs, knowing that he has lost the argument.

Lambert turns to leave and speaks as he moves to the door.

LAMBERT: Funny thing. Whittaker used to vote Conservative.

36

Interior. Hampstead pub. Day.

Dewhurst is finishing his drink. He folds the rather elegant document given to him by Garsfeld and puts it in a side pocket. Brodie and Killane are still sitting at the table.

DEWHURST: I'm off then. See you at the weekend, Sam. Perhaps you as well, Mr Killane—if we're lucky.

BRODIE (*Smiling*): Do you need any help, Ernest?

DEWHURST: I shouldn't think so. (*Grinning.*) Not yet.

Dewhurst ambles out, very much the provincial in the big city with his own strange brand of sureness.

Killane looks at Brodie, slightly puzzled.

BRODIE (*In explanation*): He gets three weeks' holiday a year. For the last twenty years he's taken them in odd days on council business. So when he gets down here he has a good meal and sees how the strip clubs are getting on. What he does after that is his own business.

KILLANE: He doesn't seem to make much of a secret of it.

BRODIE: Oh, no. Not him. He doesn't have to. Andersley's narrow-minded but that doesn't bother Ernest. It's his patch and he runs most of it. You'll see.

At that moment the barman comes from behind the bar. He is carrying an ice bucket in which there is an opened bottle of champagne and a tray with two glasses into which champagne has already been poured.

Killane looks up towards the prosperous man behind the bar who is evidently the publican. He inclines his head in acknowledgement, lifts his glass.

BRODIE: Compliments of the management. Very nice. I suppose I should congratulate you as well.

KILLANE: But you're not going to.

BRODIE: No. Why be hypocritical?

KILLANE: Fair enough.

BRODIE: What are you in this for?

KILLANE: In what?

BRODIE (*Gesturing at the champagne*): This. The MP game.

KILLANE: You want a speech or the truth?

BRODIE: I'll probably get a bit of each.

KILLANE: All right. The fast answer is I don't know. Why I'm in this, I mean. How can I? Until I've been in it.

BRODIE (*Touch of contempt*): Another hit-and-run artist. Try anything once. If you don't know why you're in it now, you never will.

KILLANE: Give me a chance to find out.

BRODIE: If it's power, forget it. Nye Bevan said once that he thought power was on the local council. Then he thought it was on the county council. Then he thought it was in Parliament. Then he thought it was in the Cabinet. He did the lot and then he said he was still looking. He still didn't know where the power was.

KILLANE: Why are you in it?

BRODIE: Because somebody's got to be. Because they want to. And not for themselves. It's a bit like a bloody lawn. You plant it, water it, and hope. And then you're twenty years older and there's just one bit of green in one corner.

KILLANE: The tomorrow business. That's not good enough. Not for me.

BRODIE: No. Not for you.

KILLANE: I was elected.

BRODIE: You beat nothing. A school teacher. He meant well but that's not enough either.

KILLANE: I might just have been the better candidate.

BRODIE: Trickier, anyway. That's why I don't like you or trust you and that's why I won't drink your champagne. Because your reasons aren't good enough and I wonder how long you'll last. (*He rises, a big man, the power showing now.*) Not very long if I have anything to do with it.

Brodie walks from the pub leaving Killane there.

Killane pushes Brodie's full glass of champagne to one side of the tray, lifts his own, sips it reflectively.

[*Credits*]

Play Two

WHO'S BEEN EATING MY PORRIDGE?

Cast

JOHN KILLANE	*Michael Gambon*
SAM BRODIE	*Colin Blakely*
ANNIE MACKINNON	*Joanna Van Gyseghem*
CLIFF LAMBERT	*Richard Hampton*
PETER CHAPMAN	*William Gaunt*
JOE GARSFELD	*Alex Scott*
HARRY KINNERSLEY	*George H. Malpas*
JOE DELANEY	*Eric Thompson*
SIR JOSEPH CONRAN	*Bill Owen*
MINISTER	*Bernard Archard*
MRS JOAN EXTON	*Kathleen Byron*
JANIE KILLANE	*Hilary Dwyer*
SAM BRODIE'S DAUGHTER, ELIZABETH	*Joanne Cookson*

Non-speaking

Policeman in uniform; Chief Whip; MP sponsoring Killane; barman in House of Commons Strangers' Bar; assorted MPs of both parties; some visitors to the House; quartet of elderly gentlemen hibernating in Andersley Conservative Club; members of the Andersley Conservative Association including seven or eight formidable and matronly ladies; barman at Andersley Conservative Club; uniformed House of Commons messenger.

Interiors

1. Sam Brodie's Parliamentary surgery which also serves as Cliff Lambert's office
2. Strangers' Bar, House of Commons
3. Conservative Club, Andersley
4. Section of British Rail dining car. All night scenes
5. Conservative Committee Rooms, Andersley
6. Section of book-lined corridor leading to library at House of Commons
7. Section of backbench of House of Commons—backdrop only

Exteriors

1. St Stephen's entrance to the Palace of Westminster
2. Exterior Labour Party Office, Andersley
3. Canal bank—Sam Brodie and daughter

ACT ONE

Titles

1

Exterior. House of Commons. Day.

Film sequence.

This is the members' entrance to the Palace of Westminster.

A taxi-cab is seen drawing to the kerb. John Killane gets out, pays the driver, stands on the pavement looking up at the façade and the building where he has just signed on to work for the next four years.

As Killane stands on the kerb, four or five press photographers arranged by the efficient party machine move in and there is a flurry of flash-bulbs. For a moment, some of Killane's elation is replaced by nervousness.

He walks slowly into the gate and a policeman moves forward, slowly, diplomatically, and there is a touch of pride about Killane as he prepares to announce his credentials for entry.

Then the Tory Chief Whip and Killane's other sponsor —a senior Tory MP from a nearby constituency—are seen as they hurry forward to meet Killane.

2

Exterior. Labour Party Office. Andersley. Day.

These premises are a converted shop in an area of Andersley that has seen better days. It is a double-fronted shop and one window is occupied by standard party posters, most of them dating from the last election and featuring photographs of party notables.

The other window exhibits some samples of the frustrated pavement artist urge in Cliff Lambert's character.

There are blackboards, neatly chalked and lettered outlining to the citizens the latest examples of Tory perfidy.

They read:
'More' under the Tories
'More Homeless'
'More Jobless'
'More Hopeless'

Another blackboard reads:
'Who Steals Free Milk From Your Children?'
'Who Charges More For Your Medicine?'
'Who Panders to Profits, Not People?'
The Tories.

A man is seen walking up to the office and hesitating, making up his mind to go in.

He looks at a notice on the door. This reads: 'Your Labour MP, Sam Brodie, is here today from 10–1. He is here to answer your questions, help with your problems.'

The man is Harry Kinnersley. He is about fifty-five, neatly dressed in dark-blue suit, boots, collar and tie, but in his hand there is a cloth cap. He is a skilled toolmaker who has been out of work for nearly two years. By now the routine of going in any door to ask

74

for anything is firmly established. He straightens his tie, squares his shoulders, buttons his jacket. Then he looks up and down the street and goes into the office.

3

Interior. Sam Brodie's Surgery. Day.

This is a cubby-hole of a room enclosed by matchboard partitioning. It serves as both Sam Brodie's surgery and Cliff Lambert's official agent's office. There is a desk, a chair, a filing cabinet. There are three photographs on the wall. One is of the Labour Cabinet which included Attlee, Bevan, Bevin and Gaitskell. Another is of the Cabinet which included Wilson, Callaghan, Jenkins, Barbara Castle. The third is of the Andersley Rugby League team with a younger Sam Brodie third from the left and with the remains of a black eye.

Cliff Lambert is sitting on the edge of the desk, talking to Sam Brodie as he gives him a folder.

LAMBERT: Old Mrs Parkinson. I told her you'd see to it. The eviction order gives her a month. I've had a word with the Housing Officer but he's this new chap. The one with the college degree who thinks everybody should live in a tent.

BRODIE: We've always known we'd have to do something about him. This might be the time.

There is a tap on the door and Harry Kinnersley comes in, quite diffidently.

KINNERSLEY: Morning, Mr Brodie. I'll come back if you're busy.

BRODIE (*Rising, obviously pleased to see the other man*): Just waiting for customers. How are you, Harry? Nice to see you.

KINNERSLEY: Not bad, Mr Brodie. I wanted a word.

He glances at Lambert, who is experienced enough to slide off the desk and unobtrusively out of the room. Brodie, who has risen to shake hands with Kinnersley, leans round to push the door closed.

BRODIE: Where did you get the *Mr* Brodie? It's been Sam for thirty years. And when you used to borrow tools from my father, it was *young* Sam.

KINNERSLEY (*Slightly ironic and without any trace of self-pity*): Bit of a habit now. When you've been out of work two years, every time you stand in front of a desk you say 'Mister'.

BRODIE: Not this desk. And I didn't know it was that bad.

KINNERSLEY: If it wasn't, I wouldn't be here. I've tried the Labour, I've written off to advertisements. I've asked and I've pestered.

BRODIE: The old story, Harry. Sit down. I'll do what I can but there's a lot of good toolmakers out of work.

Kinnersley sits down.

KINNERSLEY: I know. I'm not bothered about tool-making. What good's a trade if there's no work for it? Anything'll do. Night watchman, cleaner. So long as there's wages on the table on a Friday.

BRODIE: You worked for Conran's for twenty years.

KINNERSLEY: It's him I want you to see. If you can. You know him. He's chairman of this lot. (*Gestures round at the Party Office.*) I'll take anything he's got.

BRODIE: I can do that for you, Harry. Today, if you like.

KINNERSLEY: I'd be glad if you could. (*He rises to leave.*)

BRODIE: How's the lad?

KINNERSLEY: Doing well. Foreman at the wagon sheds. As long as that lasts.

BRODIE: Safe as houses. That's one pension you can count on. There'll always be wagon sheds in Andersley.

KINNERSLEY: I'm not so sure. Anyway, thank you very much, Mr Brodie. I'll call back. (*He bobs his head in a quite uncharacteristic gesture and leaves quickly.*)

Brodie sits back in his chair, rubs a hand over his face. This is a man he has known for a long time and he does not like the new subservience, the erosion of dignity.

Cliff Lambert comes back into the room, a look of inquiry on his face.

LAMBERT: Job?

Brodie nods.

LAMBERT: Him and a lot of others. At least he makes thirty bob a week clearing glasses at the Conservative Club.

BRODIE: That's not tradesman's work. (*His own pride in craft shows in this.*)

LAMBERT: It's thirty bob a week.

BRODIE: And he kept calling me 'Mister'. I shouldn't think Harry Kinnersley's called anybody 'Mister' since he left school. He used to borrow my father's tools to make lofts for his racing pigeons. (*Softly, reflectively, bitterly.*) And he kept calling me 'Mister'.

Lambert shrugs. At this moment there is nothing that either of them can do or say.

LAMBERT: What about Garsfeld and his new factory estate? There's five thousand jobs.

BRODIE: If we can get the terms right. If the government can get into the act.

4

Interior. Strangers' Bar. House of Commons. Day.

The distinctive and impressive feature is the fact that French windows lead on to the terrace of the house and it is possible to turn and see the riverscape over the terrace parapet, watch the boats go by and feel isolated from the Westminster Bridge bustle.

The other distinctive feature is the television set mounted above the bar which is closed-circuit and announces the debate in progress and the name of the speaker currently on his feet. The notice remains static in the same way that announcements at airports are shown.

This television screen is the first thing seen.

It reads: 'Limitation of Fisheries. The Rt Hon Frederick Peart. Lab, Workington'.

John Killane is seen at the bar, looking at the screen, on his own, very much the new boy. There are five or six other MPs in groups and in conversation.

It is evident that this is the Strangers' Bar as another MP leads a middle-aged woman and her adolescent daughter through it and out on to the showpiece of the terrace.

A man comes into the room, glances round to see if any of his cronies are present, then sees Killane and goes up to him.

The man is Joe Delaney, Labour MP for Gallowside, a constituency in one of the areas which are called depressed in normal language and special development areas in the nomenclature of the Department of Trade and Industry. These are places like Clydeside, Tyneside, the Rhondda, the scabbed regions that the Industrial Revolution despoiled and forgot.

Delaney is about forty, medium-built, fast-moving, a quiet and dangerous aggression about him. This is not personal but reflects his concern for the area he serves. His accent should be modified northern with just a hint of Durham in it. He is literate and articulate, not very popular even in his own party, very much a man on his own. There are perhaps half a dozen like him in the House and they can be extremely useful to the Party leaders because they can and do express views savagely against the Party line which need expressing and then be faintly denounced as rebels. They are nevertheless welcome and necessary.

DELANEY: You're the new boy, then. Sam Brodie's fresh sparring partner.

KILLANE: That's right. John Killane.

DELANEY: Here early like most of them and straight into the Strangers' Bar. Picking up some Dutch courage before the Chief Whip leads you down the aisle to take your little oath of allegiance.

KILLANE (*Lifting his glass*): Picking up Vitamin C. This is straight orange juice.

DELANEY: Oh, very bright. I'll take a beer off you.

Killane smiles, pushes change across the counter, and the barman—used to Delaney's habits—opens and pours a bottle of brown ale as the dialogue goes on.

DELANEY: So you're going to reform Andersley and the world.

KILLANE: Andersley, I hope. The rest may take a little time.

The tone is slightly mocking, a reaction to Delaney's own approach.

DELANEY: They reckon you've got an unemployment problem in Andersley.

KILLANE: That's right.

DELANEY: Son, they don't know they're born. I come from Gallowside. I've got generations of unemployment. When a baby's born where I come from, the first thing they do is tattoo a national assistance number on him.

KILLANE: I've heard of it. And Tyneside. And the Clyde. And the Rhondda.

DELANEY: That's good. So I'll give you a piece of advice in return for the beer. Any government handouts, I want them. Because I'm talking about malnutrition not just keeping up the payments on the car. I'm talking about good men cadging fag-ends for ten years.

KILLANE: They might need help in Andersley as well.

DELANEY: With *only* eight per cent unemployment? They don't need help. They need a thanksgiving service. Just remember it, son, any begging bowls in this place are marked for my part of the world. And I'll stop you getting them. So don't go buying Garsfeld any fancy meals. You'll be wasting your money. Sam Brodie knows that already. Ask him. (*He turns to see two men in the entrance to the Strangers' Bar.*) There's your sponsor and the Chief Whip. You'd better go and genuflect.

As Delaney drifts away, two other people enter the bar. One of them is a woman and when he sees her Killane shows shock, surprise and anger.

She turns to her companion, elderly, related, aristocratic, kisses him, walks to Killane.

The woman is Janie Killane, John Killane's ex-wife, the mother of his two children. She is about thirty-two, honey blonde, a striking angular beauty, dressed with expensive simplicity. She is unstable, unreliable, neurotic, ex-alcoholic. For this reason a judge awarded John Killane custody of the children. Janie is extremely intelligent but misapplies it. The world's best

*finishing schools have created in Janie an attractive
and dangerous human stiletto.*

KILLANE: What do you think you're doing?

JANIE: Uncle Charles smuggled me in through the
House of Lords.

KILLANE: Smuggle yourself out again.

JANIE: My, we are peevish this morning. Nervous?

KILLANE: Busy.

JANIE: As usual.

KILLANE: Well?

JANIE: Darling, it is really very simple. I have come
along to watch my ex-husband—now the distinguished
John Killane MP—make his debut in public life.
How sweet of you . . . Tomato juice please.

KILLANE: Tomato juice?

JANIE: Don't worry dear, I am still very, very much
off the sauce.

KILLANE: That's one relief.

JANIE: So you can run along. And don't trip over the
Speaker's robe or anything.

KILLANE: Don't be here when I get back.

JANIE: Of course not dear. I shall be applauding from
afar.

5

Interior. Conservative Club. Night.

*This is a Conservative Club in its old sense and dates
from about 1908. It is not one of the newer breed
where billiards, bingo and lack of political affiliation*

predominate. Its interior reflects a quiet and old-fashioned opulence and its membership includes most of the town's money.

There is a surfeit of dark wood and leather but there are also fresh flowers and the bright covers of current magazines, a good deal of well-polished brass and the patterned carpet is purpose-woven Axminster.

There is a fireplace and a raised edge-seat surrounding it with padded leather over brightly polished bars. Prominent are the customary two portraits—HM the Queen and Winston Churchill.

A man with a glass of whisky in his hand is standing in the traditional haunch-warming posture in front of the fire. He is well-dressed in a dark tweed suit and wears, in addition to this, an expression of amused contempt as he glances around the room.

The man is Sir Joseph Conran who is Chairman of the local Labour Party. He is small and whippet-like, used to authority. He is probably one of the richest men in Andersley after taking his father's small engineering business and expanding it. He remembers —and is proud of—his own origins and his socialism and, despite the money, is sincere. He and Cliff Lambert are close but incongruous friends though Sam Brodie is not too well-liked by him.

He looks up as Sam Brodie comes into the room and lifts a hand in greeting.

Two or three retired gentlemen glance up disapprovingly from armchairs in the corner. The opposition is not welcome and should know its place.

CONRAN: Hello, Sam.

BRODIE: Funny place to find you, Sir Joseph. I didn't think the Conservative Club was much on your beat.

CONRAN: Or on yours. We should get a photograph taken. Still—business is business. What'll you have?

BRODIE: Nothing, thanks. Just a chat.

CONRAN: Well, that saves money.

BRODIE: You know Harry Kinnersley?

CONRAN (*Proud of an encyclopaedic memory about his workpeople*): Toolmaker. Worked for us for twenty-three years. Had to lay him off two years ago when we started sub-contracting. If he wants a job, can't do it. We've closed the department.

BRODIE: Any job. Watchman, cleaner.

CONRAN: You're a Labour MP, not a Labour Exchange.

BRODIE: And you're Chairman of the Labour Party here. That's why Kinnersley came to me.

CONRAN: Not like you, Sam—The Old Pals Act.

BRODIE: Not like Kinnersley either. But when you've been looking for two years, you use what you've got.

CONRAN: If I were you, I'd keep out of it. Otherwise, you'll waste a lot of time. If I take Kinnersley back, how many more will you get joining the queue for old times' sake?

BRODIE: As many as I can fix up.

CONRAN: You've got better things to do. Be reasonable. We don't need men. It's nothing to do with politics. It's business. Because we're on the same side, that's no reason to ask you to pull strings.

BRODIE (*Persisting*): Think about it.

CONRAN: No need. He's out of work and so are a lot of others. I employ 800 men and that's all I've got use for. If I tried to settle the unemployment problem on my own, I'd go bankrupt. And who does that help? Sorry, Sam. (*Thinks about something, surprised.*) You know that's the first time you've ever asked me a favour.

BRODIE: I'd better change the subject while I'm in front. What are you up to in this place?

CONRAN: Business. I'm supposed to see a chap called Garsfeld. This new Tory bright spark Killane fixed it up.

At the mention of Garsfeld and Killane there is an immediate suspicion on Brodie's part—both political and personal.

BRODIE: It's not really a change of subject at all then. I'd better wait.

6

Interior. British Rail dining car. Night.

Garsfeld, Killane and Peter Chapman have just finished their meal and coffee has been poured. Killane is busy with documents and lists of figures as the other two talk.

GARSFELD: That was a pretty good piece of pie. Like the one I had last week.

CHAPMAN: Probably the same one. I have this theory about eating on trains, Mr Garsfeld. They cook enough meals to last for a year and serve what's left on New Year's Eve when nobody's in a condition to complain. Every time I travel, it's a moveable New Year's Eve.

GARSFELD: Then why travel?

CHAPMAN: My contribution to the democratic process. I'm just a humble statistician trying to run a market research agency with a lunatic partner who's decided to go into Parliament. The only time I can nail him for decisions, policy and planning is when he's rushing back to his constituency to help re-write the short and simple annals of the poor.

GARSFELD: Gray's *Elegy*.

CHAPMAN: Only the last bit. The rest is Chapman's complaint.

KILLANE (*To Garsfeld*): Don't let him give you indigestion, Mr Garsfeld. He enjoys being martyred. (*He packs his documents into a briefcase.*)

CHAPMAN: Pass me an arrow. John, we *do* need half a day this weekend. Otherwise my next market research job will be looking for one.

GARSFELD: I could tell you where *not* to go. Gallowside, for one. And the places like it. That's real soup-kitchen country. (*To Killane*) How's your new job, Johnny?

KILLANE: Slow. Lost. Bit frustrating. Very new boy at a very old school. They still have red sashes for swords on the coat-hangers and you work out of a locker about the size of an orange box. Ten MPs to one office. Kick off at 9.30 with mail and the papers, finish at 10.30 when the House rises. And then wonder what you've done in the middle except listen and walk round and chat. About 340 seats for 630 people. When it's full, the place looks like a Classic Cinema during an Ingmar Bergman season. Only noisier. There's an 83-foot periscope so the man down below in the air-conditioning chamber can check on whether you're comfortable. In the afternoon, the sun shines on the Opposition and they wave their order papers and the man twiddles a dial and then it's cooler and most of the Opposition think it's an Act of God. A lot of rules —some written, some not—and once you know the rules, you've got the system where you want it. I hope.

GARSFELD: I hope so, too. If I'm going to spend six million pounds in Andersley, you'd better.

CHAPMAN: Oh, Andersley's different. John's all right there. Mixture of pop-star, scapegoat, influence wielder and somebody to open jumble sales.

KILLANE: Andersley's not that different from Westminster. One controls the other. And *vice-versa.* Sort of tightrope act where you keep turning round to face different directions.

GARSFELD: You'd better get to the end where they take the decisions, Johnny.

KILLANE: That's why we're all here.

GARSFELD: But how much can you really *do*? That's what bothers me. How much?

Killane looks out of the dining car window into the night and his own reflection. There is no real answer to Garfeld's question about how much an MP can really influence decisions.

7

Interior. Conservative Committee Rooms. Night.

This is the room used as the Conservative election headquarters in the first play and has now resumed its function as a very comfortable billiards and card room.

Two respectable one-armed bandits have been brought back into the room and the notice board previously used for election exhortations is now covered with announcements of committee meetings, raffles and fund appeals.

Two members of the local association are playing billiards and three or four more are watching them.

Annie Mackinnon uses this room quite a lot although her office is along the hall. It is by being seen here and talking and listening that she can operate most effectively as agent to John Killane.

There is a wall telephone near the door—the coin-slot variety—and Annie Mackinnon is talking into this telephone, holding a folder in her hand.

ANNIE (*Into telephone*): All right, John. If you say so. I've been standing by. Yes, I know the train was late. There's one urgent case. Man called Perkins. Industrial injury. He's lost an arm. I'll leave the papers at your hotel. The rest can wait. Tomorrow morning? Yes, that's fine.

At the end of this conversation Cliff Lambert has come into the room and is looking warily around.

LAMBERT: Hello, Miss Mackinnon. Sam Brodie's supposed to be here. Have you seen him?

ANNIE: Not this Conservative Club. The other one.

LAMBERT: Oh. Tycoon's corner. I'd better get down there.

ANNIE: I wouldn't. We're just agents. And Garsfeld's big fish.

LAMBERT (*Mocking*): Know your place. The old Tory motto.

ANNIE: Or common politeness. It could be private.

LAMBERT (*Disbelievingly*): M'm. (*He turns to go.*)

ANNIE: Do you know anything about an accident case? Alan Perkins?

LAMBERT: Yes. Conveyor mechanic at Crabtree's. Non-union shop. So what do you expect? If you sign on for scab conditions, it's one of the penalties. Not much we can do.

ANNIE: I don't think Perkins would have joined a union anyway. He doesn't believe in them.

LAMBERT: Then he shouldn't be so bloody careless. I'd better go.

As he says this, Peter Chapman breezes into the room, right hand held up in a clenched fist.

CHAPMAN: Heil Ted.

ANNIE: Hello, Peter.

LAMBERT: I thought we'd seen the last of him.

CHAPMAN: Well, if it's not the old hot-gospeller himself. Two acres and a cow all round.

LAMBERT: And you're still licensed clown to the Andersley Conservatives.

CHAPMAN: Only at weekends, Taff. Rest of the time I earn a surtax salary so you boys can afford to plot how to take it off me.

Lambert makes a noise of disgust and leaves.

As he does so, Chapman raises his left hand with the fist clenched.

CHAPMAN: Heil Harold.

ANNIE: Traitor.

CHAPMAN (*Reasonably*): How can I be a traitor? I don't belong to either lot.

ANNIE: What are you doing here then?

CHAPMAN: Only way to get any real work out of my partner. 'I want a day,' I said, very tough. 'Or else your business is going to fall to pieces,' I said. 'See my agent,' he said. So I've come to take you to dinner.

ANNIE: John said you'd had a meal on the train.

CHAPMAN: He was using the word loosely. Besides I can eat two dinners. Easily.

ANNIE (*A show of reluctance but willing to be persuaded*): I should do some more work. John's got constituency problems as well.

CHAPMAN: I could turn into one of them. Just a simple London boy in your big northern town. Every pub I go into, it's full of Labour supporters ten foot tall and I say: 'Have a drink; vote for Killane'—force of habit—and they hit me between the eyes. That's why you've got to come with me.

ANNIE: They might hit me between the eyes.

CHAPMAN: You're younger than I am. And John's going to be busy until midnight. He said so. Come on.

ANNIE: We could go to the Linden. If you like veal.

CHAPMAN: Love veal. Very good for the gonads.

ANNIE: Mr Chapman. I'm beginning to suspect your motives.

CHAPMAN (*Taking her arm*): You needn't. They're exactly what you think they are.

She laughs and they leave, Chapman pausing only to deliver another salute to the billiards players.

CHAPMAN: Heil Ted.

8

Interior. Conservative Club. Night.

Garsfeld has been introduced to Sir Joseph Conran who is on the business end of a firm gladiatorial hand-shake.

GARSFELD: Glad to know you, sir.

Garsfeld retains Conran's hand and turns to Brodie and Killane who are standing next to him.

GARSFELD: We'll arrange the ground rules on some sordid financial details and join you later.

CONRAN: Don't waste much time, do you, Mr Garsfeld?

GARSFELD: Not when it's money.

An arm goes round Conran's shoulder and he is led away.

Brodie turns immediately to Killane.

BRODIE: Killane, the Garsfeld project covers all of Andersley. Not just your bit. Any more surprise visits,

I want to know about them. Don't pull the Tory mafia on me. Not in Andersley. It won't work.

KILLANE (*Contemptuously*): God, the jargon. Who's Garsfeld talking to? Chairman of the local Labour Association. Why? He wants to buy a piece of land. Big conspiracy.

BRODIE: If Garsfeld's here, I still like to know.

KILLANE: Annie Mackinnon's been trying to ring your agent or your home since four o'clock. If you want to keep in touch, try leaving somebody near a telephone. Elementary business rules.

BRODIE: Which you're good at. Wait till you get to the political ones.

Conran and Garsfeld are seen on a sofa with their heads together.

CONRAN: I don't know so much. We might need that land for another production line.

GARSFELD: Please don't try to snow me. I've checked. If you expand anywhere, it'll be east. Unless you turn your whole factory round.

CONRAN (*Grinning*): That's possible. Especially when you own the factory.

GARSFELD: I need a nine-acre strip for access roads. You've got an option on it and I want to buy the option. Just give me a price.

CONRAN (*Rising*): I'll think about it. Let's go and get the gossip from Westminster.

They talk as they walk across to rejoin Brodie and Killane and the end of the conversation includes the two MPs.

CONRAN: What about eight thousand?

GARSFELD: I can live with that.

CONRAN: An acre.

GARSFELD (*Exploding a little*): Come on. This isn't Alaska. I'm not buying a goldfield, Mr Conran.

CONRAN: *Sir* Joseph Conran. If you don't mind. (*Mildly.*) It's not much but it's all I've got to show for thirty years of work and a lot of money put into the Labour Party.

KILLANE: You were lucky, Sir Joseph. Just in time. Only the Tories hand out political honours now.

CONRAN: More fools us. A handle to your name isn't much to expect for a lot of unpaid slog.

GARSFELD: With the price you charge for land, who needs handles?

CONRAN: Or competition. Which is what you might give me if you come to Andersley.

KILLANE: It beats stagnation. Which is what we've got now.

CONRAN: Don't make speeches at me, lad. Save 'em for next week. Goodnight, Sam. Goodnight, Mr Garsfeld.

Conran leaves and Garsfeld glances admiringly after him.

GARSFELD: Tough old rooster. If he's a socialist, so was Ivan the Terrible.

BRODIE: Except that Conran's proved it a lot of times. Any result yet, Mr Garsfeld?

GARSFELD: Sure, the other surveys are all in. We're down to finance. I can go to a special development area—like Gallowside—get building grants, loans, big tax allowances. And trouble. These people have been screwed ever since the industrial revolution and I don't want history getting its own back on me. So they're out. My principals are opting for an inter- mediate area. Not as many incentives but we still get a twenty-five-per cent building grant and tax allowances on construction. In real money, we could qualify for a handout of about three-quarters of a million.

BRODIE: There's only one thing wrong with that. Andersley's not an intermediate area.

GARSFELD: Make it one.

KILLANE: Not as easy as that. It's up to the Minister and his advisors.

GARSFELD: So lean a little. That's why we're talking. That's how it's done. Three-quarters of a million, gentlemen. Quite an incentive and all legal. The pork barrel's there. With the lid off. Get your fist in it.

KILLANE: It's definite then. You'll come to Andersley.

GARSFELD: On those terms, yes. The town gets five thousand jobs and you get covered in glory.

BRODIE: If we can persuade the Department of Trade and Industry to zone Andersley as intermediate.

GARSFELD: That's it, gentlemen. If not (*Shrugs, turns one hand palm down*) it's been nice knowing you. See you at the hotel, John.

Killane nods as Garsfeld leaves and he and Brodie sit on the padded surround in front of the fire, side by side, thoughtfully, not speaking.

As they sit there, Harry Kinnersley comes up. He is wearing a steward's white jacket now and looks uncomfortable in it. He holds a tray on which he is collecting glasses from a nearby table.

KINNERSLEY: Hello, Mr Brodie.

BRODIE: Hello, Harry.

Brodie watches as Harry Kinnersley moves off down the room. Kinnersley is wearing working boots and looks clumsy and ill-at-ease in a job he is not used to.

END OF ACT ONE

ACT TWO

9

Interior. Library Corridor. House of Commons. Day.

This is a book-lined corridor, leading to the library, which is used as a sort of promenade for informal discussions. The protocol observed is quite strict and it is one of the unwritten rules that no conversation here should be interrupted. The value of this is that the corridor forms a venue where an MP can bring up problems informally with a minister or a Whip or one of his colleagues without being subjected to the button-holing which is frequent elsewhere.

The Minister for Trade and Industry is walking along the corridor with a senior civil servant.

The Minister is about fifty-five, quite tall and going slightly bald, an air of sharp academic distinction about him as well as a massively urbane politeness.

The senior civil servant—from the Department of Trade and Industry—is a woman, Mrs Joan Exton. She is about fifty, tall, smartly dressed in a good couturier matching coat and dress and carrying an elegant briefcase. There is an air of authority about her which reflects the intelligence necessary to acquire her present high rank. She is widowed, a career civil servant, dedicated to her job.

MINISTER: Good of you to come over, Mrs Exton. I know how busy you are at the Department.

MRS EXTON: Not at all, Minister, I enjoy the walk. And it's not far.

93

MINISTER: Sam Brodie's tabled a private question on Andersley.

MRS EXTON: So's John Killane.

MINISTER: Brodie got in first. He would, of course. Knows the ropes. How valid is Andersley's case for intermediate zoning?

MRS EXTON: Valid. But not as valid as some.

MINISTER: In that case, it's perhaps as well I'm answering Brodie and not Killane. No point in discouraging your own keen young backbenchers. (*Looks down at a slip of paper in his hand and reads as Mrs Exton takes a folder from her briefcase.*) 'Is the Minister aware of the steeply rising unemployment figures for Andersley and will he take steps to declare Andersley an intermediate area with the consequent incentives to industry that this implies?'

Mrs Exton gives him the folder.

MRS EXTON: The answer's in there, Minister. Any zoning of area and incentives to industry has to be judged in a country-wide context. The matter's receiving consideration.

MINISTER: Brodie's been around. If I know him, he'll throw in some very fast supplementaries. (*He opens folder.*)

MRS EXTON: I've thought of some of the probables. There are some figures there on population loss and a bit about duty to older industries and some comparison figures.

MINISTER: What's this about wagon sheds? No danger there, surely. One of Andersley's main industries.

MRS EXTON: I don't think so. But I think you'd be wise not to give specific assurances.

MINISTER: One of the things I admire about senior civil servants is the way they can give you an order and make it a reference to your own wisdom.

At that moment John Killane hurries along the corridor and tries to talk to the Minister. He does not know the protocol.

KILLANE: Minister, I wonder if I could . . .

MINISTER (*Gently but firmly*): Not here, Mr Killane. If you please.

The Minister takes Mrs Exton's arm and they continue their conversation. Killane turns, flustered, and leaves.

MINISTER: Your usual excellent brief, Mrs Exton. I'm much obliged. I'd offer you refreshment but I'm afraid there's a Cabinet lunch. Perhaps next week.

MRS EXTON: I look forward to that, Minister.

10

Interior. Strangers' Bar. Day.

Joe Delaney, the MP for Gallowside, is at the corner of the bar near the doors to the terrace, an empty glass in front of him.

Sam Brodie goes down the bar, moving quickly, obviously looking for someone. He reaches the french doors and looks out on the terrace and Delaney turns to speak to him.

DELANEY: You didn't score many points there, Sam. The Minister was good and ready for you.

Brodie is still looking round.

Don't worry, I saw the lobby correspondent for your part of the world on the phone. You'll make the front page of tomorrow's *Andersley Express*.

BRODIE (*Relaxing, slight grin*): I'll make today's as well. I left notice of questions with the editor.

DELANEY: The old routine. Make it look good for the constituents. Battling Brodie strikes again. What are you fighting for, Sam? The cause or your six thousand majority.

BRODIE: That doesn't bother me. I'm safe enough.

DELANEY: You won't be if Killane beats you to it and grabs the glory. There's nothing like a pile of jobs to swing votes. Not that Andersley'll get them. You're a long way down the list. And Garsfeld's after Government money.

BRODIE: I've only just started.

DELANEY: Suit yourself. It's your ulcer. You can buy me a drink.

BRODIE: Not me. Buy your own.

DELANEY: Oh, I forgot. He's just an ordinary MP now. Doesn't buy drinks. Not like when he was a Junior Minister with his car and the cares of state and twice as much money coming in.

BRODIE (*Laughing*): The job you thought you should have had. Except you made too many enemies and didn't do enough work.

DELANEY: And had a few unpopular opinions. Never mind, Sam. It can't have been bad while it lasted. Tell me. Do you still see that piece you used to cart around to receptions? The expensive one with the legs. Can't afford it now, I suppose.

BRODIE (*Still relaxed, but needing control*): You know what the messengers call you, Delaney? The vacuum cleaner for Gallowside. Because you pick up all the dirt.

DELANEY: Knowledge is power, old friend. Nothing beats it. And on the money subject, it'd be nice to have Garsfeld on your doorstep. Nice quiet consultancy for you. Couple of thousand a year. Planning and labour relations, I should think.

Brodie takes a deep breath, still retains control.

BRODIE: One day you're going to be in here on the cadge for ale and opening your big sour mouth. And somebody's going to pick you up and sling you right across that terrace. And you'll land in the river with the rest of the rubbish.

Delaney pushes his empty glass away and prepares to move.

DELANEY: It won't be you, Sam. Six, seven years ago, yes. Not now. You're that much older, that much softer, that much more frightened.

He nods to Brodie and moves away down the bar.

As he does so he passes John Killane who is being approached by the Minister.

MINISTER (*To Killane*): Didn't mean to be so abrupt this morning, Killane, but they're the rules. No Member ever interrupts anyone in conversation in the library corridor.

KILLANE: I'm sorry, Minister.

The Minister puts an avuncular hand on Killane's shoulder, senior prefect greeting the new boy.

MINISTER: Don't be. You weren't to know. One of the Whips should have told you.

KILLANE: Did you get my letter?

MINISTER: Yes, indeed. There's a reply on its way. (*Starts to move away his duty done.*) Have to encourage the new blood.

The Minister turns deftly as another MP approaches him and is quickly away, his attention still uncaught.

11

Interior. Conservative Committee Rooms. Andersley. Day.

Annie Mackinnon has five or six copies of the local paper for the last three days spread over the billiard table. She is marking some and clipping extracts from others.

Peter Chapman, carrying an overnight bag, wanders into the room with his customary salute.

CHAPMAN: Heil Ted. Hello, Annie. Looking for the crossword?

ANNIE: Wish I were.

She turns, worried, glad of the distraction and glad to see Chapman.

ANNIE: I got your postcard. Ha! 'London is empty without you.' (*The quote is in an affectionate tone of derision*).

CHAPMAN: I have them printed. Send them to all the girls. Hey, that veal we had last week was rabbit. I checked. Happens everywhere. Escalope that nips down holes and eats lettuce. Even better for the gonads.

ANNIE: Not now, Peter. Where's John?

CHAPMAN (*Changing mood quickly*): Catching the late train with some top civil servant. (*Seriously now.*) Trouble?

ANNIE (*Indicating the papers*): Look at this lot. Brodie, Brodie, Brodie all week. Private questions, supplementaries, it's starting to look as if he's representing Andersley on his own.

Chapman walks across to look at the papers and the clippings, checks the heavily ringed items.

CHAPMAN: That's a lot of coverage.

ANNIE: We managed to get John's letter to the Minister published but it was a little late.

CHAPMAN (*In an attempt to be comforting*): It's only a local paper.

ANNIE: It's the one his constituents read. And the local Association's starting to mumble. They don't like it. They think Brodie's doing all the work. And I get the playback. 'Perhaps John's a little too young. Doesn't have enough experience. We didn't really know him well enough. He was lucky to get in.'

CHAPMAN: They don't give him much of a chance, do they? He's been there two weeks and they want blood already.

ANNIE: I've had to lay on a meeting at the Club later. The full brigade.

CHAPMAN: And he shall pass among them with steely eye and words of comfort and a succession of firm handshakes. What a way to spend an evening!

ANNIE: That's politics.

CHAPMAN: I suppose. Look, Annie, there's something else. You'd better know—just in case.

Annie who has gone back to the newspapers, turns to face him as he takes the yellow slip of an office telephone message from his breast pocket.

CHAPMAN: One of the reasons I'm here early. John's ex-wife telephoned four times today. She wants to see him urgently. And some office-boy told her he was coming up here.

ANNIE: Oh. I see.

CHAPMAN: No, you don't. Until you've watched Janie Killane operate, you've not seen anything.

ANNIE: What's she like?

CHAPMAN: There's only one polite word to describe her. Bitch.

ANNIE: That's polite?

CHAPMAN: It is for her. Used to be drunken bitch. Till John spent about three thousand quid on clinics and headshrinkers. And that was *after* the divorce. Anyway, I've telephoned John's aunt and the housekeeper. They'll keep an eye on the kids.

ANNIE: She can't be as bad as that.

CHAPMAN: Don't you believe it. I remember when the twins were about three. John used to have to bring them to the office with him. She'd work her way through a bottle and then threaten carving knives. She's capable of it, too. We used to put the kids in the assessment office and the only thing that'd keep them quiet was adding machines. Those kids went through more adding machines.

During this conversation Chapman has become entirely serious, obviously quite worried. He has moved to the billiard table and started to clip newspapers around the marked items, using the scissors deftly and efficiently as a distraction to his anxiety.

12

Interior. Dining car. Night.

Killane and Mrs Exton, the senior civil servant from the Department of Trade and Industry, are facing each other at a table which still carries the reserved card.

They have not yet ordered and pre-dinner drinks are on the table before them, together with the street-fighting equipment British Rail calls cutlery.

KILLANE (*Lifting his glass*): I'm glad you could find time, Mrs Exton. I think you'll know what I mean when you've seen Andersley for yourself.

MRS EXTON: The visit's informal. I'm just breaking

my journey on a trip to the regional office in Leeds. And I know Andersley. It was my husband's last station before he was killed. We were there during the bombing. You'd see miners come off shift, help clear rubble looking for bodies and then go back to work still in their pit dirt.

KILLANE: Now they're on the dole.

MRS EXTON: Mr Killane, I know it. It would be easy to sit in a London office and just juggle the figures. That's why I take trains as often as I can. I look at the spoiled country and the terrace houses and watch the lights go on at night and wonder what sort of food's on the table. You and I trained as planners and statisticians. But we both know there's a little more to it than the figures. Which is why we do what we do.

KILLANE: They seem to be the first sympathetic words I've heard all week.

MRS EXTON: They're still just words. There's only a limited amount of mobile industry and a great many places for it to go to. When times are good, there's no problem. When there's a squeeze, everybody cuts back. I can look at the map in my office. The light green, the dark green, the shaded patches. I can add it all up in misery, old clothes and skinny children but there's only so much money and half a pint's no good for your quart pot. Oh, I can quote the figures—nearly two thousand projects in 69/70, 83 million pounds pushed out as help to provide 96 thousand jobs. It still leaves a lot.

KILLANE: That's another reason I'm glad you'll talk to the people in Andersley.

MRS EXTON: Not talk, listen. I must say I'm a little surprised at how concerned *you* are.

KILLANE: That's what they elected me for.

MRS EXTON: It's more personal than that.

101

KILLANE: Perhaps. I grew up in Dorset and the life was softer. Country vicarage. Rich uncle paying school fees. Then Andersley. And any soft life I'd had was off the backs of these people. It was funny at first. The pushbikes and the flat caps. Then the new cars and the council estates. And across it all a fairly simple doctrine. A man's hands and a pay packet and a little dignity.

MRS EXTON: Don't forget the workshy and the vicious and the agitators. The misguided and the prejudiced. If you do, they'll break your heart. (*She laughs and lifts a glass of sherry.*) Here endeth the lesson.

13

Interior. Sam Brodie's surgery. Night.

Sam Brodie is sitting at the desk—which also has newspapers spread on it—and Cliff Lambert is leaning against the wall. Lambert is looking very pleased with himself.

LAMBERT: That was a good week's work, Sam. If they'd quoted you much more, there wouldn't have been room for the football results.

BRODIE: It's something. Not much but something.

LAMBERT: It's about time that stuffed capitalist they call Minister had the facts of life pushed down his throat. And a lot of people in Andersley West are sorry we didn't keep the seat.

BRODIE: That's Killane's tough luck.

There is a tap on the door and Harry Kinnersley comes in. Over his arm is the white steward's jacket he wears for his work at the Conservative Club.

KINNERSLEY: Cliff here says you wanted to see me, Mr Brodie.

BRODIE: Yes, Harry. No luck with Conran. He says he's overstaffed as it is.

KINNERSLEY (*Forcing the stoicism*): Oh well. Thanks for trying anyway. Is it right there might be a new factory estate? I read what you'd been saying in the papers.

BRODIE: We're doing what we can.

KINNERSLEY: Is there a list I can get on?

BRODIE: Early days for that, Harry.

KINNERSLEY: But you'll let me know.

LAMBERT: You and a few thousand others.

KINNERSLEY: That's something anyway. Thanks again, Mr Brodie.

Kinnersley leaves and Lambert shakes his head.

LAMBERT: They never learn, do they? They won't read the history books. They wander along like beef to a slaughter-house and when it's their turn for the poleaxe, they wonder what they've done wrong. They've had all the years since the war to change history and they didn't take it. Well, now they know.

BRODIE (*His voice hard, resenting the doctrinaire theorising of Lambert*): Politics is about people, Cliff, not history and theories. I thought that was one thing you'd learned. If you haven't, you and me are going to fall out again.

14

Interior. Conservative Club. Night.

This is the same room seen previously but has now been reserved for a private occasion on a social basis for the dignitaries of the local Conservative Association.

Rather elegant screens have been erected and a small table bar set up. Glasses gleam on white linen, but only sherry and wine are being served. All this has been organised by Annie Mackinnon.

A barman, a young man in a white coat, is handing out sherry to the eight or nine early arrivals, including six ladies—two of them in flowered hats and one of these a very impressive specimen of Conservative matron. It is this lady who is first seen by Peter Chapman as he and Annie Mackinnon come into the room.

CHAPMAN: Puff the Magic Conservative Dragon. And her entire family by the look of it.

ANNIE: With more to come. The male variety.

At the moment a crystal, unselfconscious voice calls Chapman's name.

VOICE: Peter, darling.

Chapman turns quickly and grabs Annie's arm.

CHAPMAN: Move. Let's get in her way.

The voice belongs to Janie Killane, the ex-wife of John Killane, a visitor from another planet in a place like Andersley, and completely indifferent to any impression she may or may not make. She looks round the room with amusement, a bored child diverted for a moment.

JANIE: Faithful Peter! I should have known. Diligent right-hand to my striving ex-husband. Where *is* the public-spirited Mr Killane.

ANNIE: He may be arriving late.

JANIE: And who are you, dear?

Chapman moves in with a smooth introduction. He is still, however, wary.

CHAPMAN: Mrs Killane, Annie Mackinnon. John's agent.

JANIE: How nice for her. And who are those lugubrious ladies?

CHAPMAN: None of your business.

JANIE: Oh, they are, dear. All swigging sherry and waving their hats at each other. Are they real?

ANNIE: They're real. And quite important to Mr Killane.

JANIE: Surely it's 'John' by now. There was always a Girl Friday. But I must say that 'agent' is a new description. Does he go over the Gallup polls with you, my dear? Or do you have better things to do?

CHAPMAN (*Conversationally*): I think I preferred it when you were drunk all the time.

JANIE: Do you, dear? So did I. Except at night. But I wasn't talking to you. I was talking to this young lady agent. Just what are your duties, my dear? Perhaps we could compare notes.

Annie Mackinnon smiles. When she speaks her voice is quiet and almost bored.

ANNIE: Mrs Killane—if you still call yourself that— you're getting a little personal. Keep up this line of talk and you'll get your face slapped so hard you'll hear bells for a week.

JANIE (*Quite unperturbed*): All those muscles developed on the hockey fields of long ago.

ANNIE: Not hockey. Two years working in Glasgow slums before I came here.

JANIE: I'm so glad. I *had* heard there was a shortage of really competent lady pugilists.

During this conversation two or three or more Conservative workers have come into the room and joined those present. Out of politeness more than curiosity, a group has moved towards Janie, Annie and Peter

105

Chapman, and Janie makes a languid gesture of welcome.

JANIE: Do gather round, dears. I'm John Killane's ex-wife.

CHAPMAN (*With undisguised relief*): Here's John now.

Killane is seen coming into the room together with Mrs Exton. Janie turns, moves towards him and leaves a parting shot for the Conservative ladies.

JANIE: And do watch that sherry, darlings. You're all much too fat.

Killane waits, his face showing some shock, some anger. He glances at Peter Chapman who shrugs and lifts his hand in helplessness. Janie walks towards him as a hubbub of conversation breaks out among the Conservative ladies. Annie and Peter Chapman move swiftly in mollification, Chapman signalling vigorously at the barman.

JANIE: Hello, John darling.

KILLANE: And goodbye. Quickly.

JANIE (*Lightly, to Mrs Exton*): Impressively Victorian don't you think? And to the mother of his children, too. Are you a Conservative lady, dear?

MRS EXTON: No, I'm a civil servant.

JANIE: Ah, the secret machine behind the figureheads of power.

KILLANE: My ex-wife was never famous for tact, politeness or timing.

JANIE: But that nice judge did give me access. And he did say I could consult you whenever I was concerned about the children's welfare.

KILLANE: Or needed an excuse to make trouble.

JANIE (*Equally*): That, too.

KILLANE: I'm staying at the North-Eastern. I'll see

you there later and now I've got more important things to do.

JANIE: You always had, John darling. You always had. (*To Mrs Exton*) Goodbye, dear. Don't run short of red tape, will you?

MRS EXTON: I'll try not to.

There is another languid wave and Janie leaves, pausing once because it is an effective exit and most eyes in the room are on her.

KILLANE (*To Mrs Exton*): I used to apologise. Then I ran out of words.

MRS EXTON: No need for apology. But if she's been here long, I think you'll have fences to mend. Go and do it. Don't worry about me.

Killane nods gratefully, moves quickly into the main group of people.

15

Interior. Sam Brodie's surgery. Night.

Brodie is facing Sir Joseph Conran across the desk. Conran is authoritarian but not angry.

CONRAN: I've been reading the papers, Sam. I want to know what the hell you think you're playing at.

BRODIE (*Quietly*): If you've read the papers, you'll know. I want Garsfeld's new factory estate for Andersley.

CONRAN: *You* might do. Does everybody else?

BRODIE: If they've got any sense.

CONRAN: You should talk to a few more people. Me, for instance. Or George Pendleton.

BRODIE: I don't think the boss of the local Conservatives and me have got much to talk about.

CONRAN: If you're talking new factories, you have. So have I.

BRODIE: So spit it out. You and Pendleton own factories. A fair number of people out of work suits you. Whether you're Labour or Conservative.

CONRAN: One of each, Sam. And just as concerned about Andersley as you are.

BRODIE: It doesn't sound like it.

CONRAN: Ask Pendleton. When he's finished tearing strips off Killane. Then look at the reasons.

BRODIE: I've looked.

CONRAN: I don't think so. Times aren't good now but they'll pick up.

BRODIE (*Scoffing*): Reflation. Tony Barber's bicycle-pump. I want a steadier policy than that.

CONRAN: You want some patience as well. Six million pounds on a factory estate sounds nice. You think of the problems. You think of what it'll do to the money already invested in this town.

BRODIE: Yours and Pendleton's, you mean.

CONRAN: Among others. I'm telling you to drop this project, Sam.

Brodie stands and goes to lean against the wall shaking his head. When he speaks, the voice is full of contempt.

BRODIE: And you're the so-called bloody chairman of my local Labour Party. God help us all.

CONRAN: The principles haven't changed. I just don't want this town stretched. There's a bad patch but we'll get over it.

BRODIE: You're right there. We will. And Garsfeld'll help us.

CONRAN: No, Sam.

BRODIE: Yes. The first thing I'll do when you've gone is open a window. Then I'll call a full meeting of the Party. I want a vote on this. I want it unanimous and I want it meant. And I'll get it.

CONRAN: You've forgotten I'm chairman.

BRODIE: You won't be after that meeting. Not once I'm on my feet. I don't like lip service. I don't like penny-watchers and I don't like hypocritical neutrals. I want Garsfeld's jobs here.

CONRAN: Don't pick fights with me, Sam. You'll lose.

BRODIE: I'll chance that.

CONRAN: Don't be stupid. You've got till—when?— 1975. That gives me the best part of three years to job you. You'll be nearly fifty years old. With no savings and no prospects. I'll make sure about the prospects. If you want to end up clearing jugs like Harry Kinnersley, call that meeting. Or keep pushing for the Garsfeld project.

Conran rises, small but powerful and with Brodie's future in his hands. Brodie watches him leave.

As Brodie stands against the wall, there is also a formidable quality about him and he has every intention of following the line of action he has started.

END OF ACT TWO.

ACT THREE

16

Exterior. Canal bank. Day.

Film sequence.

Sam Brodie is sitting on a well-used fishing box, rod and line held out over the water. He watches the float drift and a peacefulness begins to replace the worry in his face.

Sitting just behind him on a small steel and canvas stool he has made for her, is his daughter, Elizabeth. She is about seven, a fair pretty child with something elfin about her and the only indication that she is in fact slightly backward is a vague placidity about her features and the stillness with which she sits. She is just the good side of sub-normal and is at a special school where her limited capacities can be trained. She has, however, a special charm and enchantment and Sam Brodie dotes on her.

Elizabeth looks solemnly at her father, stands up, touches him on the arm and waits. Brodie turns his head as she points at the box on which he is sitting.

ELIZABETH: Comics, Dad.

Brodie gets up, takes a children's comic from the box, gives it to her and watches her toddle back to sit down on the stool.

She is holding the comic upside down.

Brodie reaches across gently and reverses the comic.

BRODIE: That way up, love. Otherwise you'll think you're in Australia.

110

Elizabeth points at one of the frames in the comic.

ELIZABETH: Funny man.

BRODIE (*Ironic*): The world's full of 'em, my duck.
Including your dad.

Elizabeth nods vehemently.

ELIZABETH: Yes. Yes, my dad.

BRODIE (*Smiling*): And they reckon you're not very
bright. Special schools and all. (*Touches her face
gently.*) My little duck.

*Brodie goes back to sit on his box, watches the float
now but does not really see it, brooding about what
line of action to take following the Conran discussion.
The canal bank and the water are very still, reflecting
Brodie and the peace he needs. The little girl sits
placidly reading her comic.*

17

Interior. Sam Brodie's surgery. Day.

*Sir Joseph Conran is sitting with complete ease and
authority in the chair behind the desk which belongs
either to Brodie or Lambert.*

*Lambert, not liking this assumption of authority very
much, is sitting on the edge of the desk.*

LAMBERT: If the Member's requested a meeting of the
full Party, he's within his rights.

CONRAN: He may be. That doesn't mean they'll let
him do it.

LAMBERT: He can't for two weeks anyway. Four committee members away—one in hospital, three on
council trips. You should know. You organised the
council trips.

CONRAN: In a way. Yes, I suppose I did. Made a few suggestions. Needed the time. You can talk to a lot of people in two weeks. Count heads. Make sure they stand up in the right place. Where will you stand?

LAMBERT: I'll know that when you've finished talking. Then I might start some talking on my own. That's my chair you're sitting in and I've known Sam Brodie a long time.

CONRAN: Don't *you* start getting sentimental. Not you. You've got more sense. Look, we've had both seats in Andersley for twenty years. Now we've lost one to the Tories.

LAMBERT: We'll get it back.

CONRAN: Will we? Not if we let the town change too much. Not if we hand over the say-so to this Garsfeld and his foreign money. What sort of people will he bring in? How will they vote?

LAMBERT: Up to us to persuade them. I think you're dodging the big question.

CONRAN: Ask it then.

LAMBERT: How many of the people working for you— or Pendleton—are going to leave because they can do better at the new factories?

CONRAN (*Almost amused, but not quite liking the directness*): Right in with both feet. Just like Brodie. And just as wrong. The difference is you'll listen. So do it. Both ears. I could sell up tomorrow, never do another stroke and still die rich.

LAMBERT: Lucky old you. Except you'd go rusty in a month and be doddering in a year. You like running things too much.

CONRAN (*Lightly enough but the edge of anger under it*): Enough's enough. Watch your mouth, lad.

LAMBERT (*Unawed*): Why? Transport House pays my

wages—such as they are. I'm answerable to the Party and only the Party. Not individuals. And nationally—not just in Andersley. Persuade me what you want is for the good of the Party and I'm on your side.

CONRAN: What do you think now?

LAMBERT: I think it's big frog in little pond time. Croaking because he doesn't want change.

CONRAN: You'd better think on something else. A bit further than your nose. If new people come in and Sam Brodie's on their side, how's he going to be able to fight them? He's already joined. We're here, Mister, they'll say. Look at the money and listen to the tune. We'll tell you where to put your roads and your schools and your houses. And the Government'll help them.

LAMBERT: That's exaggerated.

CONRAN: But there's something in it?

LAMBERT: Something.

CONRAN: 20 per cent, 30 per cent?

LAMBERT: Something.

CONRAN: Even if there's only something, I'm telling you it won't be good for Andersley or the Party. And who will we have to fight it? Not Sam Brodie. Not any more. Nor any of the soft-handed lecturers Transport House send up to warble in front of selection committees. (*There is a deliberate pause here, the keystone to any deal that might be done.*) That leaves you.

LAMBERT (*Carefully*): I'm a Party agent. I'm happy at it.

CONRAN: You won't be if Sam Brodie sells out.

LAMBERT: Perhaps not.

CONRAN (*Reasonably, not over-pressing the advantage*): I'm not against change. But I want that change so I can control it.

LAMBERT (*Correcting him*): So the Party can control it.

CONRAN: Same thing. And with me as chairman and you as the local MP that's how it would work. We'd make it. Think on.

Lambert does not answer and his face is expressionless. He is too cautious to commit himself yet but Conran is shrewd enough to know that Lambert's political ambitions go a long way beyond those of party agent.

18

Interior. Strangers' Bar. House of Commons. Night.

Delaney is leaning on the bar next to Killane. The rest of the bar is half-full, a good attendance for this hour of night and obviously following an important debate.

DELANEY: Ten o'clock and all's well. (*Reaches for the glass of beer, paid for by Killane.*) Thirsty work. You try to tell a Minister who goes to Harley Street for an ingrowing toenail the real medical facts of life.

KILLANE (*Genuinely*): I was impressed. I didn't know you were a health expert.

DELANEY: I'm not. Only on slum diseases and money. Half the old dears on Gallowside are still wearing specs they bought for a shilling from a street market forty years ago and . . .

Delaney stops suddenly. He has seen the notice flash on to the closed-circuit television screen over the bar.

This reads:

Adjournment debate on intermediate areas: Samuel Brodie Lab Andersley East.

At the announcement of the adjournment debate, there

is an exodus from the bar—not a wild rush but enough to show an interest on the part of members who want to hear what Brodie has to say and—more especially—what the Minister will say in reply.

DELANEY: Cunning old sod. He's worked an adjournment debate with a Minister there, the House half full and most of the Press still floating around.

KILLANE: How? I've tried for one.

DELANEY: Know the ropes. It's supposed to be the luck of the draw, but if enough people owe you favours, you can fiddle the queue. It means doing the favours first, of course. He's right-handed you there, son.

Killane moves quickly away on his way to the chamber and Delaney moves leisurely after him.

19

Interior. Chamber. House of Commons. Night.

This need only be a backdrop showing the panelling, a section of one of the backbenches and perhaps a section of the bench in front. The scene will be dominated with the end of a solo speech from Brodie who is seen standing, holding notes which are more of a prop than anything else since he will not refer to them. . . .

BRODIE: I'll conclude by restating the main points of my case for zoning Andersley as an intermediate area so that it can attract new industry. First, the opportunity at present existing for another five thousand jobs. Second, our proximity to existing intermediate areas. One of the factors laid down by the Department of Trade and Industry is a travelling time of forty minutes. Many of my constituents used to work forty minutes away and their place of employment was in an area currently zoned to attract industry. I'm not asking for special treatment. I'm asking only for a close examination of the facts as they now exist. I *am* stressing the urgency with which a decision is required if suffering and hardship in my constituency are to be alleviated. I would like the Minister's assurance now. I would like something more tangible than his response to my previous private question. And, I'm not requesting action—I'm demanding it.

There is a hubbub of the cries heard in Parliament. Some of these are school playground standard, such as 'Come off it, Sam', 'Shut up and sit down', 'Why don't you go home to bed' as well as cries of support such as 'Hear hear' and 'Answer, answer, answer'.

20

Interior. Strangers' Bar. Night.

This bar is not quite as full as before and Delaney is reluctantly buying himself a drink.

In the doorway, a uniformed messenger is seen escorting Garsfeld.

Garsfeld enters the bar, looks round hesitantly, watched rather suspiciously by the messenger.

Delaney lifts a hand in greeting to Garsfeld, who hurries towards him, and the messenger looks less suspicious.

GARSFELD: Hello, Delaney. Brodie got me in here for his debate. Have you seen him?

DELANEY: Probably in Annie's Bar passing the good word to the lobby correspondents.

GARSFELD: I'd better go and find him.

DELANEY: You can't. Annie's is Press and MPs only. Here's the only place you're allowed.

At that moment Killane comes back in the bar and across to Garsfeld.

GARSFELD (*To Killane*): Hello, Johnnie. Glad to see you. Brodie did a good job in there. You didn't say much.

KILLANE (*Genuinely frustrated*): I didn't say anything. I must be invisible. How the hell do you make the Speaker see you? Set off fireworks? And some of Brodie's figures were wrong.

GARSFELD: Nothing wrong with his argument. Looks good, huh?

DELANEY: Don't kid yourself, Mr Garsfeld. Parliamentary shadow boxing. Just like a minuet. Sam Brodie tables a private question. Killane here sends a letter to the Minister. Sam's move. He pulls an adjournment debate. It's a ritual, full of words. Fodder for the local papers. It's got nothing to do with results.

At the end of this conversation, Sam Brodie has joined the group. He nods to Garsfeld, listens intently to Delaney.

GARSFELD: What has ?

DELANEY: The case you've got. Gallowside is where you should go, Mr Garsfeld.

GARSFELD: Sorry. I've been there. They call it special development. I call it depressed. I'm not buying trouble.

DELANEY: You wouldn't be.

GARSFELD: No? Look at the record. The big firms with the social conscience. How many of them have pulled out since? You want the names?

DELANEY: I know the names. I know the record.

GARSFELD: Like the Clyde?

DELANEY: Ha. The old song. Communists under the bed.

117

GARSFELD: Not under the bed, friend. At the mass meetings, running the show. (*Reasonable*) They're entitled to their views. They're open about it. So I'm entitled to protect the money I represent.

BRODIE: And Andersley's better.

DELANEY: Better? Luckier. You know me, Sam. I know the Parliamentary ropes as well as you do. Perhaps better. And I've done as many people favours. And if I want the big stick, I can pull in more unions than you can. If they zone Andersley, you'll hear me squawk loud enough to stop it.

BRODIE: Squawk away. You won't be on your own.

DELANEY: I've got a case.

BRODIE: Granted. No hard feelings. (*Contempt in his voice now.*) But look who else you'll have squawking with you. Some of the greedy clowns from the Midlands. They've got voters who take home more in overtime than my lot get for a full week and they're still grabbing for new development. There's union pressure there as well. More than you've got. You heard them just now. You want to join the lads with the three-car families, Joe?

DELANEY: I want what's mine.

BRODIE: That's what they say. So do I.

KILLANE (*Shaking his head, speaking softly, slightly amazed*): Who's been eating *my* porridge?

GARSFELD: It's not anybody's porridge. Not till I get an answer.

KILLANE: And I'm starting to believe you'll only get part of that answer here.

Killane is too shrewd not to acknowledge the truth of Delaney's reference to Parliamentary shadow-boxing. There are pressures to be applied elsewhere and it is the realisation of this that lends his last sentence an edge which is almost menace and certainly bears elements of disillusion.

21

Interior. Library corridor. Day.

The Minister is strolling slowly with Mrs Exton.

MRS EXTON: I read the argument Brodie put up three days ago very carefully. And John Killane turned in a set of figures that must have kept his whole agency busy for a week.

MINISTER: Better than ours?

MRS EXTON: More up-to-date. And with three sets of added factors. He's taken Andersley to pieces like a watch. I didn't realise he was so good at this particular job.

MINISTER: I could have warned you. That's how he started in politics. Sitting anonymously on the Party's top advisory committees and turning figures into people and votes. He's very clever. (*He glances at his watch.*) They'll be here in a minute. What about Andersley?

MRS EXTON (*The reluctance genuine*): We just can't recommend it. It's marginal and we know it's marginal. But, on balance, the answer has to be no.

MINISTER: At least that'll be good news for our friend from Gallowside. Sour little man. (*He takes a folder from Mrs Exton as he sees Killane and Brodie approaching.*) Thank you again, Mrs Exton.

Like all good civil servants, Mrs Exton's disappearance is unobtrusive and the Minister turns to greet Brodie and Killane.

MINISTER: Good morning, gentlemen. I won't waste your time. I'm advised that Andersley cannot be classified as an intermediate area and therefore cannot qualify for Government help to industry.

BRODIE: With respect, Minister, you've been wrongly advised.

MINISTER (*Trace of Party acerbity*): You have to say that, Mr Brodie, so I'll ignore its implications. (*More reasonably.*) There's a long queue for help and Andersley's some way down that queue.

KILLANE: Did you get my figures?

MINISTER: Yes, they were received and considered. I'm sorry, gentlemen.

He turns to go and is halted by Killane.

KILLANE: One thing, Minister. You'll keep the matter under review?

It is an assurance that Killane needs badly and obviously. This shows and Brodie and the Minister look hard at him.

MINISTER: Yes, Mr Killane. That's normal practice.

KILLANE: Thank you.

The Minister leaves and Brodie turns to Killane.

BRODIE: What's that about?

KILLANNE: We've done nothing sprawled over back-benches except make a lot of public noise. I'm going to find out who's backing Garsfeld and I'm going to make a lot of private noise instead.

22

Interior. Conservative Committee Rooms. Andersley. Night.

Janie Killane is seen working a one-armed bandit which is situated near the billiard table. As usual, she is beautifully dressed with a good fur coat draped over her shoulders.

Annie Mackinnon is pinning an announcement for a fund-raising dinner and dance to the notice board near the machines.

JANIE: Will all this money I'm losing go to Party funds?

ANNIE: Some of it.

JANIE: In that case I don't feel conscience-stricken about wasting John's money.

ANNIE: He should be here soon.

JANIE (*Stopping playing, bored again*): How terribly exciting for you, my dear. Just like High Noon every Friday. Waiting for the train to trundle in and Two-Gun Killane to step off.

ANNIE (*Equably*): Me and a lot of people who need help.

JANIE: *Very* Florence Nightingale.

Killane comes into the room, carrying his overnight bag, sees his ex-wife and stops.

ANNIE (*Trying to explain*): Mrs Killane wanted to speak to you privately.

KILLANE: That's all right, Annie.

ANNIE: And Sir George Pendleton wants to see you very urgently. He's been talking to Conran and neither of them are happy about the Garsfeld project. He says they weren't consulted enough.

KILLANE: There wasn't time.

ANNIE: I think it's an excuse. I think it's trouble. I know Conran's after Brodie. I'll be in the office.

Janie has strolled across to join them and cannot keep out of any conversation for long.

JANIE: Waiting. How romantic. With just a touch of Roneo fluid behind each ear.

ANNIE: At least *I* pay for my own perfume, Mrs Killane. It's not Roneo fluid.

Janie inclines her head in acknowledgement of the opposition as Annie leaves quickly.

KILLANE (*To Janie*): What are you doing up here?

JANIE: It's the only place I can see you. There's an injunction forbidding me to go to the house. Remember? That sweet little judge with the sniffle?

KILLANE: And the sweet little trio of psychiatrists who prophesied exactly what you might do with a match and a can of petrol and you and two children in the house.

JANIE: So where else can I talk to you?

KILLANE: Through your solicitor. Through your bank manager. Through the post. I think we've done all the talking there is. Years of it. Talking but not listening. You used to say it was dull unless it was an argument.

JANIE: But you were dull, John, dull, dull, dull. Every time I looked at you.

KILLANE: Using a bottle as a telescope.

JANIE: And now you're an MP. A public servant. You'll get even duller. You'll take to wearing long khaki shorts and going for long, tedious drizzly hikes on the moors.

KILLANE: Janie, what do you want?

His voice is gentle enough and there is a trace of anxiety in it.

When she replies, it is with an effort and the sincerity is evident as she tries—spacing the words carefully—to answer his question.

JANIE: This is not easy to say. I think I'm trying to

make friends and I don't know how. I am still neurotic but I'm no longer a drunkard. The world's a clearer place now. Too clear. I see things. I see me. And sometimes I'm frightened and I'd like somebody to know that I'm frightened and I don't really know anybody except you. There were too many years when I was hiding behind a bitchy remark and the next drink and everybody went away.

She is standing with her hands at her sides and the statement has been a simple appeal for help but with no expectation of success.

Killane starts to move forward and then Cliff Lambert crashes into the room, Annie Mackinnon trying to restrain him.

Killane turns, snarling.

KILLANE: Not now, Lambert. Get out of here.

ANNIE: That's what I told him.

LAMBERT: Sorry. Has to be. It's even your territory. Sam Brodie's at the Conservative Club waiting for you. It *has* to be urgent.

Killane looks at Janie but the mood is broken now and the façade is back.

JANIE: The public weal, the common good. Go and crusade, darling. You mustn't disappoint the avid electorate.

Killane shakes his head, frustrated, moves out after Lambert.

Janie takes a billiard cue from the rack, moves to the table where snooker balls are scattered. She makes a desultory shot and by accident pots black.... There is a harsh rattle in the pocket.

She stands upright, does not look at Annie Mackinnon although she is talking to her.

JANIE: You look like the sort of well-brought-up young

lady who would always have not one but *two* clean handkerchiefs.

ANNIE: Yes.

JANIE: Good.

Janie's face is remote but the control is difficult. Even so she will not ask for a handkerchief into which she can weep until she has to.

23

Interior. Conservative Club. Andersley. Night.

Sam Brodie, grim-faced, is sitting on the arm of one of the big leather chairs in front of the fireplace and Harry Kinnersley is standing next to the raised fender seat. Kinnersley has his white steward's jacket over one arm.

BRODIE: Sit down, Harry. It won't bite you.

Kinnersley lowers himself uneasily on to the fender seat, moves his jacket to the other arm.

KINNERSLEY: I hope he's not long. I've got to start soon.

Killane hurries into the room to face Brodie, followed by Cliff Lambert who leans easily on the mantlepiece.

KILLANE: This had better be very important, Brodie.

BRODIE: It is. (*To Kinnersley*) Tell him, Harry.

KINNERSLEY: My son's just got notice from the wagon sheds.

KILLANE (*To Kinnersley*): I'm very sorry. (*To Brodie, anger in his voice.*) But I still don't see what makes that important. It's just one man.

BRODIE: Let me spell it out for you. I'd forgotten you

124

grew up on office jobs. It was a works committee notice. The start of consultation. They're closing the wagon sheds down. First sackings next month. Get rid of the rest up to the end of the year. You're the figures man, Mr Killane. Add eight hundred to your list of unemployed.

KILLANE: I see. (*To Kinnersley*) We'll do what we can.

BRODIE (*Harsh and bitter*): We'll do more than that. This used to be a railway town. We lived on it. Wagon sheds and repair shops and big sidings. Near the river and the pits and the mills. The engineering we've got followed it. Nearly everything did. Victoria Street starts next to the cattle market and ends up in shunting yards. It runs two and a half miles and once you could take a bet with strangers. No matter what hour of the day or night it was, there'd always be a railwayman on a bike going down Victoria Street. I biked it twelve years myself.

KILLANE: It's not as big as it was. Not now. Conran's and Pendleton's are as big.

BRODIE: It's still one of the biggest we've got. And the oldest. The size doesn't matter. It's the pride in it. Coal sidings all over the world. Africa, Australia, South America, Russia even. The old steam locos chug by and the plate on them says Andersley. They're still running because they were made well. That's what this town's work stands for. Kill that and you kill this town.

On Brodie's face is a determination Killane will never be able to match in quite the same way. For Brodie the roots are deeper, the pride stronger, the feeling stemming from his own knowledge of the work and the skills and the long-ago apprenticeship.

[*Credits*]

Play Three

HISTORY DOESN'T PAY THE RENT

Cast

SAM BRODIE	*Colin Blakely*
JOHN KILLANE	*Michael Gambon*
PETER CHAPMAN	*William Gaunt*
ANNIE MACKINNON	*Joanna Van Gyseghem*
SIR JOSEPH CONRAN	*Bill Owen*
JANIE KILLANE	*Hilary Dwyer*
ELIZABETH BRODIE	*Margaret John*
ERNEST DEWHURST	*Bill Dean*
ITN NEWSCASTER	
'CALENDAR' INTERVIEWER	
RADIO NEWS READER—voice over only	
SIR GEORGE PENDLETON	*Ralph Michael*
PERCY ASKERTON	*William Moore*
SUE MARDEN	*Jacqueline Pearce*

Non-speaking

Elizabeth, Sam Brodie's daughter; Thomas Brodie, Sam Brodie's youngest son, about twelve, quiet, well-built, good looking; workers at the Andersley wagon sheds; members of the Andersley Conservative Association—preferably snooker players; members of the local Conservative Club; steward at Conservative Club; drinkers and steward at the Andersley Working Men's Club—preferably to include some wagon shed workers; assorted MPs frequenting the Strangers' Bar at the House of Commons; barman in the Strangers' Bar; high-class waiters and sommelier in a fashionable London restaurant.

Interiors

1. Conservative Committee Rooms
2. Conservative Club
3. Sam Brodie's living room
4. Working Men's Club
5. Strangers' Bar, House of Commons
6. Library corridor, House of Commons
7. Railway dining car
8. Fashionable London restaurant

Exteriors

1. Wagon sheds. With workers leaving, watched by Sam Brodie and Ernest Dewhurst
2. Closed wagon sheds featuring padlocked main gates

ACT ONE

Titles

1

Exterior. Andersley wagon sheds. Day.

Film sequence.

The main gate of the wagon sheds is seen. This can be the entrance to any large engineering works, which is adjacent to a complex of railway sidings.

Shifts are changing and a crowd of men on foot, or with bicycles, or driving cars is leaving the factory.

Ideally, they should leave and all go in the same direction, down Victoria Street, an arrow-straight thoroughfare linking the wagon sheds with the heart of the town.

Watching the men are Sam Brodie and Ernest Dewhurst. Dewhurst, who works at the wagon sheds, is in overalls and leaning on an old upright bicycle.

DEWHURST: Friday and pay-packets. But there won't be many of that lot in the pubs tonight.

As he says this, two or three of the men wave in greeting to Brodie and Dewhurst. They do not seem worried or wretched.

BRODIE: You'd never know it.

DEWHURST: It hasn't sunk in yet. In ten months' time, they'll put a padlock on those wagon shed gates and leave it there.

BRODIE: Oh, no. Not if I can help it.

DEWHURST (*Shrugging slightly*): You're a good MP,

Sam, but I work there. I'm telling you. That lot'll be on dole queues in a year.

Brodie shakes his head, stubborn.

Both men turn and walk away from the wagon sheds. Dewhurst pushing his bike one-handed with the ease of experience, fitting in with the crowds whereas Brodie— who was once part of this same stream of men—has been away too long and looks slightly out of place.

2

Interior. Conservative Committee Rooms. Day.

Set as previous plays—a large room with a billiard table and smaller tables around.

John Killane and Annie Mackinnon are sitting at one of these tables and Killane has papers in front of him— letters from constituents, invitations to attend functions, complaints or explanations from local authority officials.

On the next table, within reach, is a portable radio. There is music and then the brief hourly news bulletin —none of this for the moment audible.

Annie indicates an engraved invitation card.

ANNIE: I'd try to go to that one, John. I know it sounds boring but Richard Pryor's put in twenty years' work for the Conservatives and he doesn't have golden weddings often.

KILLANE (*Making a tick on the invitation*): If you say so.

Annie hears the news come on faintly and turns to increase the volume on the radio.

ANNOUNCER'S VOICE: ... no hesitation in condemning football rowdyism. (*Pause for breath and the next item.*) Negotiations are still taking place between management and unions on the closure of the wagon sheds at Andersley where more than five hundred men are expected to be put out of work. No official statement has been issued. Now, the weather . . .

Annie turns down the volume.

ANNIE (*Referring to the wagon sheds*): It might be useful for you to show your face there as well.

KILLANE: Sympathy and platitudes? No.

ANNIE: Sam Brodie's there. And the sympathy wouldn't hurt.

KILLANE: I was elected for Parliament—not the Samaritans. I've got other things to do. (*The tone is worried, a little sharp and then Killane relents.*) All right, Annie, I know. You're the agent, your job's to push me where the trouble in the town is.

ANNIE: You can't just keep away. Or quiet.

KILLANE: I think I can.

ANNIE: You'll need very good reasons.

KILLANE: I think I've got them.

Annie looks up as Peter Chapman ambles into the room. Chapman looks weary, a little dishevelled from travel. In one hand he carries an overnight bag with a bundle of airline tickets on the handle and in the other he is balancing a cuckoo clock.

He drops the overnight bag on a chair, lifts his right hand in the usual salute made every time he enters Conservative premises.

CHAPMAN: Heil Ted. Hello, Annie love.

Killane points at the cuckoo clock.

KILLANE: I hope you've brought back more from Switzerland than that.

133

CHAPMAN (*Rueful*): It's better than nothing.

KILLANE: And what else?

CHAPMAN (*Apologetic*): The good news is—*no* news. Everybody and his Alp know the facts. Garsfeld's got the money for a five-thousand-job factory estate. They all know Andersley's on the list. If.

KILLANE: But where's the money coming from? Who are the sources?

CHAPMAN: Nobody knows. Or if they do, they're not telling. A big fat chorus of silence. Sorry, John. Anyway, I did some work for us so at least the office rent gets paid this month.

Killane, who is still on the Garsfeld train of thought, has paid no attention to Chapman's last sentence.

KILLANE: Maybe Pendleton's found out something. I asked him to try. Perhaps that's why he wants to see me.

ANNIE (*Shaking her head*): If you think that's why he wants to see you, you're being optimistic. Our distinguished chairman made it a summons—not a request. You may need to produce the reasons you were talking about. (*She looks at her watch.*)

KILLANE: Oh. I see. Sir George and his civic pride. The wagon sheds. I'd better move. See you later.

As he talks, Killane has picked up his briefcase and is moving out of the room.

Chapman advances on Annie and gives her the cuckoo clock.

CHAPMAN (*Mock-portentous*): This is for you.

ANNIE (*Laughing*): Why me?

CHAPMAN: Symbolic. Every hour on the hour. It says cuckoo. Which is what a nice girl like you must be to do a job like this in a town like this.

ANNIE: Especially now?

CHAPMAN: Especially any time.

ANNIE: I should have done the same as Cliff Lambert.

CHAPMAN: Who? Oh. The cut-rate Keir Hardie. Sam Brodie's agent. What's he done?

ANNIE: Taken a nice quiet leave of absence while Chairman Conran puts the boot in Brodie.

CHAPMAN: I'm with Lambert. I'm squeamish myself.

3

Interior. Conservative Club. Night.

Set as previous plays—padded armchairs, the comatose elders of the tribe. There is, however, one addition which is a portable television set on a table near the fireplace and its padded seat.

Sir Joseph Conran is standing in front of the fire with Sir George Pendleton.

Sir George Pendleton is chairman of the local Conservative Association and is also a prominent local industrialist but this is all he has in common with Conran. He is about sixty, an old-style Tory who accepts power as a responsibility in almost Roman terms, public service bred into him. He is tall, stooping a little now, puzzled by the pace at which the world is moving. A farmer by inclination and hobby, he has spent his life in the family business and made a good job of it. He can be entirely ruthless where principles or ethics are concerned, but is not intolerant of human weakness or fallibility.

PENDLETON: You're Chairman of the Labour Party and it's your affair but I think you're being unduly hard on Brodie. Thank goodness it's none of my business.

CONRAN: It is. And I hope you'll be as hard on your chap Killane. That's why I'm here. Look, George, they're down in Westminster scoring points. We're up here in Andersley. We know how it works.

PENDLETON: Then we should be talking about the wagon sheds.

CONRAN: No, we shouldn't. Bigger fish frying in the pan. I've told Sam Brodie to stop pushing for this Garsfeld estate.

PENDLETON: And he won't. I've read the papers.

CONRAN: So we make him. And Killane. Both of them.

PENDLETON: I'll think about it. No more.

CONRAN: Think about the results. It all sounds nice. Big new estate, five thousand jobs. What about the rest of it? Schools, houses, roads to go with it. This town'll have to find the money for that.

PENDLETON (*Turning to look directly at Conran*): I hope that's the real reason, Joseph. You and I are both major employers here. We face competition and people won't believe us easily.

CONRAN: I'll sleep at nights. Yes or no?

PENDLETON: I'll think about it.

At the end of this Pendleton has moved to the television set. He is fiddling with it more to bring to an end a conversation he finds embarrassing than any desire to see a specific programme.

NOTE: It would be useful if the television set could have been showing an antipodean cricket match or some other harmless occupation for the elderly as a reason for its being there and if the programme could now have changed to the news.

It would also be useful if the face of an IDENTIFIABLE

ITN newscaster could be shown—continuing as voice over.

On voice over, the newscast should feature the group of men leaving the wagon sheds seen in the first film sequence.

NEWSCASTER: And now a report from the town being called angry Andersley as its most famous and longest-established industry is threatened with shut-down. Discussions are still taking place and a mass meeting will be held there tomorrow to be addressed by local union leaders and Mr Sam Brodie, Labour MP for Andersley East, who recorded this statement for us earlier.

There is a cut to Brodie and studio backcloth and Sam Brodie's anger is showing—in direct contravention of the television tutorship handed out at both Transport House and Central Office.

BRODIE (*On TV screen*): This is more than men's livelihoods. This is an industry and a tradition our whole town was built on. The wagon sheds *are* Andersley. We've built locos—diesel and steam—put rolling stock together for railways all over the world. We've had generations of craftsmen. If this Government and its nationalised bodies can get their greedy noses out of the balance sheets, they'll see that there's more to a society than words like rationalisation and figures on a graph.

The newscaster's face appears again and Pendleton turns down the volume.

CONRAN: He's getting worked up about it.

PENDLETON: He should be. We all know a lot of those men.

CONRAN: At least it'll keep him occupied while the Garsfeld project gets dropped. Better for him. Better for us. Pity it's too late for him.

PENDLETON (*The reproof obvious*): That aspect—fortunately—is not my affair.

At that moment Sam Brodie comes into the room, looks round, sees Conran and Pendleton, hesitates, then moves towards them.

CONRAN: Hello, Sam. They'll make you a member here soon. If you can afford it.

PENDLETON: Mr Brodie's been offered a guest membership several times. (*To Brodie*) You wanted to see me.

BRODIE: Yes, Sir George. (*A wry glance at Conran.*) Both of you. I'd like an all-party platform at the wagon shed meeting tomorrow.

PENDLETON: I'll be there. Of course.

BRODIE: I want a deputation as well. With everybody on it. Westminster next Thursday. Business question day. You two, the mayor, trade unions, Killane. If we've got everybody, we can nail down the Minister and the civil servants that count. They'll have to listen.

During this speech, Killane has entered the room and has joined the group at a signal from Pendleton.

Conran has also been looking in a small pocket diary.

CONRAN: Listen, they might. That's about all.

BRODIE: But you'll be there.

CONRAN (*The diary open*): No, Sam. Not me. (*Smiles.*) Too short notice.

BRODIE: I want full representation.

CONRAN: You didn't bother about full representation when you were making all the noise about Garsfeld and pushing his factory estate. You don't turn party support on and off like a tap.

BRODIE (*The anger showing*): Party support or Sir Joseph Conran support? Town-interest or self-interest?

138

(*Contempt now.*) They told me the rich were different. They didn't tell me it was childishness.

PENDLETON (*Wanting to interrupt*): Can I offer you a drink, Mr Killane? If only to inject some note of amiability.

KILLANE: I'd like that.

CONRAN (*Pressing the bell push to summon the steward*): I'll buy the drinks. But it won't change the political facts. And it might do your new boy good to listen. Who do you think does the work while the pair of you are down in London? The party machine, the party workers. Most of them unpaid. Whist drives, bingo, jumble sales. They raise the money that pays for your leaflets. They provide the solid work that gets you elected. With people like me running 'em. Sam's forgotten where his support comes from. Don't you do the same, Mr Killane.

KILLANE: I think you're being elementary, Sir Joseph. If all you wanted was a mouth-piece, you could send tape-recordings down to Westminster and save money on hotel bills.

BRODIE: And save useless arguments like this one. What about the deputation, Sir George?

PENDLETON: I'll be glad to attend.

CONRAN (*Turning to leave*): The lion shall lie down with the lamb. Hallelujah.

By now a steward has approached and Conran passes him on the way out.

CONRAN: Give those gentlemen a drink, will you? Put it on my account.

BRODIE: Somebody ought to apologise. It might as well be me.

PENDLETON: Public squabbles are never agreeable. But much as I dislike the manner of it, I have a certain belief in Conran's sincerity. He's worked—as I have—for thirty years. I think his politics are misguided but his concern for this town is genuine. And you must remember that successful businessmen develop the uncomfortable habit of always expecting their own way.

BRODIE: It shouldn't apply. This is politics. He's a good socialist but so am I. To say you're a better socialist than anybody else is a contradiction in terms.

KILLANE: Unless your names are Bevan or Gaitskell. Or their supporters.

BRODIE: A bit snide, Mr Killane.

KILLANE: Meant to be. Another way of saying nobody's perfect. Respect the individual.

BRODIE (*Mocking*): And vote Conservative.

KILLANE: That's it.

BRODIE: Let's forget the dialectic. What about this deputation? (*Gets a dig in.*) And the jobs of *your* individuals? Will you be there?

KILLANE (*Taking a deep breath, the answer flat and irrevocable*): No.

Brodie's surprise at this verges on shock. Closure of the wagon sheds is clearly a non-party issue to him and he has expected Killane to feel the same way.

BRODIE: You've got to be.

KILLANE: No. I've seen the figures. It's a lost cause. The sheds are losing money and nobody's going to keep pouring it down the drain just because of tradition. Facts of life.

PENDLETON (*Not liking Killane's flat and factual approach*): I'd rather you were more concerned. Or at least appeared to be.

KILLANE: Why waste energy?

BRODIE: You give up easily, don't you?

KILLANE: I try not to get emotional. I try to work on the figures. It's a lost cause but we can still use it. I'd like a lot of noise if they close the wagon sheds. Then we can try again to get Andersley zoned as intermediate. this time we'll make it and Garsfeld moves here. Five hundred jobs against five thousand. A necessary sacrifice.

BRODIE: Oh, yes. Only five hundred men. We can put a notice up at the Labour Exchange: 'Sorry and all that. Garsfeld or the wagon sheds.' (*Shakes his head*) Either/or. One or the other. (*His contempt for Killane's factual approach boils up.*) You wouldn't try for both, would you? That would be too bloody individual.(*He turns to leave.*) Thank you, Sir George. See you to-morrow.

PENDLETON: Good night, Mr Brodie. I'll be there.

KILLANE: Did you manage to find out anything about where Garsfeld's raising the money?

PENDLETON: I made two or three telephone calls. I think there are more important things at the moment.

KILLANE: I don't think so.

PENDLETON: That's your privilege. I also happen to think that Garsfeld and the zoning of Andersley should be the subject of normal procedure.

KILLANE: Sir George, I'm a little tired of the procedure. I watched it. All the Parliamentary shadow-boxing. The letters to the Minister, the private questions, the adjournment debate.

PENDLETON: The system works. Perhaps you're to blame for not giving it enough time.

KILLANE: I don't have the time. Garsfeld gave us three weeks. After that he'll cancel and go to Holland.

141

4

Interior. Sam Brodie's living room. Night.

Set as previous plays.

Sam Brodie is sitting on the arm of one of the big chairs with a cup of tea in his hand.

His wife, Elizabeth, is standing in front of him, showing signs of worry.

Sam Brodie's daughter is sitting in the chair next to her father. There is a board on her lap and she is busy with a simple structure of building blocks.

ELIZABETH: Sam, you can't afford to fall out with Conran.

BRODIE (*Mildly*): We've had disagreements before.

ELIZABETH: Not like this. What about the money? Only six months ago he was talking about giving you some sort of consultancy. He was talking about fixing you up if you ever left Parliament.

BRODIE: Is that what you want, love? MP for sale. Part-worn, house-trained, one owner.

ELIZABETH: You know it isn't. (*There is a rasp of anger in her voice.*)

Brodie turns to his daughter, lifts the board from her knee.

BRODIE (*To his daughter*): Go and play in your room, my duck. I'll come up before I go out and see how clever you've been.

The little girl nods and toddles obediently out.

ELIZABETH (*Her voice soft now*): No need for that, Sam. She doesn't understand.

BRODIE: She listens to the voices. Watch her face. She knows when you're upset.

ELIZABETH: I've got reason to be. I've always had to look after the money. I could go on till midnight telling you. The clothes we need, the insurance we need, the rest of it. I keep hoping it'll get better. I know what you're doing and I believe in it but I wish you'd think sometimes. Think about us.

BRODIE: I do, my duck. And Conran knows it. Perhaps he even counts on it. I don't know. (*The last phrase is one of weary bafflement, the realisation that crossing his own party chairman may not be worth the massive personal sacrifice.*)

5

Interior. Conservative Committee Rooms. Night.

There are more people in the committee room now and Chapman is one of a foursome playing snooker.

Annie Mackinnon is seen turning on a television set in another corner of the room and calls across to Chapman.

ANNIE: Peter. Come and look.

The programme she is watching is a news magazine—Yorkshire Television's 'Calendar'.

Chapman, still holding the billiard cue, joins Annie and they watch the programme.

ANNOUNCER: Our interviewer asked Mr Ernest Dewhurst, leader of the Labour majority on Andersley Town Council and himself a worker and union representative at the wagon sheds, his views on this massive closure.

The interviewer is seen with Ernest Dewhurst against a back-drop of wagon sheds and shunting yards.

143

INTERVIEWER: First of all, Mr Dewhurst, do you think there's any chance of a workers' takeover?

DEWHURST: Lad, if you're baiting traps, use better cheese. No, there isn't. No chance at all.

INTERVIEWER (*Persisting*): I've heard rumours to that effect.

DEWHURST: I've heard rumours to the effect that the missis next door's pregnant. Trouble is, she's eighty-three.

INTERVIEWER: And how will the closure of the wagon sheds affect the attraction of new industry to Andersley?

DEWHURST: I'm the wrong person to answer that question. Try Sam Brodie. Or the other chap, the Tory fella, what's-his-name? That's one of the jobs they're supposed to do down in London.

At that moment Killane hustles into the room, carrying an overnight bag and in a hurry.

KILLANE: Thank you, Mr Dewhurst. I'm on my way.

ANNIE: You can't. There's a pile of work.

KILLANE: You watch me. Come on, Peter. I'll drive you back.

Chapman bounces the billiard cue from hand to hand, looks longingly at his interrupted snooker game, makes up his mind.

CHAPMAN: Oh, no, you won't. Not if you're in a hurry. I'll take the train tomorrow morning. Where I don't have to clutch a St Christopher medal and close my eyes. Besides, I can drink on trains. And work. For money. What's the rush, anyway?

KILLANE: You couldn't find out and Pendleton can't or won't. And I need to know where the Garsfeld money's coming from. (*He turns to leave.*)

ANNIE: John, there really is a lot of work.

KILLANE (*On his way*): Tell Peter. He can bring the papers back with him.

CHAPMAN: The only shadow MP in the business.

By now, Killane has left and Chapman is suddenly very serious.

He replaces the cue in the rack and turns towards Annie.

CHAPMAN: That tears it. Human-sacrifice time. Come on, let's go to the pictures. Something cheerful. 'I was Dracula's ex-husband', 'Why I married a lady werewolf'. Something.

ANNIE: Make sense. What's wrong?

CHAPMAN: Love, I've seen John go after information before. And he never stops to wonder if it's worth it. He's gone to see his cannibal ex-wife. Janie's got to be the only person likely to know.

ANNIE: How can she?

CHAPMAN: It's who she knows. That lady is so well connected her address book looks like a wiring diagram. Merchant bank? Three uncles. Top military brass? A cousin or two. Swiss gnomes? A page and a half of them. By marriage on her step-mother's side. Whew! (*Drops his hands in a gesture of futility.*) Not the pictures, love. Let's go and get drunk instead.

Annie looks at him puzzled, appreciates his evident distress, then nods.

6

Interior. Working Men's Club. Night.

Set as previous plays.

Dewhurst is at his usual table and Brodie is facing him. Beer in pint glasses is in front of both men.

DEWHURST: He ran out of questions. So I offered to give him a banjo solo.

BRODIE: I didn't hear that bit. And you can't play the banjo, Ernest.

DEWHURST (*A trace of hard sadness*): I couldn't answer the bloody questions either. Not properly. What about this deputation of yours?

BRODIE: I've got Pendleton, the mayor, some councillors, union people. I'm still rounding them up. We should be all right.

DEWHURST: Free advice, Sam. Stick up here and keep playing sheepdog. Just in case Conran puts the word about.

BRODIE: I don't think I can. I wish Cliff Lambert hadn't gone away.

DEWHURST: You're better off without him. Who do you think arranged for him to attend a training course he didn't need?

BRODIE: Your friend and my friend. The gent with the money in his wallet. Conran. You can't blame Cliff. You don't argue with the man who pays the wages.

DEWHURST: I do.

BRODIE: It doesn't matter.

DEWHURST: You're big enough to fight your own battles but there's no need to get charitable about it as well.

BRODIE: I wonder when the purse-strings'll get tightened on me.

DEWHURST: When he's ready.

BRODIE: That's what Elizabeth says. She's worried to

146

death about it. Anyway, that's my look-out. You'll be on this deputation, Ernest?

DEWHURST: No, Sam. Sorry.

BRODIE: You've got to be. The other union boys are coming.

DEWHURST: That's just it. We've got three or four herberts at the sheds making speeches here and there. You know them. Sent in for the job. The lads with chips on their shoulders and snow on their boots. Leave the union office empty and that's when they'll start the bother. I've got to stay here.

BRODIE (*With some relief*): I thought for a minute there you'd joined Conran.

DEWHURST (*Hard*): You know better than that. I've joined nobody.

BRODIE: Perhaps as well. Between the two of you I'd be a prize gammon in the bacon machine. Sliced to bits. (*His own hardness showing.*) *If* you could get me on the machine.

DEWHURST: I'll keep out of it as long as I can. Then I'll join.

BRODIE: But I don't see how I can stay up here. There's a Whip on and I'm not paired.

DEWHURST: It depends who you're standing for. The Whips or Andersley.

BRODIE: That's a damn fool question.

DEWHURST (*Mildly*): Lots of people have been asking it lately. 'Junior Minister once, you know. Getting a bit too big for us now'. (*Hesitates, is gentle with the next phrase.*) And they reckon there used to be at least one good reason for you wanting to stay in London.

BRODIE: Don't tell me you've been soft enough to listen to Delaney and his Strangers' Bar muck-peddling.

DEWHURST (*Still mildly*): Last time I was down. An expensive piece with long legs, he said. Slavering a bit. Marsden or some such name. I'm not criticising, Sam. Just telling you.

BRODIE: And I'm not denying it. But it was a long time ago. (*Reflectively.*) When all the leaves were green. And it was going to stay summer for ever. (*Note of bitterness in his voice.*) Don't worry, Ernest. I'll stick up here. Buy the beer, kiss the babies, chat the people. All nice and normal. With my agent shifted, you neutral and the party chairman after me with his hatchet. Sometimes I wonder whether it's all bloody worth it.

END OF ACT ONE

ACT TWO

7

Interior. Strangers' Bar. House of Commons. Day.

Set as previous plays.

It is the following Tuesday and Janie Killane and Peter Chapman are standing at the bar. Chapman looks rather nervous, is still not used to being at the House but Janie's crystal voice shows all her usual uncaring self-confidence. She is, however, still drinking orange juice. Janie is elegantly dressed and the object of a good deal of attention from the MPs around the room and near the terrace windows.

As she speaks, she rubs her ear.

JANIE: I should really have this bandaged, you know. All those telephone calls to my tedious relatives. Saturday till Tuesday. I shall send John the bill. And all those fiendish foreign operators. In the end I had to start using a title.

CHAPMAN: I can think of several for you.

JANIE: Dear Peter, you always could. I'm a reformed character now.

CHAPMAN: That was the excuse Charlotte Corday used.

JANIE: Who, dear?

CHAPMAN: Before she stabbed Marat in his bath.

JANIE: At least it didn't make a mess on the carpet. (*Turns, surveys the room in her best junior dowager fashion.*) I do like this place. All these little men looking deadly serious. What did Tom Driberg call it? 'A four-ale bar.' Whatever that is.

CHAPMAN: That was six months ago—before it was rebuilt.

JANIE: And where's John? I thought he wasn't supposed to leave us unescorted in case we blew up the place.

On the last sentence, there is an exodus from the bar, not hurried, the usual departure when someone controversial is on his feet.

Janie glances up at the closed circuit television screen which reads.

(EEC Finance)
(Mr N A F St John-Stevas)
(Cons. Chelmsford)

JANIE: Oh, does he talk about money too? How clever of him.

CHAPMAN: Janie Killane, I really wonder about you. Especially when I remember all the damage you've done.

JANIE (*Both hands round her glass, very serious*): I wonder about me, too. And about the damage.

8

Interior. Library corridor, House of Commons. Day.

Set as previous plays.

Mrs Joan Exton is walking along the corridor as Killane hurries after her.

KILLANE: Mrs Exton.

She turns and stops.

MRS EXTON: Good morning, Mr Killane. (*There is a note of surprise in her voice but there is a sort of protocol which means that she will stop.*) How did *you* know I was seeing the Minister this morning?

KILLANE: Looked at the Questions down for him. You're the senior civil servant on that subject. So I lurked.

MRS EXTON: You're learning. You lurk very well.

KILLANE: Mrs Exton, how final was the decision not to zone Andersley as intermediate?

MRS EXTON: Oh, no, Mr Killane. No answer. Completely outside my discretion.

KILLANE (*Taking a chance*): So stop being discreet.

MRS EXTON (*Not offended*): I've been in it too long for that. Even with your Mr Garsfeld's three-quarter million in incentives at stake.

KILLANE: If we zone Andersley.

MRS EXTON: If. You had a fair hearing, you know.

KILLANE: And we'll get another one if the wagon sheds close.

MRS EXTON: I would think so.

KILLANE: And will the Minister be in town for the next two weeks?

MRS EXTON: Really, Mr Killane, he has secretaries for that. Ask them.

KILLANE: I did. They were vague.

MRS EXTON (*Philosophically*): Well, there *are* rules.

KILLANE: I've had my share of the rules in this place. Too many of them.

MRS EXTON: And now you're using your own.

KILLANE: I have to.

MRS EXTON: It could be dangerous (*Picks up a second thought*.) I don't know though. There seem to be five standard routes for ambitious young politicians looking for office. You can be clever, be very noisy, be around all the time, be extremely amiable or be a persistent nuisance.

KILLANE (*Grinning, starting to move off*): I'll start with the nuisance side.

MRS EXTON: Don't overdo it. There are three known nuisances on your front bench already.

9

Interior. Strangers' Bar. Day.

Janie Killane and Peter Chapman are still waiting.

CHAPMAN: John's probably lost. You need a blood-hound to trap round all these corridors. They once lost a whole coach party for three weeks.

JANIE: Don't exaggerate, Peter. There aren't enough loos for a *whole* coach party.

John Killane hurries into the bar and across to them.

KILLANE: Sorry I'm late. I had to see somebody.

JANIE: Don't worry, dear. We're quite comfortable watching your little friends playing.

KILLANE (*To Chapman*): I had a Telex from Garsfeld. 'Tell Peter he'd starve as a snooper. But don't worry about the money. It's there.'

CHAPMAN: In a suitcase under the bed.

JANIE: Oh, but it's not. I have a list.

CHAPMAN : You can't have.

JANIE: Oh, yes. It's very simple. People were so delighted I didn't want something outrageous they told me all about your Garfunkle or whatever his name is. And where he's getting his money. Very respectable indeed.

As she talks, Janie is fumbling in a fashionable handbag and produces, uncharacteristically, seven or eight index cards with neat handwriting on them.

KILLANE: Did you do those?

JANIE: Yes, dear. It's something they taught us at my last clinic. We used to use them for recall of symptoms. We put times on them.

KILLANE: Oh. Janie, I'm very grateful. I know it's been a lot of trouble but it's very important. Not just for me.

Janie inclines her head in acknowledgement of the thanks.

As she does this, a man called Percy Askerton bustles up to them.

Askerton is a burly man of about fifty, a trade union MP for one of the West Midland constituencies. He has an air of small authority about him which stems from his position as assistant whip. He is a conscientious man, painstaking but not clever, punctilious in his attendance at the house, unswerving in his adherence to the party line, a solid wheel-horse MP whose ambitions have been realised and who will serve as long as he can and for as long as he is allowed. He is at the moment slightly agitated and this shows through as petty officiousness.

ASKERTON (*To Killane*): Don't want to interrupt, Mr Killane.

JANIE: But you are doing, dear.

ASKERTON (*Ignoring her*): Have you seen Sam Brodie?

153

KILLANE: Not here. He was in the constituency last weekend.

ASKERTON: And he should be bloody here today. There's a Whip on.

KILLANE: Sorry, can't help.

JANIE (*To Askerton*): Oh, you're a Whip, are you? How Dickensian.

KILLANE (*To Askerton*): If it's any help, I know that Brodie was trying to get a deputation together. It may be taking longer than he thinks.

ASKERTON (*Turning to leave*): I'll give him deputation if he's not in the lobby for this division.

JANIE: I'm sure you will, dear.

At that moment the division bell rings and the bar empties completely and hurriedly.

KILLANE: I'd better go. There's the vote.

He leaves and Chapman shakes his head at Janie.

CHAPMAN: I suppose you can vote without listening.

JANIE: You can do anything without listening, dear. Most people do. I did it once for a very long time.

10

Interior. Working Men's Club. Andersley. Night.

Conran and Dewhurst are sitting, at ease with each other, at Dewhurst's normal table.

CONRAN: I thought I'd talk to you, Ernest, before the ward chairmen get here.

DEWHURST (*Touch of irony*): That's good of you, Sir Joseph.

CONRAN: They tell me you're not going on this deputation of Sam Brodie's.

DEWHURST: He'll manage on his own.

CONRAN: Do you believe that? Or are you trying to prove something else?

DEWHURST: That's too crafty for me. Such as what?

CONRAN: You know well enough. Two men run the Party in this place. You and me.

DEWHURST: I've heard people say that.

CONRAN: And we've run it for—what?—twenty odd years.

DEWHURST: I've been in it longer than that.

CONRAN (*Rising to leave*): It's something I think Brodie's forgotten. I'm glad you're ready to remind him as well.

DEWHURST: In that case, I'm glad you're glad.

Dewhurst's attitude is interested, non-committal. If Conran wishes to believe that he, Dewhurst, is willing to join forces in the attempt to influence Sam Brodie, a good politician's instinctive reaction is to allow the assumption to continue.

11

Interior. Sam Brodie's living room. Night.

Sam Brodie, still wearing a topcoat, has just come in and is standing by his desk looking at the messages on the telephone note pad.

Elizabeth is sewing on the sofa.

ELIZABETH: I went to the bank. There's the money you asked for in the envelope under the clock.

BRODIE (*Puzzled, having forgotten*): What?

ELIZABETH: The twenty-five pounds. For a suit and some shoes.

BRODIE: Oh. Thanks. love. (*He crosses, puts the envelope in his inside pocket.*)

ELIZABETH: The Whips' Office called three times.

BRODIE: Who was it?

ELIZABETH: Percy Askerton, by the sound of it. He wasn't very friendly.

BRODIE: He's not supposed to be. That's his job.

ELIZABETH: He gave me a couple of chances to say you were off sick.

BRODIE: And you took them?

ELIZABETH: No. More fool me. I told him you were busy up here.

BRODIE: I can see him putting the black mark in his little book. (*Shrugs quite philosophically.*) Him and Conran. Local party, national party. Oh, well. If you're going to get in trouble, you may as well do it properly.

12

Interior. Conservative Club. Night.

Annie MacKinnon is sitting with Sir George Pendleton on one of the very comfortable leather sofas. In front of them is a silver coffee tray with silver pot and good china cups and Annie is pouring coffee for Sir George. They are continuing a subject begun at dinner.

PENDLETON: No, my dear, I'm not a bit worried about the local association. Largely thanks to you. Funds, publicity, events. The Young Conservatives are working like beavers and even the Women's Association seems to have taken to you. Which isn't as easy as it sounds. Most of the time they're more comfortable with lady agents who look like professional footballers.

ANNIE (*Laughing*): I think Mrs Gresham deserves the credit there. She's managed to persuade them that their sons and husbands are safe.

PENDLETON: I wonder if she consulted the sons and husbands first (*Reverts to the original subject.*) No, it's Killane I'm a little worried about.

ANNIE: You shouldn't be, Sir George. He's working very hard. If anything, too hard.

PENDLETON: But on his own. That wasn't what he was elected for.

ANNIE: We all had a lot of time to find out about him before he was adopted. He knows the snags as well as I do. John and I are both outsiders. We're accepted in Andersley but only up to a point. He knows all this.

PENDLETON: I would still like you—if you would—to bring the subject up with him sometime. The conservatism with a small 'c'.

ANNIE: Sir George, are we talking about morale in the association, political policy or consultation on the Garsfeld project?

PENDLETON: All three. I don't think they can be separated. If John thinks they can, I'd like very much to hear his reasons. I wouldn't want him to run the same risks as Sam Brodie.

13

Exterior. Westminster. Day.

Film Sequence.

It may be feasible to stage this against a simulated back-drop rather than in London but the scene should feature the approach and steps to 10 Downing Street with Sam Brodie leading a deputation of seven or eight men. Alternatively, the approach could be to the Palace of Westminster.

He nods to the uniformed policeman and then turns and nods towards the camera of a television news unit as he knocks on the door of Number 10 or moves into the St. Stephen's entrance of the House.

The door is opened and the deputation led by Sam Brodie files inside.

14

Interior. Strangers' Bar. House of Commons. Day.

Askerton is standing at the bar as Brodie comes in and puts a hand out to detain him.

ASKERTON: Hello, Sam. Good of you to drop in.

BRODIE: Don't get sarky with me, Perce. I wasn't elected yesterday.

ASKERTON: Then you should know better. There's been a Whip on for two days and no vote from Brodie.

BRODIE: Constituency business. I had a deputation to get up.

ASKERTON: It could have waited. Part-time MPs are no good to us.

BRODIE: Don't kid me, Perce. And don't hang that label

on me. We've got too many real part-timers. Barristers and accountants who drop in when the whip's on or when they feel like it.

ASKERTON: The Whips' Office would still like to see you, Sam. Question of solidarity.

BRODIE: You're really trotting them out today. Old-time music-hall. Solidarity? Don't make me laugh.

ASKERTON: I'm sorry, Sam. I know all about your deputation but there are more important things.

BRODIE: Not to me. My constituency comes first.

ASKERTON: Then it shouldn't. The party should. Above all other interests.

BRODIE: When you've managed to convince all the trade-union Members and the special-interest boys that they're sitting here for the sake of Party unity, you might manage to convince me. But don't waste too much breath on the job.

ASKERTON: I believe it.

Brodie's attitude up to now reflects his anger and upset at the wagon sheds closure and his resentment that party discipline—which he does regard as important— should currently be added to his problems.

As he is faced with Askerton's evident sincerity, his manner softens.

BRODIE: I know you do, Perce. But I've got a lot on now and not much of it good.

ASKERTON: Quite a few of us could say that. The job's not as easy as it looks.

BRODIE: It is for some.

ASKERTON: Not you, Sam. Nor me.

BRODIE: No. Have a drink?

Askerton nods and Brodie signals to the barman who puts beer in glasses on the counter.

The train of thought started by Askerton added to Brodie's other worries brings on an almost subconscious realisation in Brodie of the dangers in his own self-imposed loneliness. He broke the loneliness of being away from Andersley once when he was a minister and the pressures are now great enough for him to want to break it again. The name of the break was Sue Marden.

He finishes his beer quickly.

BRODIE: I think I'll make a telephone call.

There is a moment of indecision and then he moves away very quickly.

15

Interior. Working Men's Club. Andersley. Night.

Dewhurst is at his usual table and there are four or five men sitting with him, two of them in working clothes, the rest neatly dressed for an evening out. Two of the men are quite young and obviously sedentary workers. The others are of Dewhurst's stamp, middle-aged engineering or building tradesmen. They are there because they are the chairmen of the ward committees which make up the local party.

Dewhurst, at the head of the table, is the obvious chairman and he is just bringing proceedings to a close. The beer on the table in no way detracts from a business-like manner or an odd, if incongruous, formality.

DEWHURST: I think that's about it, brothers. I only wanted to talk money. Any self-respecting Labour constituency with a full-time agent needs at least £2,000 a year just to exist. Another £2,000 for recruiting and propaganda and we're happy. You're the Ward Chairmen who raise the money and you tell me we're all right. So if Conran's cheque every six months is just marzipan, I reckon we can eat plain cake for a bit.

Sir Joseph Conran comes into the club straight to Dewhurst's table and angry.

CONRAN: What the hell do you think you're playing at, Ernest?

Dewhurst, by pre-arrangement, dismisses his meeting before replying.

DEWHURST (*To the ward chairmen*): Thank you, gentlemen.

The ward chairmen leave and Dewhurst addresses Conran directly.

DEWHURST: You picked tonight for the annual meeting. I've just postponed it.

CONRAN: Without consulting me.

DEWHURST: It's possible. (*Takes a small blue rule book from his pocket and taps it on the table.*) Not polite but possible. And according to the rules. I don't like Item 4 on the Agenda. If we're going to put the knife in Sam Brodie, I'd rather have him facing us when we do it.

16

Interior. Restaurant. Night.

This is a very good restaurant in terms of decor, service and food. Although the opulence is quiet, it is unmistakable. A luncheon bill for two is of the order of £20.

Seated at a table for two with pre-dinner drinks in front of them are Sam Brodie and Sue Marden.

Sue Marden is about twenty-nine, poised and assured,

161

a fashion buyer for a large chain of stores and with a veneer of sophistication and code of conduct which Brodie is twenty years too late to understand fully. She is not immoral but independent. From a fairly glossy world of inherent flimsiness she was attracted to Brodie by reason of the difference between them and was quite content to be worn as an ornament at diplomatic receptions. It flattered her and she thought she was learning. Under the veneer, however, is a good quality of warmth and she made the mistake of becoming very fond of Brodie. Women like Sue Marden do not make mistakes twice. She lifts her glass at Brodie.

SUE: Long time, Sam.

BRODIE: Long time.

Brodie lifts his glass to that and at that moment John Killane comes into the restaurant with Mrs Exton, causing Brodie to look up quite sharply—first with surprise and then a touch of guilt.

Killane sees Brodie and nods in recognition. The nod is returned and then Brodie half-rises in recognition of Mrs Exton.

Sue Marden sees the look and turns.

BRODIE (*In explanation*): My neighbouring MP and a top civil servant.

SUE: He must have a lot of money if this is where he does his persuading.

She continued to remain turned, examining Killane.

BRODIE: Take a good look. He's single. Divorced, anyway.

SUE: I am doing (*She turns back to Brodie, shakes her head.*) Not for me. One of the distant ones. Too many scars on him. Nobody gets closer than ten feet away with that one.

162

Killane and Mrs Exton are seen at their table being discreetly ushered by a bevy of immaculate waiters.

Mrs Exton looks round impressed.

MRS EXTON: Very lavish.

KILLANE: It's meant to be. By way of apology. I was in a tearing hurry the other morning. (*To the hovering sommelier.*) Sherry, manzanilla, please, and gin and tonic for me.

MRS EXTON: I wanted to see you, anyway. You really took me seriously on the nuisance-making.

KILLANE: Only indirectly.

MRS EXTON (*Emphatic*): Only very effectively.

Killane produces Janie's index cards from his inside pocket, fans them neatly like a hand of cards. They have now been further annotated with Killane's own handwriting giving details of letters written or telephone calls made. Every card represents someone with a financial interest in Garsfeld's venture and they have all been asked to have a quiet word with Mrs Exton's Minister.

KILLANE: These?

MRS EXTON: I imagine so. One private telephone call from the treasurer of an international trade union.

KILLANE: He said he'd write.

MRS EXTON: Too cautious. One merchant banker. *He* collared the Minister at a charity reception and hung on to him long enough to annoy the organisers.

KILLANE: That's good. Charity begins at home.

MRS EXTON: Your other people wrote. The property man and the gentleman who went to school with my Minister and the retired NATO general. A strange similarity about the letters. Rather more emphasis on public service than I would have expected.

163

KILLANE: I didn't write the letters. Just asked them not to rattle the cash box too much.

MRS EXTON: Fortunately, my Minister has some humour and a respect for research. He says he's only waiting for a plumber with money in the Garsfeld scheme to catch him in the bath.

KILLANE: I might try and find one.

MRS EXTON: I wouldn't. You've made the point about influential money and made it well.

Killane smiles, watches her accept an embossed menu only slightly less impressive than the Book of Kells.

17

Interior. Working Men's Club. Andersley. Night.

Conran is still sitting at Dewhurst's table. He is talking as Dewhurst moves to switch on a television set in an alcove near them.

CONRAN: I've been half an hour trying to tell you and you still don't see it.

DEWHURST: I see it. But not your way. Just a minute.

By now the television set has warmed up.

An ITN newscaster's face is seen and then film inserts taken, if possible, from previous clips used in this play —wagon sheds exterior and Sam Brodie's deputation in Downing Street or approaching the House of Commons.

NEWSCASTER: There was an orderly demonstration at Andersley wagon sheds today but no threats of strike or workers' takeover.

DEWHURST: Not bloody much there wasn't. We missed it by one of our cat's whiskers.

The film continues and at one stage there will be a still of Sam Brodie against a wagon-shed backdrop.

NEWSCASTER: Meanwhile, Mr Sam Brodie, Labour MP for Andersley East, led a deputation of the town's leaders and union officials to Westminster. Mr Brodie said that he was ashamed and disgusted that any government—Labour or Conservative—could even contemplate dismantling an industrial complex which has contributed so much to this country over the last hundred years. (*Pause for breath, change of item.*) In Washington, further news of important regulations . . .

This has been faded as Conran and Dewhurst move away from the set.

CONRAN: That's the sort of work Sam Brodie *should* be up to.

DEWHURST (*Mildly*): I don't think it's our job to tell him.

CONRAN: It is while I'm Chairman. And don't forget it, Ernest. You won't stop me. The meeting's just postponed—not cancelled.

18

Interior. Restaurant. Night.

Killane and Mrs Exton are at the coffee and brandy stage and Killane is gesturing for the bill.

KILLANE: Sorry to rush but my Association chairman was on this deputation. He's probably still at the House and I'd like to catch him.

MRS EXTON: And make your explanations. You weren't much help to Mr Brodie.

KILLANE: On purpose. Lost cause. Brass band in an

empty hall. There are bigger things to do. Were you there?

MRS EXTON: Oh, yes. I'm usually there to hold hands on the industrial ones. About two a month. Some of them year after year. After a while you get to know the deputation members quite well. Ask about their wives, how the roses are this year. Two or three even send me Christmas cards.

KILLANE: So much for deputations.

MRS EXTON: They make a case. I think what's more important they let people feel they're making a case. Not marooned on some island away from all the decisions.

KILLANE (*Flat, a statement*): But basically they are. Marooned. Just that.

MRS EXTON: You're the figures man, Mr Killane. Look at the record.

She means yes but will not say so and Killane smiles as he signs the bill.

Sam Brodie and Sue Marden are seen at their table. They, too, are at the coffee and brandy stage and are looking at each other.

Brodie turns his head slightly to watch Mrs. Exton and Killane leave the restaurant. This time there is no exchange of nods since Killane is tactful enough to respect Brodie's privacy.

SUE: Why dig it all up again, Sam? Nothing for nearly three years. Then, bang, a telephone call. 'Come to dinner. Tonight. Where you like.' I could have been in Honolulu, married, anything.

BRODIE: But you weren't. I still read about you in the papers. London's shrewdest fashion buyer. Making big decisions on what piece of daftness is in this year. This month even. You're doing very well.

SUE: Not badly. A year of eighteen-hour days when you waved goodbye was a big help.

BRODIE: Love, you did the waving.

SUE: Because you wouldn't. You're too soft-hearted. A granite realist in every way but one—women.

BRODIE: Woman. Just one. You.

SUE: Oh, I know that. It's a reasonable record. Eleven years with four nights a week on your own in London and you only stepped out of line once. Being you, the step had to be drastic. So I had to be just as drastic.

BRODIE: I remember. 'The summer's over, Sam.' Once upon a time there was a Junior Minister with an official car and tickets to the plush receptions. And the lady was flattered. He was important. Ha! (*The noise is one of ironic disparagement. No self-pity in it.*) And the lady was available.

SUE: He was—is—important.

BRODIE: Compared with?

SUE: Anybody. Not just the neutral young men I work with in the lavender blouses and the love bracelets.

BRODIE: I could always try a lavender blouse. Borrow one of yours?

She laughs.

SUE: And he knew exactly where he was going. Except in one direction. Then there was an election and he couldn't afford me any more.

BRODIE: We didn't try very long.

SUE: The great realist. I told you then. Why watch it go sour? Make it quick. Leave a good taste. How long would we have lasted? Sitting over cups of coffee for an hour and a half because it was raining, picking up sandwiches from a Pimlico delicatessen, kidding ourselves that river walks were romantic. That's for the starry-eyed eighteen-year-olds, Sam. Not for us.

BRODIE (*Gesturing round the restaurant's opulence*): This?

SUE (*Flatly*): Yes. This. (*She finishes her brandy.*) So he was better off going back to the bank manager's daughter he married. Who gives him money out of the jug every Monday morning. Did you ever tell her?

BRODIE: No.

SUE: I shouldn't think you'd have to. She'd know.

BRODIE: Not Elizabeth.

SUE: She'd know.

At that moment a waiter who has seen Brodie's previous gesture brings the bill.

The shock shows on Brodie's face.

SUE: Stiff?

BRODIE: Twenty-four quid. For two.

SUE: You said dinner. You said choose the place. Summer's over, Sam. You wanted a ribbon to wear in your coat and this piece of ribbon is too expensive. Somebody had to prove it.

Brodie takes out an envelope, empties it to pay the bill, then, unexpectedly, he smiles at her. He appreciates the lesson, bears no grudge.

BRODIE: They serve a good chip here, anyway.

SUE: Why the call, Sam? Trouble?

BRODIE: Not really.

There is trouble—Garsfeld, Conran, the summons to the Whips' Office—but it is not trouble he is now prepared to share. He will face it on his own.

19

Interior. Strangers' Bar. House of Commons. Night.

Sir George Pendleton and Killane are standing at the bar. This is not one of Sir George's habits. He does not like it very much and some of the disapproval shows.

PENDLETON (*With finality*): First things first, Mr Killane. Keep the wagon sheds open. I believe we've been successful with our deputation.

Killane cannot hide his scepticism about the deputation's value.

PENDLETON: Whatever your opinion. Then Garsfeld, if we so desire.

KILLANE: We?

PENDLETON: All of us. The constituents you represent. No matter what their political persuasion.

KILLANE: Such as Conran.

PENDLETON: He's a constituent.

KILLANE (*Quite gently*): Sir George, I was elected. Presumably that implies trust in my judgement.

PENDLETON: It does.

KILLANE: Then let me get on with it. Your family's been in Andersley for three hundred years. Good farms, good engineering business. You care about the place. But so do I. And I care about it enough to give up a good job to represent it in Parliament. All right, there are other reasons but that's one of them. While you and Conran *stay* in Andersley. Let's use the words, Sir George. Neither you nor Conran can be an MP by proxy. Not if you elect anybody who's any good.

PENDLETON: I agree with all that. I'm not sure Conran does but that's not our affair. I'm offering advice, not warnings. Garsfeld means change. Change is not necessarily progress. And some people are frightened. They require explanations, tact, patience. It's not enough merely to treat them as an audience while you perform as a brilliant parliamentarian. I heard from the Minister of your adept piece of lobbying. An accomplished solo. I congratulate you. But you have three clearly defined responsibilities, Mr Killane. To your Party, to your own conscience and to your constituents. These responsibilities co-exist equally and you neglect any one of them at your peril.

The advice is well meant. It is also sound, deriving from Sir George's own sense of civic responsibility and his experience of it. Killane would be foolish to resent or ignore it. He can only nod in acceptance—thoughtful and with a hint of gratitude.

END OF ACT TWO

ACT THREE

20

Interior. Restaurant. Day.

The restaurant is the same one seen previously. Killane and Janie have just finished lunch and Killane is noticeably relaxed. It has been a pleasant, chatty lunch. When she decides to be, his ex-wife can be very good company.

JANIE: That was very good.

KILLANE: It ought to be. And you would pick the most expensive place in town.

JANIE: I earned it. All that telephoning. Did it work?

KILLANE: We'll know soon. At least I scored a few small personal points. Which cheers me up. Even if they're not tailored to Pendleton's definition of civic responsibility.

JANIE: I've met him. He's sweet. Like some old borzoi that no one has ever, ever left out in the rain.

KILLANE (*Laughing*): I'd forgotten how shrewd you can be when you're trying.

JANIE: Bitchy. Bitchy is easier. And what does your Mrs Flugelhorn think? The civil service lady. The one with the pearls.

KILLANE: Professionally non-committal.

JANIE: You should get Napoleonic. Masterful. Fix up an illicit weekend somewhere. Feather bed. Thatched roof. Sexy tweeds. She'd like that.

171

KILLANE: I've thought of it. I like her.

JANIE: That's no excuse.

KILLANE: Popular fallacy though. State secrets across a shared pillow.

JANIE: Nonsense. What about Lloyd George?

KILLANE (*Laughing*): I'm working on it. Why else do you think I'm in Parliament?

JANIE: I wish I knew. It's not really like you.

KILLANE: Not like you to ask.

JANIE: Morbid interest. What was it you used to sing in the bath?

KILLANE: 'Change and decay in all around I see.' Over and over again. In different keys.

JANIE: That's it. So I wonder what it is in you. Change or decay? Change, I think. We used to talk about it.

KILLANE: You did. Putting the needle in.

JANIE: That's why I never knew about the change, I suppose. That's why I don't know now. Peter's coming in a minute, isn't he?

KILLANE: Yes. We're off up to Andersley.

JANIE: So I'll go. Thank you very much for luncheon.

Over the last few sentences, Janie's manner has changed to a strange and almost shy formality. Until now the lunch has been relaxed and happy but she has been nerving herself to make a statement.

She gets up and leans gracefully on the gilt chair.

Killane picks up the change in manner.

KILLANE: Janie, what is it?

JANIE: I think I want you to take me back and I can't think of one single good reason why you should.

There is a pause and then she turns to greet Chapman who is moving through the tables towards them.

JANIE (*To Chapman*): And here's our own, our very own Blondel. Lute in hand. The ever-present troubadour to our new crusader.

CHAPMAN: That's it. Only the lute's broken, I've got a sore throat and the Saracens can have Jerusalem.

JANIE: You mustn't be disenchanted, dear. Very bad for the complexion. (*To Killane*) Goodbye, John.

KILLANE: I'll ring you.

JANIE: That would be nice.

She drifts elegantly away through the restaurant, people turning to look as they will always turn to look at Janie Killane. Chapman sits down.

KILLANE: Coffee?

CHAPMAN: Oh, yes. It's a good excuse for brandy. They can leave the bottle.

KILLANE: Janie was right.

CHAPMAN: She knows blood when she smells it. We didn't get the Masefield business. They called a full meeting. And old man Masefield was there. Rumbling on about where was young Killane and really this particular research needed Mr Killane's special aptitudes. In the circumstances he thought—and he was sure we would understand—that Masefield's would be better off with ELC. So there it went. A nice fifteen-grand account and I thought we'd got it all sewn up.

KILLANE: There'll be others, Peter. We've missed a few before. Law of averages. Pitch for five, get two.

CHAPMAN: On those figures, we're due for four in a row. And young Simon's leaving.

KILLANE: Why?

CHAPMAN: Ambition. He joined an expanding research agency, was offered a piece of it if he was good enough. He's good enough but the shop's stagnant. He's not going to hang around while fungus grows on his pension fund. And while one of the senior partners is donating his all for Queen and Country.

During this dialogue, coffee and brandy have been served and Chapman sits moodily with the brandy glass in both hands.

CHAPMAN: Sorry, John. I'm a big boy. I should be able to cope. You're right. We've missed a few before.

21

Interior. Dining car. Night.

Mrs Exton is sitting at one of the tables as Sam Brodie, carrying his overnight bag, comes down the aisle.

MRS EXTON: Hello, Mr Brodie. Won't you join me?

BRODIE (*Hesitating*): Yes. Thank you.

He puts his bag on the rack and sits down. He picks up the menu by instinct, realises that he does not have enough money to pay for the meal and there is food waiting for him at home.

He pushes the cutlery to one side.

BRODIE: I'll just have coffee. Andersley or Leeds this time, Mrs Exton?

MRS EXTON: Both. Not curiosity this time. Official.

BRODIE: That sounds hopeful.

MRS EXTON: About the wagon sheds? We'll see. I'm up against the figures, Mr Brodie. And they're not being cooked. If Andersley stays open, somewhere else closes down. Question of choice. Somebody's got to suffer but who'll suffer least.

BRODIE: Not a choice I'd fancy making.

MRS EXTON: You can't avoid it. Or part of it. Somebody has to do the explaining. You.

BRODIE: I'm not good at abstracts. I see five hundred men out of work and a padlock on the gates and Victoria Street empty, and I can smell the hopelessness. It's not a bit of good your saying to me if it isn't my town it'll be somebody else's. I don't want to understand any of that. I want to declare a special interest and stick to it. (*A thought strikes him and he leans back in his seat.*) Funny. I suppose that's just how Conran feels.

Mrs Exton looks at him enquiringly and he shakes his head, not wanting to explain.

22

Interior. Another part of the dining car. Night.

Chapman and Killane are sitting facing each other.

There are papers and folders over the table and Killane closes one of them with an air of finality.

KILLANE: That should do it. Simon can get it tabulated on Monday.

CHAPMAN: Good. Thanks, John.

Killane leans back, rubs his eyes.

CHAPMAN: What about the lunch with Janie?

KILLANE: You mean why? Repaying favours. I enjoyed it.

CHAPMAN: That's what I thought. (*Hesitates.*) Watch it, John. She's a vampire with a radar fix on your particular blood group. I've seen you come in too many mornings with one hand clutching your jugular and the rest of you shaking.

KILLANE: She's settled down now. And I'm still fond of her. And she has a sort of need.

CHAPMAN: So get your running boots on. Let her find some other carcass.

KILLANE: Peter, you're pushing it.

CHAPMAN: I know. But I'm the only one who can. I bought it. I'm the clown you read medical reports to. Late at night over the office bottle. 'Your wife, Mr Killane, requires more care, and attention than you can afford to give her.' And you walking up and down asking who's failed. You? The shrink? Janie? They pick the words, these boys. And the words to latch on to are 'care' and 'afford'. John, if you couldn't afford the care then, you sure as hell can't now. Not with the business on the skids and a whole town of your own to care about.

KILLANE: She's still my responsibility.

CHAPMAN: That's not what the judge said.

Chapman's concern is obvious and it has not been easy for him to put in his small warning. He is a realist and knows that warnings are like help or advice. There is very seldom any gratitude forthcoming for them and it is foolish to expect any.

23

Interior. Working Men's Club. Andersley. Night.

Dewhurst is sitting, still in working clothes, at his usual table. In front of him is a pay-packet.

176

Sir Joseph Conran is sitting opposite and Dewhurst is tipping notes and money out of the pay-packet to produce a small typed slip of paper which he hands to Conran.

CONRAN: I've seen one of those before. A redundancy slip.

DEWHURST: Otherwise known as the bullet. 'Regret to inform you, tra-la. And a special office will be set up to assist in redeployment of personnel.' Redeployment, ha! Straight down to the dole office, quick march.

CONRAN: It's official then? The sheds are closing down?

DEWHURST (*Flicking the redundancy slip*): This isn't a five-pound note. The official statement comes out on Monday. I've just been to the works committee meeting.

CONRAN: I'm sorry, Ernest, but there isn't much I can do now. As you know, we tried.

DEWHURST: Sam Brodie did. And there is something. Garsfeld.

CONRAN: You know what I think about that.

DEWHURST (*Flicking the redundancy slip again*): And this makes no difference? Five hundred men out of work?

CONRAN: I'll need to go into it.

DEWHURST: Yes or no? Now. Garsfeld or not?

CONRAN (*Authoritarian*): I've told you I'll need to go into it.

DEWHURST: I can't take the chance. You've done a lot for the Party and for the town. And a lot for you. Which comes first?

CONRAN: You're getting a bit cheeky, Councillor Dewhurst. None of your bloody business.

DEWHURST: So I'll make it. And I'll tell you first. Which is more than you did for Sam Brodie. The annual meeting is called for tomorrow. First item on the agenda is replacement of you as chairman.

CONRAN: You try it. You don't stand a chance.

DEWHURST: Yes, I do, Brother Conran. (*Takes the ever-present blue rule book from his pocket, taps it on the table.*) It's in the rule book and nothing beats the rules.

CONRAN: I know the rule about electing chairmen.

DEWHURST: I don't see how. We've never used it. You should rotate with a vice-chairman. Instead, you've got in every year on the nod. By agreement. Not this year. This time tomorrow, you'll be ex-chairman Conran.

CONRAN: Oh, no. I've got too much support.

DEWHURST: Try counting it.

CONRAN: What if I change my mind on Garsfeld?

DEWHURST: Tomorrow night you could change it back (*Hard now, disliking turncoats.*) Man, if you believe something, stick to it.

CONRAN: You know, I think I will. And I can still push a lot of people in this town.

DEWHURST: But not very far. And not as chairman of my Party. (*His true opinion shows, flat and factual.*) You're like a Mablethorpe fan-dancer. Neither built for the job nor value for money.

24

Interior. Sam Brodie's living room. Night.

Elizabeth is putting the telephone down as Sam Brodie comes into the room carrying his overnight bag.

Their younger son, Thomas, is sitting on the sofa completely absorbed in a paperback thriller—not lurid— probably a Penguin Chandler in the green cover. Thomas is about twelve, a quiet intelligent boy, quite well-built and good-looking.

As Sam passes the sofa, he touches the boy lightly, a hand on his shoulder. Thomas turns and smiles, then resumes his avid reading.

Brodie puts down his bag, kisses Elizabeth and then holds her by the shoulders for a moment longer than usual, looking at her.

BRODIE (*To Elizabeth*): Hello, my love. (*Turns to Thomas.*) Time you were in bed.

Thomas nods and rises, still glued to the book and wanders out still reading it.

ELIZABETH (*Calling after him*): And don't get reading till midnight.

BRODIE: He didn't hear a word of that. I'll go up in a minute. Where's our Andrew?

ELIZABETH: Youth Club. There's a dance. I told him he could be a bit late.

BRODIE: Dance, she calls it.

ELIZABETH: Just because you got a silver medal for the fox-trot.

BRODIE: Oh, I was young and graceful then.

ELIZABETH: Your meal's in the oven, but I turned it down. Ernest Dewhurst wants to see you for ten minutes. Tonight, if you can. He just rang.

BRODIE: The character who said woman's work was never done should try being an MP.

ELIZABETH: It's just gossip, isn't it? So it's the same thing.

BRODIE (*Laughing*): Don't you get brassfaced with me.
I've got enough with the Whip's Office.

Elizabeth picks up his holdall.

ELIZABETH: Are they in there? Can I see them?

BRODIE: What?

ELIZABETH: The shoes, the suit.

BRODIE: I thought I wouldn't bother.

ELIZABETH: I'll have the money back, then. There's a
sale at Griffin's and I can get new raincoats for the
boys.

BRODIE: I've spent it.

ELIZABETH: Sam, you can't have. How?

BRODIE: I had to see these business people and there
was a lunch and I ended up with the bill.

ELIZABETH: Not twenty-five pounds. Not for one meal.
How many of you were there?

BRODIE: I don't know. I don't remember.

ELIZABETH: It's still not fair. If it's business, they get
expenses. You don't.

BRODIE: They don't know that. And I can't scrounge
all the time.

ELIZABETH: Bit different from scrounging, Sam. We
don't have money like that.

BRODIE: I know, love. I'm sorry. I probably had a
couple of drinks, felt generous.

*Elizabeth is mollified very quickly by Brodie's evident
guilt and regret over the money. She realises that it is
not easy for him in London to watch the pennies as
carefully as she does in Andersley.*

180

ELIZABETH: Never mind. It's not often. You're entitled to a few mad moments.

Brodie grins, touches her face, turns to leave.

BRODIE: Later. (*The meaning obvious but with no leer in it.*) When I've seen Ernest Dewhurst and had something to eat.

25

Interior. Conservative Committee Rooms. Night.

Killane and Chapman have just arrived and are talking to Annie Mackinnon. In the background Conservative party members mingle and chat. The billiard balls click, the glasses clink, the quiet Friday enjoyment.

ANNIE: There's a rumour the wagon sheds are definitely closing. It'll be official Monday. So they say.

KILLANE: Could be why Mrs Exton was on the train.

CHAPMAN: Perhaps she just likes trains. She can have my share.

ANNIE: The Housing Officer's coming in for coffee to-morrow morning. And there's the Wallingridge fête in the afternoon. Abbey Fields. I said you'd be there. Peter?

CHAPMAN: I'll be working.

KILLANE: Besides, he's too heathen to chat to the vicar and too old for toffee apples and rides on the local pony.

ANNIE: In that case I'll only borrow one pair of gum boots. Nine and a half?

KILLANE: That's it.

ANNIE: It always rains for the Wallingridge fête. And

Councillor Dewhurst wants to see you as soon as you can.

KILLANE: I want to see him as well.

ANNIE: You know where?

KILLANE: Oh, yes. Just follow the queue of pint mugs. See you later. (*He leaves quickly.*)

ANNIE (*To Chapman*): He seems in good form.

CHAPMAN: Lucky old him. He says he's had a good week.

ANNIE: And you?

CHAPMAN: Lady, don't ask. The minstrel boy to the wars has been. How's my cuckoo clock?

ANNIE: Still there. Just. Midnight's the worst time. Last night I counted up to thirty-three before it stopped and it took me an hour to get back to sleep.

CHAPMAN: Oh, I asked for that. It's special. What he does is take twelve to six all together. So he can keep quiet until breakfast. Hell, even a cuckoo's entitled to its sleep. And nobody I know goes to bed before midnight.

ANNIE: Somebody you know now does. Me.

CHAPMAN (*Ruminatively*): What an interesting idea.

26

Interior. Working Men's Club. Andersley. Night.

Dewhurst and Brodie are sitting at Dewhurst's table. Brodie has a sheet of paper in front of him.

BRODIE: Item One. Replacement of Chairman. Does Conran know?

DEWHURST: I've just told him.

BRODIE: Why, Ernest? You don't need Conran as an enemy.

DEWHURST: I don't need him as a friend.

BRODIE: But why?

DEWHURST: Wait till your Tory pal turns up.

The steward arrives at the table with a tray on which two pint mugs of beer have been joined by an alien gin and tonic.

He is followed by Killane and Dewhurst points at the gin and tonic.

DEWHURST: Who ordered that?

KILLANE (*Sitting down*): I did. Why pretend? I don't like beer. So I bribed the steward on my way in.

DEWHURST: It looks like Ladies Night at Montmorency Manor.

This is said completely without offence and Killane laughs.

DEWHURST: You'll have heard the sheds are closing.

KILLANE: Only rumours.

BRODIE: And Ernest just told me. I'll keep hammering till it's official.

DEWHURST: Save your energy, Sam. That milk's been spilt. And there are bigger things to do. We can't stop the sheds closing so let's use it. History doesn't pay the rent.

BRODIE: You sound like him. (*Meaning Killane.*)

DEWHURST: That makes him brighter than you are. Perhaps for the wrong reasons.

KILLANE: It'll work on the figures now. Percentage of unemployed goes up. And they'll have to zone Andersley as intermediate.

DEWHURST: There's no 'have to' about it. It'll be up to you two.

Killane takes Janie's index cards from his pocket again.

KILLANE: I think the time has come for long telegrams. Not just me. All of us.

BRODIE (*Looking at the cards*): What's that lot?

KILLANE: The money behind Garsfeld.

DEWHURST: If they'll help.

KILLANE: They are doing.

BRODIE: They should. If Andersley's zoned, Garsfeld is on to a three-quarter million hand-out.

KILLANE: An incentive, Mr Brodie. Sanctioned by Parliament.

BRODIE (*Again not offensively, the mockery gentle*): Listen to him. The ink on his Oath of Allegiance still wet.

DEWHURST: And five thousand jobs. I don't care if they rob a bank to find the money. I'll leave it to you two then. I'd better get off.

BRODIE: How long have you got, Ernest?

DEWHURST: I'll be out in a month. Just in time to dig the bloody garden.

BRODIE: Will you be all right?

DEWHURST: I should think so. (*Grins.*) Unless I try for a job at Conran's. (*He nods and leaves.*)

KILLANE: Will he be all right?

BRODIE (*No bitterness in the voice, the delivery*

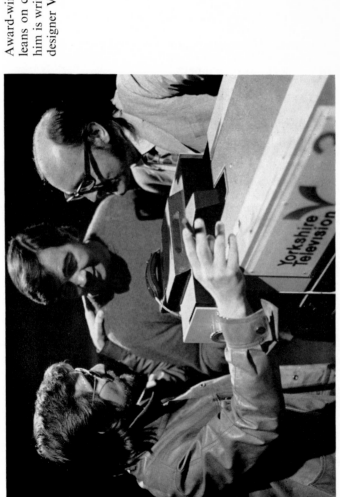

Award-winning director Marc Miller leans on camera and explains. Next to him is writer Edmund Ward and (right) designer Vic Symonds.

Representation of the People Act and the strict limits imposed on the amount an MP can spend on his campaign. Labour agent Cliff Lambert (Richard Hampton) seen left, accuses newly elected Conservative MP John Killane (Michael Gambon) of breaking the law—and perhaps forfeiting the election.

The back benches of the House of Commons. Labour MP Sam Brodie (Colin Blakely) during the adjournment debate in 'Who's been eating my porridge?'

'The Salesmen'. Westminster and the constituency used as sales offices to attract industry. Sam Brodie (Colin Blakely), his wife (Margaret John) and Peter Chapman (William Gaunt) forget sectarian differences among the canapes and the persuasion.

factual): Oh yes. He's got two sons he brought up properly. And while there's food on their table, he'll eat. They'll bury him on the Co-op. And the divi can pay for some of the ale. His friends'll bring the rest. I'll be there.

It is a simple statement of Dewhurst's values and ambitions and it is something which Killane may never quite understand. Brodie accepts it implicitly and understands it without admiration or comment. It is the way Ernest Dewhurst is.

27

Interior. Strangers' Bar. House of Commons. Day.

Killane is sitting at one of the tables with a pile of work in front of him.

At the bar, Sam Brodie is talking to Percy Askerton, one of his party's Assistant Whips.

ASKERTON (*Obviously at the end of his persuasive powers*): Sam, we want you on that committee. Lad, it was your Department when you were in government.

BRODIE: I can't, Perce. Honestly. I'm on two committees as it is. Three mornings a week.

ASKERTON: That's where the work's done. In committee. Mini-parliaments. Well, I can't do more than ask. It won't help you very much if you turn it down, you know. Not after that shemozzle the other week.

BRODIE: I've had my fortune told for that. The full carpet.

ASKERTON: When we get back in, it's that sort of record that gets looked at. It could make the difference between your being given office or not.

BRODIE: I'll have to chance that. I've told you why.

ASKERTON: I know. Andersley zoning. Tearing round ministries. But I've got to find somebody.

BRODIE: So tread on it, Perce. And next time round they'll make you a full whip and you'll get an extra thousand a year.

ASKERTON: I'll earn it. It's all right for the Tories. They tell their Members to do committee work. We have to ask our lot for volunteers.

A liveried messenger comes into the door with five or six green cards in his hand. These indicate that there is a visitor waiting in the central lobby who wishes to see his MP. It is up to the MP whether or not he sees the visitor and quite often the messenger returns with a circle on the card. This indicates that they have been round the House and have not been able to find the member concerned. Quite often the member does not wish to be found.

The messenger proffers a green card towards Brodie so that he can read it without accepting it.

BRODIE (*Taking the card*): Thank you. Yes, I'll take it.

ASKERTON: If you've got time for visitors, I should think . . . (*He is about to say . . . 'You've got time for committees' but it is too late and Brodie is already moving.*)

BRODIE: Sorry, Perce.

As Brodie leaves, he passes Mrs Exton who looks with some surprise as he goes quickly past her. She sees Killane and goes over to him. Killane rises.

KILLANE: Hello Mrs Exton. Can I get you something?

MRS EXTON: No, thank you. Just a meeting you might like to know about. Especially after the way you and Mr Brodie have been rushing round this last two weeks.

186

KILLANE: Is there a decision? Do we know?

MRS EXTON: You must be the least patient MP in the House. Usually they slow down after the first three months. Just to tell you the official meeting on the zoning of Andersley is this afternoon.

KILLANE: I'll be here.

MRS EXTON: No. It's Friday. You go to Andersley. The Minister's agreed—in view of your Garsfeld time element—to letting me send a telegram.

KILLANE: I'll tell my agent. And thank you. (*The impatience again.*) What are the chances?

MRS EXTON (*Shaking her head*): Really, Mr Killane. (*She shakes her head again and walks away.*)

Askerton comes up to Killane.

ASKERTON: What was that about a telegram?

KILLANE (*Surprised*): What? Do all Whips have big ears?

ASKERTON (*Equably*): Everybody in this place has. You'll learn.

KILLANE: And I'd have told Sam Brodie anyway.

ASKERTON: You might. There's some wouldn't. I wouldn't. If I had to tell you, say.

KILLANE: I'll remember.

He looks up to see Sam Brodie coming in the door and starts to move towards him then stops—as does Askerton. The reason is that Brodie is escorting Sue Marden.

Killane sits down again, still looking at Askerton, registering the faint frown of disapproval on the Assistant Whip's face, another potential black mark on the Brodie record.

Killane shrugs, gets on with his work.

Brodie has moved to the quiet end of the bar with Sue Marden.

BRODIE: You'd written 'Important' on the card.

SUE: I thought the name might not be enough.

BRODIE: Why not? Old times' sake, even.

Sue Marden produces an envelope from her bag, puts it quietly on the bar, pushes it towards Brodie, her hand over it.

SUE: So for old times' sake, take this.

BRODIE: What is it?

SUE: Money for the stupid, stinking expensive meal we had. Chosen by me, picked by me. Out of spite and nastiness.

BRODIE: It wasn't like you.

SUE: Then take it.

BRODIE: No. Thanks all the same. The point needed making. And experience is never free.

SUE: It was more than the money.

BRODIE: I know.

SUE: I thought this was going to be easy and it isn't. You're a good man, Sam. Stay where you belong. And that's not what I meant at all. If ever you want to buy a girl a cup of coffee . . . Goodbye, Sam.

She puts the envelope in her bag, turns and leaves, watched as always by the MPs in the bar.

188

28

Interior. Conservative Club. Andersley. Night.

Sir Joseph Conran and Sir George Pendleton are standing in front of the fire, side by side, talking.

PENDLETON : No decision has yet been taken.

CONRAN : What if it is?

PENDLETON : The chances are slight—in my opinion. Other parts of the country are far more deserving.

CONRAN : But Garsfeld doesn't—won't—go there.

PENDLETON : I share your concern, Sir Joseph, but I think the issues can be negotiated as they crop up.

CONRAN : There'll be new union agreements—which'll spread to our factories. There'll be priority claims for housing lists—which'll affect some of our workers.

PENDLETON : And the good of the community? The country, if you like?

CONRAN : My political views haven't changed. We've had disagreements in the Party before. I'm still Labour. You're still Conservative. But we're both businessmen.

PENDLETON : Both with strong political views. You may be right. The views may be unimportant in the context of the change coming to this town.

CONRAN : And we'll need something a lot tougher than the Chamber of Commerce.

PENDLETON : Perhaps. But let me finish. I believe you to be sincere. I also believe Brodie and Dewhurst to be sincere. I've always preferred collaboration to vendettas.

CONRAN : Then I don't think we'll get very far.

PENDLETON: I disagree. If our concern is really for Andersley, it's up to us to try.

29

Interior. Conservative Committee Rooms. Night.

Brodie, Annie Mackinnon and Peter Chapman are sitting at a table. Killane is on his feet, hands in pockets, repressing an urge to walk up and down. Chapman is nursing, rather disconsolately, the cuckoo-clock.

KILLANE: For God's sake, how long do these meetings go on? They should have finished by now. Annie, what did the Post Office say when you rang them?

ANNIE: I've told you twice. Nothing yet. When the telegram arrives, they'll rush it over.

CHAPMAN: It's tough on a bicycle with all these hills.

Killane almost glares at him.

BRODIE: That's the best reason I've heard all night. Sit down, Mr Killane. Before they charge you for holes in the carpet.

Killane pulls a chair towards him and then a Post Office boy comes into the room.

Killane takes the telegram from him, starts to tear it open and then recognises protocol and turns to Brodie.

BRODIE: Go on.

Killane takes out the telegram, reads it, hands it to Brodie. Brodie nods.

BRODIE: Let's go and find Ernest Dewhurst.

The reactions have been hidden and there is only relief

that the telegram should have arrived. It is impossible to tell whether the decision is favourable or not.

Annie turns in bafflement to Peter Chapman as Brodie and Killane leave.

ANNIE: What's in the telegram?

CHAPMAN: Does it matter? Yes or no. It's trouble. At least for us. The helots on the fringe of the mighty.

Annie grins at him and at that moment the cuckoo clock on Peter Chapman's knee chooses to pop out with its warbled bisyllable, repeated to announce nine o'clock.

Chapman pats the cuckoo fondly on the head.

CHAPMAN: I'm on your side, pally.

30

Interior. Working Men's Club. Andersley. Night.

Dewhurst is sitting alone at his usual table as Brodie and Killane hurry towards him. There is still no indication on their faces of the telegram decision.

Dewhurst is leaning back, happy. The reason for his happiness is the performance of a close-harmony duet of 'Bye, Bye, Blackbird'.

As Killane and Brodie come in, the lines have been reached:

'Sugar's sweet,
So is she,
Bye, bye, blackbird.'

Brodie talks over this.

BRODIE: Ernest, the telegram's arrived.

191

DEWHURST: Listen a minute. I like this song.

Here is a man who has learned patience and Killane recognises it. He sits down and, as the duet continues, Killane joins in softly.

'There's no one to love or understand me.
Oh, the hard-luck stories they all hand me.
Make my bed, light the light,
I'll be home late tonight,
Blackbird, bye bye
Blackbird, bye, bye'

Dewhurst turns to him.

DEWHURST: Didn't think you'd know the words to that.

KILLANE: Also to four hundred-odd assorted hymns.

DEWHURST: That's always handy. If ever you're near a big accident sometime.

BRODIE: They said yes, Ernest. Andersley's been zoned. We'll get the jobs.

Dewhurst nods, lifts his glass, drinks.

DEWHURST: That's good news, Sam. That's very good news.

KILLANE: We thought we'd send a telegram to Garsfeld. I'd like your name on it.

DEWHURST: That's a kind thought, lad. With your politics, I shouldn't make a habit of it.

BRODIE: He'll learn. (*To Dewhurst*) No more word on the wagon sheds, Ernest? No hope?

DEWHURST: No. No hope at all.

KILLANE: We'd better go and tell Garsfeld.

BRODIE: Yes. Just don't tell him the price. Just don't

tell him Victoria Street's always going to look empty without a railwayman on it.

They sit for a moment and in Brodie's eyes can almost be seen the final padlock on the wagon shed gates. Then these fade in.

31

Exterior. Andersley wagon sheds. Day.

Film sequences.

The padlocked gates, the empty sheds, the price Andersley has paid for a hypothetical future prosperity.

[*Credits*]

Play Four

WHOSE LAW?
WHOSE ORDER?

Cast

S A M B R O D I E	*Colin Blakely*
J O H N K I L L A N E	*Michael Gambon*
P E T E R C H A P M A N	*William Gaunt*
A N N I E M A C K I N N O N	*Joanna Van Gyseghem*
C L I F F L A M B E R T	*Richard Hampton*
E R N E S T D E W H U R S T	*Bill Dean*
P E R C Y A S K E R T O N	*William Moore*
S I R G E O R G E P E N D L E T O N	*Ralph Michael*
J O E G A R S F E L D	*Alex Scott*
M R S E L L E R B Y	*Gwen Cherrell*
S I R R O B E R T W E N S L E Y	*Colin Gordon*
S A M M Y B R I G G	*Andrew McCulloch*
H E N R Y P A R K E R	*Mark Dignam*
E L I Z A B E T H B R O D I E	*Margaret John*

Non-speaking

Elizabeth, Sam Brodie's daughter; women and children
on their way home from school; construction and
machinery installation workers; local Andersley
workers; stewards at Andersley Working Men's Club
and Conservative Club; a uniformed police sergeant;
two other uniformed policemen; Members of Parliament.

Interiors

1. Labour Party surgery
2. Conservative Committee Rooms
3. Conservative Club
4. Working Men's Club
5. Strangers' Bar, House of Commons
6. Library corridor, House of Commons
7. Backdrop of Back Benches
8. Railway dining car
9. Interior of Rose Ellerby's pub

Exteriors

1. Hill in Andersley. Stone-walled to one side, featuring heavy lorry and women and children
2. Exterior. Andersley Labour Party Office
3. Exterior. Andersley public house in narrow street, featuring men fighting and policeman
4. The same street with Andersley workers moving down it towards the pub
5. John Killane getting out of a taxi outside the House of Commons
6. Canal bank, featuring Sam Brodie, his young daughter and football supporters crossing a bridge

ACT ONE

Titles.

1

Exterior. Road in Andersley. Day.

Film sequence.

This should be a fairly narrow road on a hill with a stone wall on one side leading from Andersley Abbey and through one of the new housing estates to the large site where the Garsfeld factory estate is in the process of construction.

A heavy construction lorry is seen coming down the hill too fast, the gears grating. It can be loaded with removed spoil or reject prefabricated concrete elements. It is obviously loaded above its legal capacity.

A group of people is then seen walking on the narrow pavement up the hill towards a curve. There are four or five women, two of them pushing prams and a gaggle of about ten children—between five and seven years old—just collected from primary school.

The lorry rounds the bend, careers towards them, and they flatten themselves against the wall, the mothers grabbing at their children.

One of the women, about thirty-five, Mrs Harris, stares after the lorry and then runs to a junction where a uniformed policeman is standing.

She points after the lorry, her face angry, mouthing a complaint.

The policeman shrugs, turns and walks away.

Two small children who have followed Mrs Harris are seen staring after the policeman.

2

Interior. Labour Party surgery. Day.

Set as previous plays.

Brodie is standing behind the desk with Cliff Lambert leaning on the wall at the side of him.

BRODIE: If this is happening every day, Mrs Harris, we'd better look into it. I'll do what I can and Mr Lambert will let you know.

Mrs Harris is then seen tight-lipped. With her is another of the women seen in the procession home from school.

They both nod and leave and Brodie shrugs much as the policeman shrugged.

3

Exterior. Andersley Labour Party Office. Day.

Film sequence.

This exterior with its slogans and exhortations has been seen in previous plays.

Mrs Harris and her companion are seen leaving the office and stand for a moment near the sign which reads: 'Andersley Labour Party'. There is some satisfaction on their faces. It was not easy for them to summon up enough courage to see their Member of Parliament and now they are confident that something will be done.

4

Interior. Labour Party surgery. Day.

Brodie sits on the desk.

BRODIE: They ought to close that Abbey Road. It's always been a menace. They built it for tired pilgrims, not 30-ton trucks.

LAMBERT: Not much chance of that. Not now it's the fastest road to the Garsfeld job. (*Flash of anger.*) He was only supposed to move into the town. Nobody said anything about him taking it over.

BRODIE: It won't last for ever. Another six months and it'll all be built.

LAMBERT: That's why the coppers let him get away with it. Magic Garsfeld and his magic factory estate and his magic five thousand jobs. He's bloody hypnotised everybody.

BRODIE: He was promised co-operation. That's why he moved here.

LAMBERT: And one day one of those bloody great lorries is going to get out of control on that hill. And it's going to smear half a dozen women and kids along fifty yards of stone wall. And, as usual, (*His voice breaks into fruity BBC announcer's diction*) 'The driver of the lorry was unhurt but is in hospital being treated for shock'. (*In his normal voice.*) While he counts his bloody time bonus.

BRODIE: I'll look at it. Especially if the police are keeping their backs turned.

LAMBERT: Looking's not much good. Doing's better.

BRODIE (*Mildly*): You aren't running things yet, Cliff. How was the training course?

LAMBERT: Not bad.

BRODIE: Pity it won't do you any good.

201

LAMBERT: So Conran isn't Chairman any more. (*Philosophically.*) I managed to stay neutral. So it was worth a try.

BRODIE: Why?

LAMBERT: I've told you before. You're the MP but I think you've forgotten what the Party stands for. I haven't. And I'm not going to stay a political agent all my life.

BRODIE (*Smiling*): Cards face up.

LAMBERT: That's right.

BRODIE: You'll never make a politician that way, Cliff.

LAMBERT: Oh, but I will. (*Hard.*) I believe in the cards.

BRODIE: Good.

LAMBERT (*A little puzzled by Brodie's seemingly easy acceptance of his previous defection*): No hard feelings?

BRODIE: Not this time. Is there any more trouble from this Garsfeld project?

LAMBERT: Nothing but. It's Friday. Pay day. Wait till tonight, walk round, see for yourself.

5

Exterior. Andersley public house in a narrow street. Night.

Film sequence.

This is a street in one of the rougher parts of Andersley and the first impression is one of noise, angry shouts and breaking glass.

In the street outside the pub, three or four men are fighting and another four men slam the pub doors open

*and join in. The fight is brief and brutal, the odds five
to three. It lasts no more than five seconds and then
five men run down the street.*

*Two others lean against the wall, one of them mopping
blood from his face.*

*The other man is on the floor in the pub doorway and
the owner of the pub—a woman—comes out, kneels by
him and lifts his head.*

*Then his two friends pick the man up, wait until his
groggy legs start to function, and move away.*

*The landlady is then seen clearly in the light from the
door. She is Mrs Rose Ellerby, a young-looking fifty
and not the stereotype brassy pub landlady. She is
attractive in a hard buxom sort of way and like all good
barmaids has a chameleon quality which will make her
all things to all customers. She is, however, shrewd
enough to own and run a pub in a fairly rough quarter,
and authoritative enough for there to have been—until
the Garsfeld project—very little trouble. The three men
who have lost the fight are then seen twenty yards from
the pub. They pass a uniformed policeman who looks
at them equably, makes no attempt to stop or question
them.*

*This is seen by Mrs Ellerby who starts to move towards
the policeman and then stops as he crosses to the other
side of the street.*

6

Interior. Conservative Committee Rooms. Day.

*This is the part of the committee rooms which serves as
Annie Mackinnon's office.*

*Peter Chapman is on his own in the room, standing
under a large photograph of Mr Heath. He is pretend-
ing to steer a boat.*

The door is thrown open and Chapman turns guiltily.

Mrs Ellerby stalks into the room, neatly dressed, an element of successful business-woman about her, no dyed fox-fur accessories.

MRS ELLERBY: I want to see you.

CHAPMAN: I don't think you do.

MRS ELLERBY: All right, I voted Labour. But you're the MP and I've got a complaint.

CHAPMAN: Madam, I'm not the MP. I wouldn't be the MP if they gave me a scale model of the Houses of Parliament in solid gold.

MRS ELLERBY: What are you then?

CHAPMAN: One of Mr Killane's business partners. He should be here soon. Won't you sit down?

MRS ELLERBY: No, thank you. I've got a pub to open in ten minutes. Some of us have to work to keep your lot going. Will you tell Mr Killane I want to see him. My name's Mrs Ellerby and I run the 'Crown' in Wellington Street.

CHAPMAN: Mr Killane is very busy.

MRS ELLERBY: It doesn't look like it. Tell him I want to know what he's going to do about my pub being half-wrecked every Friday by a load of foreigners and Scotchmen and all sorts building these new factories. And why you never see a policeman lift a finger.

CHAPMAN: I'll certainly do that, madam. One of the few things I manage to feel strongly about is the idea of any pub being wrecked. If that happens, nothing's sacred.

He is, however, writing down Mrs Ellerby's name and the address of the pub and this stops her rising in anger at his flippancy. Displeasure is evinced only by a forceful exit.

As she leaves, the telephone rings and Chapman, shaking his head, picks it up.

CHAPMAN (*Into telephone*): Yes. No, I'm sorry Miss Mackinnon isn't here. What? No, this is the window-cleaner. Mr Killane should be back in a minute. He's down at the Town Hall with the Welfare Officer. Yes, it's about Mrs Donaldson. (*Puts phone down.*) Of course, I'm well-informed. I'm a Conservative window-cleaner.

During the conversation he has been scribbling on the telephone message pad full details of the call. John Killane comes into the room.

CHAPMAN: That was the legal aid people about Mrs Donaldson. I said you'd ring back.

KILLANE: Thanks, Peter. You'd make a good agent but where's the proper one? Where the hell is Annie?

CHAPMAN: Search me. (*Thinks about this.*) That's an interesting thought. I wouldn't mind Annie Mackinnon concealed about my person.

Killane has crossed to the desk where folders and files are arranged neatly.

CHAPMAN: It's in better shape than our office. And Mrs Gresham rang to say she'd be standing by if you needed help.

Killane has pulled the telephone message pad across to him.

KILLANE: Who's Mrs Ellerby?

CHAPMAN: A lady publican.

KILLANE: Trouble with some of the hooligans from the Garsfeld job?

CHAPMAN: That's it.

Killane thumbs through three or four of the case folders.

KILLANE: That makes the fourth this week.

CHAPMAN: She was a shade bitter about the police.

KILLANE: They all are. I'd better go and see her. We signed on with Garsfeld for five thousand jobs—not the old-time Wild West.

CHAPMAN: Can *you* lean on the police?

KILLANE: Oh, yes. If they're not doing their job. That's what I was elected for.

7

Interior. Andersley public house. Day.

This is the 'Crown', the free house owned and run by Mrs Ellerby.

The saloon bar is cosier than the exterior of the building would suggest. There is a good deal of fretted polished woodwork and red velvet upholstery on the seats of the bent-wood chairs.

The public bar is functional but the wood is scrubbed to newness on the benches and tables. There is pine sawdust on the floor, sprinkled lightly, a rare hygienic custom which only publicans' idleness has failed to perpetuate.

Mrs Ellerby, again neatly dressed, a bright gingham overall over her good clothes, is standing behind the bar talking to Sam Brodie.

MRS ELLERBY: I've asked the other chap to come in as well. It's getting past a joke, Sam.

BRODIE (*Looking round the pub*): I've had a few rough nights in here myself.

MRS ELLERBY: That's when you were playing Rugby League and you'd won and you wanted to smash something else besides other people's faces. But you'd come

206

round Sunday and apologise and pay for it. And those days I could have had four coppers here in minutes.

Killane comes into the pub, sees Brodie and walks across to join him.

KILLANE: Mrs Ellerby?

MRS ELLERBY: Yes.

KILLANE: I'm John Killane. You wanted to see me.

MRS ELLERBY: More than that. I want something doing. I'm having to close this bar every Friday and Saturday and the public next door's a shambles.

BRODIE: Good for business though, Rose.

MRS ELLERBY: Not with all my regulars gone. And not the sort of pub I want to run. I'll worry about the trade, Sam Brodie. You worry about getting the police to do something.

KILLANE: Have you complained to the police yourself?

MRS ELLERBY: Every Saturday and Sunday morning. And nothing happens.

BRODIE: I thought Charlie kept an eye on things for you.

MRS ELLERBY: He's packed it in. I don't blame him.

BRODIE: I can't see Charlie being frightened of much.

MRS ELLERBY: He was frightened of this lot. What's worst is you can't talk to them. They don't come from round here. They don't care what happens. God help us if this lot stays in Andersley. It'll be blackies next and that's when I close this pub.

BRODIE: You're worse than your mother. I remember her saying once that a foreigner was anybody born in the next street.

MRS ELLERBY: She'd pack up her grave and move if she could see this lot.

BRODIE: You don't bring a factory estate this size in without a bit of bother. It'll be good for Andersley in the long run.

MRS ELLERBY: Easy for you to talk. You don't work behind that bar when they're throwing pint pots.

KILLANE: And I don't agree with Mr Brodie. I think something should be done.

BRODIE: Such as what?

KILLANE: Stop the police negligence. We can see the Chief Constable.

BRODIE: You can if you want. Up to you.

MRS ELLERBY (*To Brodie*): Can't you do anything?

BRODIE: I'll think about it.

Killane looks at Brodie, slightly contemptuous.

KILLANE: We need more than that. I'll be in touch, Mrs Ellerby.

Killane leaves and Brodie leans on the bar, his face quiet, slightly amused.

BRODIE: All the young crusaders charging into battle.

MRS ELLERBY: At least he's trying.

BRODIE: Oh, yes. I'll give him that.

8

Interior. Conservative Club. Night.

Set as previous plays.

Sir George Pendleton, Chairman of the local Conservative Association, is standing in front of the fireplace with the Chief Constable of Andersley, Henry Parker.

Henry Parker is about fifty-five, a big man who has not run to fat. There is a slow and quiet authority about him and his origins in the lower ranks of the force are still obvious in the trace of local accent, in the hard lines of experience on his face and in his delivery and voice.

PENDLETON: Have you met John Killane?

PARKER: Only once. He came in to thank me for the police arrangements during the Election. Seemed a nice keen lad.

Killane comes into the club and directly across to Pendleton.

KILLANE: Hello, Sir George.

PENDLETON: Mr Killane, Chief Constable Parker. Though I believe you've met.

KILLANE: Once. Briefly. And I was a lot happier then. (*His attitude reflects both anger and intention to express it.*)

PENDLETON: I'll leave you to it then.

PARKER: I'd rather you stayed, George. You're Chairman of this gentleman's Party Association and you're also on the Watch Committee. What's it about, Mr Killane?

KILLANE: Why wrap it up? Police negligence.

PARKER: Fact or gossip?

KILLANE: Fact. Lorries charging down Abbey Road. Overloaded and badly driven. And the junction policeman waving them by. The complaints made by my constituents and the facts confirmed by my agent.

PARKER: Overloading, I've yet to prove. We've made a few checks. Abbey Road? It's always been dangerous. We've been on to the Borough Engineer for five years. Widen it or close it. You can see the correspondence at the Town Hall or in my office. Negligence, no.

KILLANE: I don't think you avoid responsibility by writing a few letters. Not good enough.

PARKER: And what else?

KILLANE: At least one public-house being smashed up on pay-nights. And policemen cross the road to avoid trouble.

PARKER: I can answer that. My instructions.

KILLANE: Then I want those instructions cancelled.

PARKER: Perhaps you'd like my job as well. Nothing to it. Only thirty years as a policeman.

PENDLETON: Mr Killane, I think requests are always more viable than demands.

KILLANE: Not in this case. Not without reason.

PARKER: I'll give you reasons. (*His voice hard now.*) I'm short-staffed. Every police force in the country is. And we've got enough to do sorting out villains without putting special squads on punch-ups. Especially this sort of punch-up. I also happen to care about what men I've got. In that area, I've mostly the older ones on night duty, and I'm not having half a dozen good coppers in the infirmary every Monday morning because a gang of jocks or paddywacks or some other rag-tag and bobtail get too much ale in them. It'll sort itself out.

KILLANE: It won't unless you do something.

PARKER: I was a super in this town during the war. Free French, Poles, Yanks. I know one or two coppers on disability pension with bayonet wounds. Not again. Not now I'm Chief Constable. This lot can take it out on each other.

KILLANE: And that isn't good enough either.

PARKER: It is for me.

KILLANE: So I'll make noises elsewhere.

PARKER: Such as the Home Office.

KILLANE: That's right. But I'll get something done.

PARKER: You do that, Mr Killane. And I appreciate the warning.

KILLANE: I have to. It seems to me I'm the only person able or willing to do anything.

PARKER: Willing, yes. Able might be another thing.

KILLANE: I'm the Member of Parliament for this area.

PARKER: Funny. I've worked here and other places. I suppose I've known—what?—twenty, thirty MPs. They all think they're something special. They're not, you know. They're citizens—just like anybody else.

KILLANE: With special powers and privileges. Including the right to . . .

PARKER (*Interrupting quickly*): . . . To do what? To dictate. Not to the police, Mr Killane. Not ever. You stick to theories. I've seen too much blood. You gave me a warning so I'll give you one. As Chief Constable, I'm responsible to the Watch Committee in this town and only to the Watch Committee. It pays my wages. There's a special committee of chief constables and any Home Office instructions come down to me through it. Whether I take these instructions is up to my Watch Committee and then me. The system works, Mr Killane. It might not suit you when you can't do anything about it. But I'm a citizen in uniform controlled by other citizens. And the people that elected you depend on me to keep them safe at night. (*Turns to Pendleton.*) Thanks for the drink, George. Good night, Mr Killane.

Parker's delivery has been flat and factual, some of it almost as if he were giving evidence in court. There has been very little anger in it but occasionally hard determination has shown through. Parker is proud of his position and the way it was reached. He is the last man in Andersley to succumb to any outside pressures.

211

PENDLETON: I suppose it's youth and enthusiasm but I wish you'd thought to have a word with me first. You were very lucky to have used words like police negligence in front of Henry Parker and got away with it as easily as you did.

KILLANE: I can see that.

PENDLETON: Not your fault. As Henry said, it's easy to develop an elitist mentality when you're an MP—especially a new one. But that's Westminster and this is Andersley. A different set of machinery.

KILLANE: I promised Mrs Ellerby I'd do something.

PENDLETON: And you've tried. Parker won't blame you for it.

KILLANE: And Sam Brodie sat there and listened. Then let me tear off and make a fool of myself.

PENDLETON: That won't do you any harm occasionally. (*Presses the bell push near the fire place.*) Let me get you a drink.

9

Interior. Conservative Committee Rooms. Day.

Chapman is at Annie's desk. It is covered with charts and graphs. Chapman is using a slide rule, extracting statistics and writing summary figures on a clipboard.

It is mid-afternoon and Annie Mackinnon comes into the office carrying a small suitcase. There is a newspaper in her other hand.

Chapman looks up, pleased to see her.

CHAPMAN: Hey, Cinderella. The ball must have ended early.

ANNIE: They always do, Peter. They always do.

CHAPMAN: Well. That was a nice elegaic note.

ANNIE: Where's John?

CHAPMAN: Out. He's been trying to reorganise the local fuzz. CS gas and rubber bullet time. All for use on Garsfeld's roustabouts.

Annie puts the newspaper on the desk, indicates an item in it.

ANNIE: I can see why. One of his lorries knocked down three children this morning.

Chapman picks up the newspaper.

CHAPMAN: Rush job. Eight-month contract. (*Shakes his head, genuinely sad.*) Poor little sods. And for what?

ANNIE (*Moving to a filing cabinet*): We had complaint files on Abbey Road. I'm glad John did something before this happened.

CHAPMAN: The mothers'll be glad, too. That's politics for you.

Annie looks at Chapman sharply but he has gone back to his imaginary ship's wheel under the photo of Heath and is spinning it as he sings a shanty.

CHAPMAN (*Singing*): 'And we'll drink tonight to the midshipmate. So belay, me lads, yo-ho!' John's a bit fed up with you, too.

ANNIE: Why? Everything was in order. Mrs Gresham was on stand-by.

CHAPMAN: He ran into a brick wall called Chief Constable Henry Parker. And bounced. You could have told him it was there.

ANNIE: Yes, indeed. Anybody could. He could also have looked in the files.

On this, Killane has come into the room. He is also carrying the newspaper.

KILLANE: They were locked.

ANNIE: Mrs Gresham has a key.

KILLANE: There wasn't time. And, Miss Mackinnon, if you're going to disappear, I think I'm entitled to a little notice of it. And how to get in touch with you.

Killane's tone is sharp and Annie's first reaction is to reply with the same sharpness. Instead she speaks quietly, some of the control showing.

ANNIE: Mr Killane, how many weekends have I had off since you were elected?

KILLANE: None. (*He flicks the newspaper.*) But you could have picked a better weekend than this one.

ANNIE: I've seen it. That's why I came in. But I'm not clairvoyant. I'll practise.

CHAPMAN: Seconds out.

Killane realises that he has been over-irritable.

KILLANE: Sorry, Annie. Four late sittings this week. Then Garsfeld, then that bone-headed Chief Constable. (*Flicks the newspaper again.*) Now this.

CHAPMAN: That's better. If you don't watch it, you could turn into a bit of a pig. And I remember when you were human. A perfectionist. But human.

ANNIE: And you can't take too much of the responsibility on yourself. (*There is a flicker here of some private thought as she adds.*) Believe me.

CHAPMAN: There she goes again. I may sing 'Misty'.

This brings a sharp reaction from Annie. Chapman has scored an unwitting point by the reference to romance and Chapman himself is quick enough to realise this and look at her curiously.

KILLANE (*To Annie*): What happened to you anyway?

ANNIE: My private life.

CHAPMAN: John doesn't have any. He won't know what you're talking about.

KILLANE: Try me.

ANNIE: Sounds silly. I know what being an agent's about. Work most evenings, be sociable, organise. Public, public, public. Watching everything I do and say. I just got tired of the faces. Tired of smiling at the people. Tired of being on show all the time. I wondered what had happened to me. (*Shrugs.*) Perhaps I'm in the wrong job.

KILLANE: Oh no, you're not. But don't take off again, Annie. Not without telling me.

ANNIE (*With reserve*): I'll try.

She is too honest to give any firm assurance and Killane would have liked one. He frowns slightly and Chapman steps in again, starting to gather the graphs and records from the desk.

CHAPMAN: The pubs are open and I'm prepared to spring for large glasses of tonic wine. Vitamin-fortified, guaranteed to restore enthusiasm and remove dandruff. I drink it by the quart. I have to.

KILLANE (*Picking up the newspaper again and shaking his head*): Not for me, Peter. I'm going back to London. I'm going to make a lot of noise and you won't really have to listen to hear it all up in Andersley. I'm going to nail Parker.

10

Interior. Working Men's Club. Andersley. Night.

Lambert and Brodie are sitting at Ernest Dewhurst's table. They each have a pint of beer and there is a spare one placed in front of Dewhurst's usual seat.

LAMBERT: Bad news about those kids.

BRODIE: Yes.

215

LAMBERT: What are you going to do about it?

BRODIE: Nothing. Nothing I can do.

LAMBERT: It still makes me sick. But that's the trouble with a Tory police force. Still, I suppose you have to be Tory to be a policeman.

BRODIE: Stalin's lot didn't do so bad. And the police aren't political.

LAMBERT: The Watch Committee is.

BRODIE: With a Labour majority.

LAMBERT: Forget it. Two of them have never been to the meetings. Old Pendleton as good as runs it. And he stands to make money out of Garsfeld.

BRODIE: So does half this town.

LAMBERT: They'll laugh on the other side of their cash boxes when Andersley's full of bloody foreigners.

BRODIE: You sound like Rose Ellerby. Come to that, you're a foreigner yourself.

LAMBERT: But I don't get special privileges from the police.

BRODIE: You're sure about the Watch Committee set-up, Cliff?

LAMBERT: Oh, yes. Check the minutes.

Brodie nods, thinks about this.

Ernest Dewhurst ambles up to the table.

BRODIE: Evening, Councillor Dewhurst.

DEWHURST: Evening, Mr Brodie.

Dewhurst sits, reaches with automatic precision for his pint.

LAMBERT: Hey, Ernest, you're on the Watch Committee. How about lighting a fire under old jackboots Parker?

216

DEWHURST: No reason. Best Chief this town's ever had. You can't buy him, frighten him or tell him how to do his job.

LAMBERT: Not in Committee, you can't. They just pull the old quiet strings over at the Club.

DEWHURST: Try telling George Pendleton that. Last month his son got a hundred-pound fine and his licence taken away for being drunk in charge.

BRODIE: He's not quite as drastic with—what do you call them, Cliff?—Garsfeld's Foreign Legion.

DEWHURST: Bit of rope there. Not much. Simple. The faster the job's over, the faster the town gets back to normal.

LAMBERT: I think it's political. Tory money.

DEWHURST: You would. You can make anything political if you chew at it long enough. You even reckon Little Noddy was the first Young Conservative.

As he says this and takes a drink, the club starts to empty. Glasses are slammed down and a rush of men converge on the door. Three or four of the faces are recognisable, men in their thirties, neatly dressed, respectable. Their faces are hard and angry.

BRODIE: What's to do, then?

DEWHURST: I heard it on the way here. One of the kids they ran over this morning just died.

Lambert half-turns in his chair as more men leave the club. When he speaks, there is just a trace of satisfaction in his voice.

LAMBERT: Now somebody's going to do something about it.

He is tempted to rise and Brodie puts a hand on his arm.

BRODIE (*Hard*): And settle nothing. All that mob'll do is pull in every hooligan and boot-artist from fifty

217

miles round here. Then the police will really have something to do. (*To Dewhurst, urgently.*) Better make a phone call, Ernest.

Dewhurst nods, rises, moves away quickly, fumbling in his pocket for telephone change.

11

Exterior. Andersley public house, in narrow street. Night.

Film sequence.

The men who have been seen leaving the Working Men's Club are moving down the street, orderly but determined. One of the men waits at the door of the pub, looks round to check on the dozen or so men with him and then pushes the pub door open with a crash.

END OF ACT ONE

ACT TWO

12

Interior. Conservative Club. Day.

It is now Monday morning. Sir George Pendleton and Henry Parker are standing near the fireplace with coffee cups in their hands.

There is a contusion on Parker's forehead from the disturbances of the weekend. This is not an Alan Ladd cosmetic bruise but an ugly welt. Parker is a working Chief Constable and quite capable of joining in with his officers to subdue trouble.

PENDLETON: Do you want a Watch Committee meeting, Henry?

PARKER: No need. We're over Friday and Saturday and last night was quiet enough. We've isolated the trouble spots and I've put on extra patrols. And we've got a couple of dozen bright sparks in the jug. (*He touches the contusion on his head.*)

PENDLETON: All local people?

PARKER: All locals.

PENDLETON: I'm not too happy about that.

PARKER: Seven of them for thieving. There's a barney on, so break some shop windows and help yourself.

PENDLETON: I'm still not happy.

PARKER: You can't pinch somebody for defending himself. And if the hairy political lads want to shout persecution they're welcome. Same applies if they

219

shout privilege for Garsfeld's lot—like your chap Killane. I'm running a police force. Investment, penalty clauses, construction time are none of my business. Mob-handed street fights are. I'm not looking forward to next Saturday. The football match and two local teams.

PENDLETON: I see Sam Brodie's staying well out of it.

PARKER: He's got sense. And he knows this town. Better than Killane does.

13

Exterior. House of Commons. Day.

Film sequence.

A taxi is seen driving into the central courtyard.

Killane gets out, nods to the policeman, hurries into the house.

14

Interior. Strangers' Bar. House of Commons. Day.

Set as previous plays.

Percy Askerton is talking to Sam Brodie. The two men's attitudes reflect argument and disagreement.

BRODIE: I won't do it, Perce.

ASKERTON: Then you're an even bigger fool than you've been acting lately.

BRODIE: I won't do it. I want it left alone.

ASKERTON: You can't. Not when it's been handed to us on a plate.

220

BRODIE: Perce, you're just an Assistant Whip. When I take orders, I'll get them a bit higher up.

ASKERTON: I'm also a friend of yours. And if you have to wait for orders or something like this, they'll really start to wonder how much Sam Brodie bothers about supporting his own Party these days.

There is no rebuttal for this. It is true enough to make Brodie stop and think. Askerton presses the advantage.

ASKERTON: Score some points, Sam. For your own sake as well as ours.

BRODIE: On what? A few street fights.

ASKERTON: On police negligence.

BRODIE: They've not been negligent.

ASKERTON (*Heavily ironic*): Oh, no. They've just leaned over backwards. (*Harsh now*). And why? To protect new Tory investment. The money behind this Garsfeld project sounds like a capitalist Who's Who.

BRODIE: I'm bound to get a daft answer. The Home Secretary's away. With bigger troubles.

ASKERTON: That's just it. You've got Andersley on every front page. Keep it there. Use it.

BRODIE (*Touch of bitterness*): Use it. Is that what they elected me for?

ASKERTON (*Quickly, discipline showing*): It's why you got full party support.

BRODIE (*Wearily*): Makes sense, I suppose. If you want to clout any Government, there are two easy targets—the Chancellor of the Exchequer and the Home Secretary. That's where politics gets personal for John Citizen. He can blame one for his tax deductions and the other when he gets pinched for speeding or a police horse treads on his foot.

ASKERTON: Use it, Sam. For your own good. If ever

you want office again. Get a question in. And kick that soft lot on the other side to bits.

BRODIE: I'd feel better believing it.

ASKERTON (*A touch of rather sad cynicism*): We're both a bit past that. You or the Party, Sam. Sort it out.

BRODIE: All right, Perce. I've soldiered too long to argue.

15

Interior. Library corridor. House of Commons. Day.

Set as previous plays.

A man is seen replacing an old-fashioned pocket watch in his waistcoat as Killane hurries towards him.

The man is a Conservative Whip, Sir Robert Wensley. He is about fifty-five, a deceptively avuncular and owlish man with a neat military moustache. During the war he was a very good major in intelligence and there is a very keen mind under the slightly self-deprecating manner. Authority shows in brief flashes and is all the more effective for being used rarely to cut through the avuncular manner.

WENSLEY: Ah, Killane. There you are. How's it going?

KILLANE: Uphill at the moment.

WENSLEY: So I hear, so I hear. I sometimes think that's the only reason I'm a Party Whip. I hear things and remember faces. Probably why they made me a prefect at school, too. Same sort of job. Been here six months now, haven't you?

KILLANE: And three days. (*Genuinely puzzled.*) And how do you hear it's uphill?

WENSLEY: Be difficult not to, the amount of noise you're making. Won't do, Mr Killane, won't do. You really can't tell a senior civil servant at the Home Office he should be back on the beat, trying shop doors.

KILLANE: I apologised for it.

WENSLEY: Mind you, he should. Know exactly what you mean. It's got to stop though. Now, Mr Killane. This moment.

KILLANE: No, Sir Robert. I've a Chief Constable doing his job badly. The Watch Committee won't stop him. So I have to.

WENSLEY: Normal channels, my boy. Have you used them?

KILLANE: The string-pulling? Too slow, too inbred, too cosy.

WENSLEY: Then draw up legislation. Table a Private Member's Bill.

KILLANE: Known in the Strangers' Bar as the parliamentary Premium Bond. With about the same chance of coming up.

WENSLEY (*Some of the authority showing now*): From that opinion I can draw only two conclusions. You're either concerned simply with one narrow individual issue—which is never enough to justify legislation—or you lack persistence.

KILLANE: I'm persistent enough to chase up and down Home Office corridors until something gets done.

WENSLEY: And in so doing to give the Opposition a good deal of political ammunition. In an area where the Conservative Party has always been vulnerable. Killane, you're a new boy and, politically, you've been skating along very nicely. You've now reached the thin ice. So stop and watch the experts.

Sir Robert nods abruptly and walks away. Killane shakes his head. He is not going to accept the advice.

16

Interior. Back Benches. House of Commons. Day.

Back-drop set as previous plays.

Sam Brodie is on his feet, an order paper and some notes in his hand.

BRODIE: May I ask the Home Secretary or whichever shrewd adviser he has deputised today—whom I would also like to ask to pass on my best wishes to the Home Secretary and to hope we shall be seeing him in the House over the next few months . . .

There are cries of: 'Get on with it', 'Snide, Sam Brodie', 'You try doing his job', 'Order, order order'.

BRODIE (*Continuing*): . . . if he's aware of the situation in my constituency whereby the police force, with the apparent connivance of its Chief Constable would seem to be affording special privileges to a special group of people—the building and machinery installation force in our large new factory estate. I have received complaints from my constituents—mainly on dangerous traffic violation and gross disorderly conduct—on which no police action has been taken. The same complaints have been received by the Member for the constituency adjoining mine—who, I understand, has confirmed my charges by making personal representation to your department . . .

Killane is seen on the other side of the House. As Brodie's speech continues, he is being made very much aware of Sir Robert Wensley's judgement. Wensley is seen shaking his head slightly.

There is another outburst from members in the house. These are cries of: 'Shame' 'Stop police-bashing', Get to the point'.

The cries are loud enough and mainly from the government side for Sam Brodie to comment on them.

BRODIE: ... Yes, gentlemen, just be patient and in a minute you can all sing the Eton Boating Song. (*The voice reaches its firm political pitch now.*) First, may I have the Home Secretary's assurance that the reason for this police negligence is *not* the fact that a great deal of Tory investment—albeit at second hand—is financing this new estate? Second, may I have the Home Secretary's assurance that immediate steps will be taken to ensure that the situation—and I'm referring to recent disturbances in Andersley—in which my townspeople were forced to take the law into their own hands does not recur?

Brodie sits down and Percy Askerton is seen nodding, his face full of satisfaction. He leans down to clap Sam Brodie on the shoulder. Brodie's face is quite expressionless.

17

Interior. Strangers' Bar. House of Commons. Day.

Killane, chastened and puzzled, is accepting a drink from Sir Robert Wensley.

KILLANE: That has to be the neatest bit of coat-changing I've ever seen. Instant conversion on one train journey down from Andersley.

WENSLEY: Or a chat with a Party Whip. About political expediency. When in Opposition, oppose. Use the weapons you're handed.

KILLANE: Including buckets of mud, Brodie was solid on it. What are you going to do, I said. Nothing, he said, not a thing. And then this. Oh well, at least he'll have the Chief Constable jumping around now and that's all I want.

WENSLEY: We can't leave it as it is.

KILLANE: I don't like the attack on the Party but...

WENSLEY: And you can't countenance it.

KILLANE: Sir Robert, I'm a simple mathematician. An equation has several factors. They can be juggled anyway you like to resolve the equation—provided you come up with the right answer. Which Brodie has done.

WENSLEY: The right answer for Brodie.

KILLANE: And for me.

WENSLEY: But not for this Party. So let's examine the problem. A great deal of your noisy progress through the Home Office could have been due—shall we say? —to the understandable resentment of a new MP at being unable to influence civil authority, i.e. the police. Since then you've had time for a further look at the situation.

KILLANE (*Ironic*): And I've come up with some other conclusions.

WENSLEY: That sounds a very sensible idea.

KILLANE: Not to me it doesn't. Same equation, same factors, same answer.

WENSLEY: In politics there's very often more than one answer. (*The authority shows again.*) A note to the Speaker should do it. I'll have a word. Usual formula 'I promise to be brief etc., etc.'

There is no mistaking the instruction now as Sir Robert produces a small note pad from his waistcoat pocket and pencils a reminder in it.

18

Interior. Railway dining car. Night.

Peter Chapman is sitting opposite Joe Garsfeld. The meal is finished and Garsfeld is working busily at papers spread from his black and glossy Madison Avenue briefcase.

Peter Chapman has a glass, an ice bucket and two or three miniatures of whisky in front of him.

CHAPMAN: You're travelling up a day early, Mr Garsfeld.

GARSFELD: No, it's Thursday. Your Johnnie Killane is going to be a day late.

CHAPMAN: That's politics for you. You could have waited for him.

GARSFELD: No time. I need too many facts before I start talking to lawyers.

CHAPMAN: Bad as that?

GARSFELD: Worse.

CHAPMAN: But lawyers! All that gets you is paragraphs a yard long and no commas.

GARSFELD: Mr Chapman, I'm a very angry man. I don't think John Killane realises how angry. So you'd better tell him. And tell him I don't want any horseradish about local and national influence. I want people leaned on. Right across the board. Dewhurst, Brodie, this police chief, anybody else who needs it.

CHAPMAN: I thought you had a saying: 'You can't fight City Hall.'

GARSFELD: You don't fight City Hall. You buy it. In this case with a six million pound development. On a tight time schedule. With tough penalty clauses. I don't want key technicians beaten up. I don't want machinery wrecked. I don't need roads blocking with some dizzy procession and babies in prams. I want proper police protection. If I don't get it and this contract runs over time, I want to know who to sue.

CHAPMAN: The way I hear it, the fuzz is leaning over backwards. On your side.

GARSFELD: So what happened last Saturday? If somebody changes the rules, I want to know about it. And change them back. And anyway, what are *you* doing up here a day early?

CHAPMAN: Talking to you.

GARSFELD: Besides that.

CHAPMAN: Nothing. It's the only reason. A tight grip on your lapels. You've got two factories built and rented and a list of international firms interested in leasing the rest. I'd like that list.

GARSFELD: I'd like the keys to Fort Knox. Why?

CHAPMAN: Same reason. Money. John and I still run a market-research agency. Some of these firms will need research. Why not ours?

GARSFELD: Why should I hand over a fairly confidential list?

CHAPMAN: That old elusive intangible, Mr Garsfeld. Goodwill.

GARSFELD: And what's it worth.

CHAPMAN: Now? Nothing. But if and when we do any research, it might be worth more than you think. We need the business. You might need some information sometime. (*A confident salesman's smile and Chapman lifts his hand, tugs his sleeve, an expansive gesture of sincerity.*) Nothing up my sleeve except my elbow.

Garsfeld grins, shrugs, opens the black briefcase, gives Chapman a folder from it.

GARSFELD: Where's the harm? (*Looks at Chapman.*) You're brighter than you let people know. That act of yours is very good.

CHAPMAN (*A touch of self-mockery, knowing his own chameleon quality*): Which one? (*He unscrews one of the miniatures of whisky, pours it into the glass, adds ice.*)

Garsfeld's readiness to provide the list is not altruistic. It stems from a realisation that if he provides Killane's agency with business, it may afford an opportunity, sometime in the future, to put pressure—political or otherwise—on Killane.

19

Interior. Working Men's Club. Andersley. Night.

Lambert and Dewhurst are sitting at Dewhurst's table and Lambert is gloating over the local newspaper account of Brodie's recent question in the House.

LAMBERT: I told Sam it was the usual Tory set-up. One law for the rich, one for the poor. I thought he wasn't listening.

DEWHURST: I wish he hadn't. And I wish sometimes you'd stop sounding like one of the pamphlets we dished out during the General Strike.

LAMBERT: It's still true. Why not say it? Mealy mouths and hedging and milk-and-water socialism cost us the last Election.

DEWHURST (*Wearily*): You're a good lad, Cliff, and you work hard but sometimes you can't see the facts for the slogans.

LAMBERT (*Quoting, ironic*): 'Old men forget.'

DEWHURST: No, they don't. They're just more selective.

LAMBERT: You've got to agree with Sam.

DEWHURST: Have I?

LAMBERT: Any good party man has.

DEWHURST: I just hope it wasn't Sam's own idea. (*As he says this, his face is grim.*)

20

Interior. Conservative Committee Rooms. Day.

Annie Mackinnon is working busily and is noticeably better dressed than usual—smart travelling clothes, elegant accessories. At the side of the desk, there is a pair of small matched suitcases.

Chapman comes into the room with his usual salute.

CHAPMAN: Heil, Ted. Hello, Annie. You're up early.

ANNIE: Not by Andersley standards. This isn't the sluggish metropolis.

CHAPMAN: Articulate, too. You know, that hotel serves the smallest eggs I've ever seen. Must have hens the size of sparrows.

ANNIE (*Still working*): Biscuits in the drawer.

Chapman opens the desk drawer, takes out a packet of biscuits and starts to eat one, sees the suitcases. He taps one of them with his foot.

CHAPMAN: Off to the launderette in your lunch-hour?

All this gets him is a pitying smile from Annie.

CHAPMAN (*Shrugging*): That's how my secretary carries hers.

ANNIE: No. I'm going away for the weekend.

CHAPMAN: John didn't say anything.

ANNIE: He didn't know.

CHAPMAN: Oops. Chancing it a bit, aren't you?

ANNIE (*Unperturbed*): If you tell him, then he'll know.

CHAPMAN: Portrait of stout Christian descending to lions. OK.

ANNIE: Don't you want reasons?

CHAPMAN (*Seriously*): Annie, the one thing I never ask for is reasons. None of my business. Or John's. You're a big girl and you're supposed to know what you're doing.

ANNIE: Thanks. You've got crumbs in your moustache.

CHAPMAN: That's not crumbs, love. It's grey hair. And I've earned it. Every single silver thread among the gold.

ANNIE: How?

Chapman performs a small and satisfied tap dance.

CHAPMAN: Garsfeld. A lovely accurate double-level con job.

ANNIE: Speak English.

CHAPMAN: I now have a confidential list of firms interested in coming to Andersley. Big and international and very probably in need of some highly expensive market research. Mine. Jobs for the boys.

ANNIE: It doesn't sound like Garsfeld. Charitable is the one thing I'd never call him.

Chapman does his little dance again.

CHAPMAN: He thinks John put me up to it. You could see his little eyes shining at the thought of some more political leverage. (*Stops his shuffling, suddenly glum.*) Trouble is, John didn't put me up to it. But we need the business.

21

Interior. Back Benches. House of Commons. Day.

Killane is on his feet, his voice clear and impassioned and apparently completely sincere.

KILLANE: May I ask the Home Secretary to affirm his complete confidence—as I do mine—in the police force of Andersley and its Chief Constable. May I further ask him to express his appreciation—and that of all responsible authority—of the exemplary manner in which the Andersley police force has carried out its duties of maintaining law and order in the face of extreme civil provocation—both local and immigrant. *There are the usual cries from the house: 'Hear, Hear' and 'What do you know about it?*

22

Interior. Conservative Club. Night.

Sir George Pendleton and Chief Constable Henry Parker are talking in front of the fireplace. Parker is on duty and keeps glancing towards the door.

PARKER: Usually I'm glad it's Friday. Not this one. Not with a town full of football mobs tomorrow.

PENDLETON: Some of them have already arrived.

PARKER: I know. Another late night.

PENDLETON: You enjoy it. You never got used to a desk job.

PARKER: I see your friend Killane's changed his mind about wicked coppers.

PENDLETON: Politics. After what Sam Brodie said, Killane couldn't have done much else.

PARKER: Oh. If that's the reason, it's a pity.

PENDLETON: He'll learn.

PARKER: Not until he spends a few weekends sitting in that radio car I've got outside. Instead of just collecting complaints.

Ernest Dewhurst comes into the room and across to them.

PENDLETON: Hello, Councillor Dewhurst. Glad you could come. Garsfeld is due in a minute.

Dewhurst stares round the room with the frank curiosity he always exhibits when he is in this bastion of enemy territory. He pats one of the large and bulbous armchairs.

DEWHURST: Not my sort of pub. Is it true you need a whole hippopotamus to make one of these chairs?

PENDLETON: Not quite. It has to be a Conservative one. I'll get you a drink. (*To Parker*) You, Henry?

PARKER: Not tonight.

Over this, Garsfeld and Sam Brodie have come into the room and there is a purposefulness about Garsfeld, a quiet steamroller determination.

PENDLETON: Good evening, Mr Garsfeld. I understand you have some problems.

GARSFELD: That's right. And I need them solved.

PENDLETON: We'll do what we can.

GARSFELD: I've already put the squawk in to Mr Brodie here. He says to go through channels—whatever they are. (*To Parker*) Are you the Chief of Police?

PARKER: I'm the Chief Constable. Yes.

GARSFELD: So you'll know I've had machinery wrecked and you'll know I've had access roads blocked.

PARKER: It's being looked into.

GARSFELD: Looking isn't enough. And I'm just installing some very expensive plant in Building Two. Or I was until yesterday. Then three of the technicians got beaten up because they were German.

DEWHURST (*Mildly*): They shouldn't have told anybody then. A lot of people round here got into the habit of fighting Germans.

Before Garsfeld can reply, a uniformed police sergeant has approached the group. He gives a radio message to Parker who reacts quickly.

PARKER (*To sergeant*): Pull two of the cars in from Ashcroft. I'll be out in a minute.

The sergeant nods and leaves.

PARKER: Mr Garsfeld, Sir George Pendleton here is Chairman of the Watch Committee. Councillor Dewhurst is also a member. Any specific complaints you wish to put in will be considered and passed on to me.

Parker moves away from the group and looks across the room. The Sergeant has returned and is standing in the doorway, glancing at his watch. Parker nods to him. Then Parker turns to Brodie.

PARKER: Word with you before I go, Mr Brodie.

BRODIE: Good. I want to talk to you as well.

They have moved away from Pendleton, Dewhurst and Garsfeld.

PARKER: I'm sure you do. But I'm in a hurry so you'll just have to listen. For the first time in my career this weekend, I've had to pull in outside police forces to keep a grip on this town. Because, according to you, our own force is sloppy and soft on immigrants. Which means you've given every hooligan around a licence to play Wyatt Earp. That speech of yours was more than mischievous, Mr Brodie. It was criminal. On Monday, there's going to be a few coppers in hospital and a few people locked up. And we both know why. But if anybody ought to be locked up, it's you.

Parker turns and moves away, not quickly but with purpose, a man on his way to do a night's work at a job he is good at.

Brodie watches him leave, knows that what he has just said is true and knows, too, that there was nothing else he could have done.

END OF ACT TWO

ACT THREE

23

Exterior. Canal bank. Andersley. Day.

Film sequence.

It is Saturday morning and Brodie is fishing, his small daughter Elizabeth reading her comics on the tackle box at his side.

Brodie has pitched about twenty yards from the canal bridge and he looks up to see ten or twelve youths wearing football scarves and rosettes cross the bridge.

Out of malice and because fishermen need peace, three or four of the youths in the group start to throw stones which splash in the water around Brodie's float.

Brodie moves to stand between his daughter and the bridge, pulls her head gently against his leg and the youths move on.

24

Interior. Conservative Committee Rooms. Day.

Chapman has work spread all over the desk but has left room at the side of the telephone for a message pad. He is quietly substituting for Annie Mackinnon.

Chapman is talking into the telephone and scribbling as he does so.

CHAPMAN (*Into telephone*): No, I'm sorry, Miss Mackinnon's not here. No, sorry, we're not expecting her. Housing Officer? Yes, I'll tell her you called.

Killane enters on the end of the conversation as Chapman puts the telephone down.

KILLANE: No Annie?

CHAPMAN (*Casually*): Away for the weekend. There's not much doing.

KILLANE: I think I'd rather decide that. I've got three circulars I need typing and distributing and I want a meeting of ward chairmen.

CHAPMAN: I'll ring Mrs Gresham.

KILLANE: You're very co-operative all of a sudden.

CHAPMAN: I've seen the light. Heil Ted, Heil Enoch, Heil Alec.

Killane starts to move some of Chapman's graphs.

KILLANE: And what's all this junk? Peter, I wish you'd work in the hotel.

CHAPMAN: Furniture trouble. The table keeps falling over. (*He stands upright, his tolerance starting to wear thin.*) And this 'junk' is a survey on heating preferences with a fee of £1,800 and computer time booked for Tuesday. I had hoped for some of your esteemed advice on it. And you're getting just a little short in the fuse, boy.

KILLANE: Sorry. I know. But it's idiot time. Last weekend I was slamming the police. Yesterday I was on my feet, all sweetness and light, praise and glory. Thanks be for our trusty local coppers.

CHAPMAN: Politics. The way it's played.

KILLANE: Two faces. I'm not good at it. And the police still need slamming but how the hell do I do it now? They'll laugh.

CHAPMAN: Quietly, I should think. Pull strings. Tell you one thing. You're getting skinny and you're starting to worry too much and you're starting to blame people. Ease the world off your back. Let the trouble come to you.

KILLANE: You make it sound so easy.

Chapman has not succeeded in slowing Killane down and he shrugs.

There is a fast and peremptory knock at the door and Mrs Ellerby bustles in.

She shows signs of anxiety and haste.

MRS ELLERBY: There *is* somebody here then.

CHAPMAN (*Quickly*): Scotch and gin and tonic. Both large.

MRS ELLERBY: I telephoned early on but there was no answer.

KILLANE (*Gently*): We're here now. What can we do for you?

MRS ELLERBY: I want to know where I stand. After what Sam Brodie said and then you said about the police. Will they look after me or won't they?

KILLANE: I'm sure they will.

MRS ELLERBY: I want to know. I've got to know. If only for the insurance. It was quiet enough yesterday because the foreigners stayed away. But it's football today and they'll have read which pub to go to. And there's going to be a tallyho to play in this town to-night.

CHAPMAN: You can stay closed.

MRS ELLERBY: No, Mister. I've got to open. By law. Otherwise I lose my licence. And I'll have no staff tonight. They've told me so. They're not risking a bottle in the face and I don't blame them.

KILLANE: I'll talk to the Chief Constable.

MRS ELLERBY: You did that last week. Then changed your mind when you were making speeches.

237

KILLANE: I'll ring you when I've talked to him, Mrs. Ellerby.

She nods and leaves and Killane starts to pull the desk drawers open.

KILLANE: I like Annie's idea of a weekend when there isn't much doing.

24

Interior. Working Men's Club. Andersley. Night.

Garsfeld, Brodie and Lambert are sitting at Ernest Dewhurst's table.

Garsfeld is wearing a topcoat and is packed, ready to leave Andersley.

GARSFELD: According to my rules, Mr Brodie, you put the chisel in. We agreed special privileges, Then you get up and squawk about these privileges.

LAMBERT: The old story. Tory money and what it'll buy. They've always expected it and they always will.

GARSFELD: Tell your boy to stop quoting the funny papers at me, Brodie. I'd like a reason from you.

BRODIE: I can give you a reason. Question of balance. A lot of people vote for me who don't want to know about concessions to you.

GARSFELD: That's the point. There haven't been any damn concessions. Ask that tombstone of a police chief you've got. So why invent any?

LAMBERT (*High, incredulous*): Abbey Road. Tearaway lorries. Weekend punch-ups. Invent?

GARSFELD: You mean you didn't have fights and traffic problems before?

BRODIE: Oh, yes. But nothing as large and specific as your job. Nothing people could blame them on.

GARSFELD: I don't think you believe that. You've been around too long. But I like the word. 'Blame.' That's sweet. What word are you going to use for the five thousand jobs and the new houses and a school or two and better roads? Blame?

BRODIE: They're two separate issues.

GARSFELD: Oh no, they're not. Not with the six million pound investment that'll bring them in. Get off my back, Brodie. (*He starts to rise.*) Some things are too important for politics and money is one of them.

Garsfeld nods curtly to Lambert and leaves quickly.

25

Interior. Conservative Committee Rooms. Day.

Chapman is working at Annie's desk. Annie has just come into the room and is standing at the side of him. Next to her are the neat travelling cases.

ANNIE: You were very clever to find me.

CHAPMAN: Not clever. Lucky. A hotel phone number in the back of the address book.

ANNIE: Even then. The message was clever.

CHAPMAN: I called the number I found. Nobody named Mackinnon staying there. I did my halfwit act and it was one of those nice country hotels where they're very helpful but not discreet. They described the only lady they had—Mrs Marshall. You.

ANNIE: Better than Mr and Mrs Smith. Does John know?

CHAPMAN: No.

ANNIE: Good.

CHAPMAN: Why?

ANNIE: Some of it would rub off on him. You never get away from politics. Conservative agent on illicit weekend. So what's the MP up to? So I'm furtive about it. I tried to tell you last weekend. I get tired of being Caesar's wife. Especially when there's no Caesar.

CHAPMAN: I'll deputise. Let my hair grow, brush it forward. Oh. Sorry. I forgot Mr Marshall.

ANNIE: I wish I could.

CHAPMAN: None of my business but couldn't he come courting in the approved manner round here—freshly-ironed flat hat and a large vegetable marrow for your mother under his arm?

ANNIE: You don't know Mr Marshall. He's a physics lecturer from Manchester. And marriage is not on the curriculum. And he's going to America next week on a three-year contract. So you take what you can while you can.

CHAPMAN: And disappear suddenly.

ANNIE: That's it. 'Gather ye rosebuds.' Oh, well. The garden's closed now.

CHAPMAN: You could have told John. He would have understood.

ANNIE: I thought I'd explained that. Politics, the public face. What he doesn't know can't land him in the scandal and the gossip.

CHAPMAN: Queen Victoria's dead, love.

ANNIE: She left an awful lot of descendants in this town.

Killane comes into the room, looks at Annie, sees the suitcases, wants an explanation.

KILLANE: Well?

ANNIE: I'm not making excuses. There aren't any.

CHAPMAN (*Quietly*): How about reasons? Why do it the hard way?

240

ANNIE: I'd rather not. I'm sorry, John.

KILLANE: Me, too. Look, I'm still fairly new. I'm still struggling a little. I need all the help I can get. You're supposed to be a full-time agent, screened by a pile of selection committees, picked for—what?—a sense of vocation, specially trained for a year. We get a couple of weeks with Andersley in every newspaper and Sam Brodie scoring points left, right and centre and you just pack your little bags. It's not on, Annie.

ANNIE: There didn't seem much we could do.

KILLANE: Perhaps not. But it's too late to back out now. I started it and there are too many complaints in the files.

ANNIE: On local knowledge, I'd say do it gently.

KILLANE: Oh, yes. Sunday morning, sherry at the Club. Be impressed by Pendleton's golf score, admire Parker's peaked cap. The right word in the right ear. No, thanks.

CHAPMAN: What's wrong with it if it works?

KILLANE: My vanity, I suppose. And it's sloppy. I like things neater than that. (*He picks up one of the graphs on which Chapman has been working.*) The figures, the conclusions, the lines on a chart where everybody can see them.

ANNIE: What do you want me to do?

KILLANE: Round up the ward chairmen. Say I'd like a chat here tonight. Explain what we're doing, see what they can do.

KILLANE: And Annie . . .

ANNIE (*Turning*): Yes?

KILLANE: I'm going to have to talk to the Chairman of the Association. Perhaps Central Office. I don't need a disappearing agent.

241

ANNIE: I realise that.

Chapman has moved to open the door for Annie.

CHAPMAN: See you later, love. Buy you a drink.

He closes the door and walks back to the desk.

KILLANE: You're getting very thick with Annie. How did you manage to find her?

Chapman taps his temple with his forefinger to indicate profound deduction. There is no flippancy in the gesture and his face is serious.

KILLANE: And you know why she went?

Chapman nods.

KILLANE: Well? Come on, I want to know.

Chapman puts down his papers, leans on the desk.

CHAPMAN: Then try asking her yourself. Quietly. As if she's a woman. Which she is. It's really very easy. First, you take off your big representative of the people hat. Then, you climb down from the top of the mountain where you think you're running the world. Just be John Killane. Not John Killane MP. You were only elected, boy. Nobody made you the Lord's anointed.

KILLANE: You've seen me work, Peter.

CHAPMAN: For fifteen years.

KILLANE: I can only do it one way. Head down. Keep going.

CHAPMAN: I've seen that, too.

Killane's attitude now reflects some of his sincerity and some of his frustration.

KILLANE: And this job's important. At least to me. I know what you think about it. But it's the most important there is. To me. So. No part-timers. No sloppy disappearing acts. There's too much to do.

There is almost an appeal in Killane's voice. And there is no trace of argument between the two men. They have been friends for a long time.

CHAPMAN (*Quietly*): And how much achievement is there? How much are you really doing?

KILLANE: That's the crunch. Peter, I don't know. If I'm honest—not very much. Especially now.

26

Interior. Library corridor. House of Commons. Day.

Percy Askerton and Sir Robert Wensley are strolling through.

WENSLEY: Hello, Mr Askerton. Catching up on the paperwork?

ASKERTON: Saturday's the best day for it.

WENSLEY: I've found that. I wanted your opinion on something anyway. Informally, you understand. This report on police recruitment. Well down. And a lot of chaps leaving.

ASKERTON: Bit worrying. They're well under strength in my constituency.

WENSLEY: Everywhere. Will you talk to your masters about it?

ASKERTON: No need. They're just as worried.

WENSLEY: Good, good. We can agree then.

ASKERTON: I should think so. No bother at all.

WENSLEY: No one minds legitimate criticism of the police but I think we'd all be well advised to soft-pedal for a while.

ASKERTON: I'll see to it for our side.

WENSLEY: Andersley was a fair point, mind.

ASKERTON: It'd better be the last one. None of us can afford to hammer law and order too much. Not these days.

27

Interior. Working Men's Club. Andersley. Night.

Ernest Dewhurst is sitting at his table, talking to a youth of about nineteen. This is Sammy Brigg who has been Dewhurst's apprentice at the wagon sheds. He is stockily built with a cheerful, intelligent face and, at this stage in his life, could be picked out very easily as a provincial. There is a combination of some innocence, some gullibility, some lack experience.

It is noticeable that he has a half pint of beer in front of him, not the full pints which are Dewhurst's normal order.

BRIGG: Quiet in here.

DEWHURST: Likely to be. This is one night anybody with any sense stays at home.

As they talk, sirens are heard faintly outside from either police vehicles or ambulances.

DEWHURST: Did you go to the match?

BRIGG: Not this one. I didn't want a free thumping.

Sam Brodie comes into the club and across to the table.

DEWHURST: Evening, Mr Brodie.

BRODIE: Evening, Councillor.

There is a slight formality between the two men—who have been using Christian names for a long time now.

Brodie sits down.

244

DEWHURST: This is Sammy Brigg. Used to be my apprentice at the wagon sheds before they laid the pair of us off. He's going to London tomorrow.

BRODIE: That's a pity.

BRIGG: You go where the work is. If there's any down there.

DEWHURST (*To Brigg*): You remember what I've told you.

BRIGG (*Almost reciting*): Yes, Mr Dewhurst. Leave my big suitcase in the cloakroom at the station. Not a locker. Leave it there till I see how the lodgings shape up. And don't give the landlady my right address. When I get a job, tell the gaffer my insurance cards are in the post. Don't part with them till I see what the job's like. Ask for a sub on my wages halfway through the week and not the first day. So I stand a better chance of getting it. Keep my dues paid up and keep telephoning the union.

DEWHURST: Good lad. That's it.

BRIGG: Pal of mine went down last month. He's got a job labouring. He might get me taken on.

DEWHURST: Try the factories first. (*Brigg rises to leave.*) Take care of yourself, lad.

BRIGG: Thank you, Mr Dewhurst. And you.

Dewhurst watches him go and there is some quiet anger in the face.

DEWHURST (*Quite softly*): He's done four years of his time learning to be a tradesman. And he would have been a good one. He is now, near enough. You should see him use tools. Now, he's going down south bloody labouring.

BRODIE: It's happening all over, Ernest.

DEWHURST: That's no consolation. Just one of the reasons Garsfeld's getting a bit of rope. And we could have done without your speeches about it.

245

Dewhurst signals to the steward.

BRODIE: I wanted to see you about that.

DEWHURST: Oh, I know why you did it. Nobody's blaming you. We're both good Party men. But if you want to spend your time playing with the big lads down in Westminster you can't expect to run our little game up here as well.

BRODIE: It wasn't that. I wanted to ask you to see Parker for me. Get him to keep an eye on Rose Ellerby's place.

DEWHURST: No need to ask. He's doing it already.

Police and ambulance sirens are heard again, a little nearer this time, as the steward arrives with a tray of drinks.

Dewhurst pushes one of the pints towards Brodie.

DEWHURST: Get that down you. We can't let you push us and we can't let Garsfeld push us. We'll sort it out somehow. As usual.

28

Interior. Conservative Club. Day.

The time is nine o'clock on Sunday morning and the interior of the club has been slightly modified by the addition of a table with five chairs round it. On the table are two trays, one with coffee pot and cups, the other with tea. In each case, the pots are silver and the china is good. The table itself is a rather handsome small refectory table and possibly a screen serves to divide this area from the rest of the room.

Sitting at one end of the table is Chief Constable Henry Parker. He looks weary but happy and is working his way through a plate of excellent sandwiches in which the ham is equal in thickness to the thin bread surrounding it. Sir George Pendleton comes into the room, checks the trays on the table, nods to a hovering white-coated steward who promptly leaves.

At this hour, the rest of the club is empty.

PENDLETON: Breakfast, Henry?

PARKER: Last night's supper.

PENDLETON: It was quieter than we thought.

PARKER: Still too noisy for me.

Ernest Dewhurst comes into the room, knowing he is punctual and therefore glancing at his watch.

PENDLETON (*To Parker*): I've asked Killane and Brodie to look in.

PARKER (*Ironic, wiping his mouth with a good damask napkin*): I can't wait.

PENDLETON (*To Dewhurst*): Morning, Councillor. Tea or coffee?

DEWHURST: What's coffee?

PENDLETON (*Smiling*): I should have known.

He pushes the tea tray across to Dewhurst as Killane and Brodie enter.

PENDLETON: Good morning, gentlemen.

Brodie takes in the room, the table, the appurtenances of a formal meeting.

BRODIE: The gang's all here. Official or unofficial?

PENDLETON: Come, come, Mr Brodie. At nine o'clock on a Sunday morning? A completely informal discussion among interested parties.

PARKER: A short one. So I can get home to bed. Can I say my piece first, George?

PENDLETON: By all means.

247

PARKER (*Deceptively mild*): This force has been accused of negligence. By you, Mr Killane, privately. By you, Mr Brodie, publicly. I have, therefore, asked for and been granted a full and official enquiry to be carried out by a senior officer from another division. According to the usual procedure.

KILLANE: There was no need for that, Chief Constable. None at all.

PARKER: Never start arguments you can't finish. I'm not a politician. I've got my reputation to think about.

BRODIE: You're making this very personal.

PARKER: Case of having to. You named the names.

PENDLETON (*Interrupting smoothly*): I think it's a question here of clarification. No more. You pass the laws, we enforce them. Enforcement is no part of your elected position. Nor is attempting to influence that enforcement—except by legislation. It's the fundamental difference between the power of Parliament and that of the civil authority.

KILLANE: Then what are we doing here?

DEWHURST: Sorting it out.

PENDLETON: A situation has arisen which creates problems. They need solving. We thought you might like to hear some suggested solutions.

BRODIE: You mean letting Garsfeld have it his own way?

DEWHURST: No, Sam. Only when he's right.

KILLANE: And when he's wrong?

DEWHURST: Do it quietly. I'm Chairman of the Roads and Transport Committee. I've had a word with the Borough Engineer. Next Tuesday, we close Abbey Road. Stop the big traffic. Put two or three men on and take six months to re-surface it. Normal maintenance work.

Killane is forced to shake his head in admiration.

PENDLETON: I happen to be concerned with one of the companies providing insurance cover for the Garsfeld site. A properly worded note to our Chief Constable here will, I'm sure, be favourably received.

PARKER: And I can put dogs round the site and a few more patrols than we've got. Not on hearsay. On proved felonies. Backed by insurance evidence.

BRODIE: And what about the public fights? You can't enrol coppers as potmen.

PARKER: Not their job to stop arguments in boozers. Get that straight for a start.

PENDLETON: What we can do is have a word with the magistrates. The men who attacked Mr Garsfeld's Germans have been found and charged. I hardly think they'll be put on probation.

BRODIE: And there's nothing like six months inside to make you keep your hands to yourself.

DEWHURST: Satisfied, gentlemen?

Both Killane and Brodie have to nod.

PENDLETON: And so, apparently, is Mr Garsfeld. (*To Dewhurst*) I don't see any need for a full Watch Committee meeting. Do you, Councillor?

Dewhurst shakes his head.

PENDLETON: Good. Well, I don't know about you but I could do with some breakfast.

He gets up, walks across to the fireplace, presses the bell for the steward.

Brodie and Killane look at each other. They have been out-manoeuvred by a smooth and knowledgeable machine whose function is action and not theory and whose action is immediate.

29

Interior. Railway dining car. Night.

Brodie and Killane are seen putting overnight bags on the rack.

They sit down, facing each other.

KILLANE: I suppose we should be delighted. We both got what we wanted.

BRODIE: Oh, yes. But let's not kid ourselves. It wasn't anything to do with us.

KILLANE: It might have been in a small way. We'll never know.

BRODIE: We know all right. We're Members of Parliament. We're not shabby men but sometimes we're made out to be. And sometimes we are. We serve too many masters. A party. A constituency. Our own beliefs. Too many. And the days of the free vote are over—except on trivialities to keep the vocal minorities quiet. The major facts still exist and they come first. Positive and negative. Government and Opposition. The facts of political life. They still don't stop the shabbiness from tasting like green apples sometimes—sour and acid and likely to keep you awake at night.

[Credits]

Play Five

THE SALESMEN

Cast

SAM BRODIE	*Colin Blakely*
JOHN KILLANE	*Michael Gambon*
PETER CHAPMAN	*William Gaunt*
JANIE KILLANE	*Hilary Dwyer*
ELIZABETH BRODIE	*Margaret John*
CLIFF LAMBERT	*Richard Hampton*
SIR JOSEPH CONRAN	*Bill Owen*
JOE DELANEY	*Eric Thompson*
JOE GARSFELD	*Alex Scott*
SIR GEORGE PENDLETON	*Ralph Michael*
MINISTER	*Bernard Archard*
BILL FROEBEL	*Edward Hardwicke*
EDDY VANDERGRAF	*David Waller*
ANDREW BRODIE	*Nicholas Hoye*

Non-speaking

Head porter and bell boy at London hotel; waiters at House of Lords reception; a cross-section of both Labour and Conservative peers; some MPs; some trade union leaders; stewards in white coats at an Andersley reception and a cross-section of Andersley dignitaries and councillors, again of both parties; a PPS to the Minister; assorted civil servants; uniformed policeman; British Rail dining car stewards.

Interiors

1. Conservative Club, Andersley
2. Strangers' Bar, House of Commons
3. Sam Brodie's living room
4. Killane's hotel room, Andersley
5. British Rail dining car
6. Tented reception area on House of Lords terrace
7. Luxurious suite at London hotel

Exteriors

1. House of Commons from Westminster Bridge
2. St Stephen's Entrance to the House of Commons, Policeman, Sir Joseph Conran, Sir George Pendleton and chauffeur of limousine
3. St Stephen's Entrance. Reception guests leaving, chauffeurs and cars
4. Westminster Bridge showing Houses of Parliament and Lambeth Palace. Featuring Sam Brodie
5. As above. Featuring John Killane

ACT ONE

1

Interior. London hotel room. Day.

This is part of a suite in one of the new and very expensive London hotels. Many of the clientêle are businessmen who use the accommodation as offices.

This particular suite is comparatively tastefully decorated but the fittings are harsh, angular and efficient. Since it is one of the larger suites, there is space for a small conference area—the usual low-slung chairs and sofa round a table. There is also a small bar— the type that can be wheeled in and out—set up against one wall.

The room is high up over London, quiet being part of the price, and Joe Garsfeld is looking moodily at the view, drumming his fingers on the window.

John Killane is standing near him, reading a cable.

Sam Brodie is half-sitting on the back of one of the low-slung chairs.

KILLANE: Your problem, Mr Garsfeld. Not ours. (*He hands the cable to Brodie.*)

GARSFELD: Think about it. You got over here fast enough. Mr Brodie?

BRODIE (*Reading the cable*): 'Confirm finally that we shall not be taking up our previous commitment for industrial space in Andersley. Regrets. Ellatt.'

KILLANE (*To Garsfeld*): I thought you spent a week with them. I thought you had a firm promise.

GARSFELD: I had. And a letter of intent. I've got

enough to sue the bastards but law-suits don't fill factory space. Or pay rent.

BRODIE: Did they give a reason?

GARSFELD: The usual ones. Times are hard in the States. A board shake-up. Bad attack of caution. (*Spins round, angry, worried, depressed.*) And Ellatt was the big one. (*Turns his hand over in a card player's gesture.*) The full house.

Killane has taken a small notebook from his pocket, checks one of the pages.

KILLANE: Forty per cent of the whole estate. The south-west end, due to start installation in two weeks. All the rest is leased, most of it operational.

GARSFELD: You should be working for me. You don't miss much.

KILLANE: Joe, I've known you a long time. The one thing I've learned is to watch you.

BRODIE: If it's forty per cent, that's about fifteen hundred jobs.

GARSFELD: The figure was sixteen hundred. That's why it's your problem, Mr Brodie. And yours, Johnnie.

KILLANE: Not necessarily. We're MPs, not factory salesmen.

GARSFELD: What about Andersley? What about its unemployment rate?

KILLANE: You mean: 'What about Garsfeld?' You're in the tightrope business, Joe. One mistake and it's a long way to fall. And nobody picks you up. Ever.

Killane's attitude is hard and factual, the analytical discussion of the commercial problem. Brodie misunderstands this.

BRODIE: Mr Killane, we started this lot. Andersley needs jobs and we promised co-operation. Your attitude isn't going to get us anywhere.

KILLANE: No?

BRODIE: No.

KILLANE: This is business. We're not playing parliamentary rules now. If I enlist, it'll be on that basis—and as an equal. All the facts, all the information, all the figures. (*To Garsfeld*) As I hear it, Ellatt was prepared to talk other terms. And you wouldn't cut the asking price.

GARSFELD: Not wouldn't. Couldn't.

KILLANE: Can we see the books?

GARSFELD: If you have to. (*The manner conciliatory now.*) Look, I don't want to kid anybody . . .

KILLANE: Much.

GARSFELD: . . . OK, I'm in a bind. Fine, I admit it. But so are you. Unless I can fill factory space in a month, I stand to take a personal loss of thirty thousand pounds on contract clauses. And you stand to lose a pile of jobs and end up with a big record for broken promises.

KILLANE: That's better. 'Joe Garsfeld, businessman' beats any act you put on. Leave the public-servant approach to us.

As Killane is speaking, Garsfeld has moved to the small bar. He laughs, accepts a sort of defeat, looks at Brodie and points to Killane.

GARSFELD: I'd forgotten this guy. Being an MP was supposed to soften him up. (*To Killane*) All right, Johnnie. I'll play cards.

KILLANE: Good. Who's the prospect we're selling to? There has to be one or we wouldn't be here.

GARSFELD: Two. Froebel's one. Vandergraf's the other.

KILLANE (*Impressed*): They're big enough.

257

Garsfeld has poured drinks and walked from the bar to hand them to Brodie and Killane.

GARSFELD: And they can take decisions. Fast. (*His confidence returning.*) We'll operate from here. To start. I've booked suites for them, organised telex, secretaries, the usual status hoo-hah. Private plane on standby.

BRODIE: It must be costing you a lot of money.

GARSFELD: Investment never comes cheap, Mr Brodie. The rest of it's your end. I'll pick up the bill. I want a royal progress. Hirohito without the demonstrators. Well?

Killane sips his drink, looks at Brodie and waits for him to answer.

BRODIE: I've seen it done. Using the Palace of Westminster as a sales office. There's a pattern.

There is indeed a pattern but it is one which Brodie has never used and does not like very much. His face shows this.

GARSFELD: Can you do it?

BRODIE: Some of it. (*To Killane*) You'll have to do the rest.

Killane nods, finishes his drink.

GARSFELD (*Once more the expansive entrepreneur*): So go to it, gentlemen. Your prospective Andersley industrialists are flying in tomorrow.

Brodie picks up a briefcase and a coat and prepares to leave. Killane is already by the door.

BRODIE (*To Garsfeld*): You reckon they're both big. What if they both want all the space? Or most of it? What if it turns into an auction?

GARSFELD (*Beaming*): That's their problem. I'm happy.

BRODIE (*To Killane*): Now I see what you mean.

Killane smiles wryly and opens the door for him.

2

Interior. Andersley Conservative Club. Day.

Set as previous plays.

Sir George Pendleton and Sir Joseph Conran are standing in front of the fireplace.

PENDLETON: The Ellatt cancellation is still bad news—whatever one's politics.

CONRAN: Worse for you though. You're Conservative Chairman. Our side's used to private enterprise welshing.

On this Cliff Lambert hurries quickly into the Club and across to them.

LAMBERT (*To Conran*): I've just had Sam Brodie on the phone, Sir Joseph. Can you ring him? It's urgent.

CONRAN: Mr Killane's got a faster messenger service. (*Nods towards Pendleton.*) I've already heard. (*Touch of irony, not displeased.*) Now is the time for all good men to come to the aid of whichever party's nearest.

LAMBERT: You don't seem very bothered.

CONRAN: I'm not. I'm only Vice-Chairman of our Labour Party now. That was Sam Brodie's idea. So why should I do him any favours?

PENDLETON (*The civic pride showing*): Because the issue is much too important for personalities. And both our MPs will need all the support they can get. Especially locally.

CONRAN: 'Steadily, shoulder to shoulder.' Never one

259

of my favourite songs. And I've got my own business to run. I'll think about it. (*To Lambert*) Tell Sam Brodie that.

He nods to Pendleton and leaves. Pendleton shakes his head, turns to Cliff Lambert.

PENDLETON: What about you, Mr Lambert?

LAMBERT: It means jobs. And I'm Sam Brodie's agent. If he wants red carpet rolled out up here for visiting capitalists, I'll roll it. If he wants local councillors whipped in wearing their best suits, I'll knock on doors. If he wants the mayor on show in his full rigout, I'll polish the municipal chain of office. The same way you'll get whatever gentry we own to uncork the last few bottles of vintage port.

PENDLETON: We'd both find life much easier though if Sir Joseph Conran could be persuaded to help.

LAMBERT: He's a bit disenchanted with politics at the moment. You can't blame him. It was always a hobby with him. Bit like you. You're both businessmen first. Everything else is second. The committees and the cause just keep your conscience quiet.

This is said as a true and simple statement and there is no offence meant or taken.

3

Interior. Strangers' Bar. House of Commons. Day.

Set as previous plays.

Janie Killane—John Killane's ex-wife—and Joe Delaney, the Member of Parliament for Gallowside, are standing at the bar, looking towards the door.

DELANEY: He said he'd be back in a minute. He's gone with Sam Brodie to try and see the Minister.

JANIE: Killane and Brodie meet the Minister. It sounds like a very old Abbott and Costello film.

DELANEY: You don't seem very impressed with it all.

JANIE: Oh, but I am, Mr Delaney. It's just that I'm only John's ex-wife. I have absolutely no intention of writing his memoirs.

DELANEY: That makes a change round here.

At that moment Brodie and Killane come into the bar together. Both of them glance by instinct at the closed circuit television screen which shows:

Welfare allowances—Rt Hon. A. E. U. Maude—Cons. Stratford.

Brodie waits for Delaney to join him and they move to one of the tables.

Killane goes up to Janie at the Bar.

KILLANE: Sorry. These corridors are longer than you think. (*He looks a bit harassed, turns to the barman.*) Tomato juice. Two, please.

JANIE (*Noticing the fraught look*): One tomato juice and one quite large gin and tonic. (*To Killane*) Don't worry, dear. I can be teetotal on my own. My nose doesn't twitch any more at the fumes of other people's alcohol.

Killane grins, accepts the gin and tonic.

KILLANE: And I need this.

JANIE: You sound like Peter Chapman. How is dear Peter?

KILLANE: Very quiet these days. Very busy. (*Frowns at this.*) I should telephone him.

JANIE: Devoted partners are hard to come by.

KILLANE: So are devoted ex-partners.

261

There is a small and gracefully sketched-in curtsey from Janie and then a flash of seriousness.

JANIE: I'd like to think you meant that, dear.

KILLANE: I meant I'm grateful for what you're trying to do.

JANIE: It's all done. I marched into the House of Lords, waited until Uncle Charles and that sweet old life peer of Sam Brodie's had finished talking about their operations and just asked.

KILLANE (*Quickly*): And?

JANIE: They're perfectly willing to sponsor a reception in the House of Lords for any visiting millionaires you care to invite. Will it do any good?

KILLANE: It should do. Now we just make sure the right people turn out.

He glances across at Sam Brodie who is seen carrying two glasses of beer towards the table where Delaney is sitting.

JANIE: And tell the caterers to dust their little rubber sandwiches and keep the cloth round the champagne so that people can't see it was estate-bottled in Wigan.

KILLANE (*Laughing*): We'll do a little better than that. Don't judge all receptions by the business ones we used to go to.

JANIE (*Hesitantly*): Uncle Charles seemed to take it for granted I'd be there. Is that all right?

Instinctively Killane does not like the idea but it would be graceless to refuse and he realises that he must force some warmth into agreement.

KILLANE: If you'd like to come. Of course.

JANIE: Thank you.

Killane looks towards Brodie again.

262

Brodie is leaning on the table and Delaney is sitting back in his chair.

DELANEY: Tell me one thing, Sam. Why should I?

BRODIE: These two are big-time industrialists. One's Dutch, one's American and all tycoons get nightmares when you mention unions.

DELANEY: I don't mean that. I can round up some union bosses, some other trade union MPs for this reception of yours. We can prove we're not raving lunatics. That's no bother. They'll come for the ale if not for the sound of their own voices giving advice. I meant, why should I? Me, personally, Joe Delaney.

BRODIE: I'll talk to Garsfeld. He's paying the bills.

DELANEY: Take the sneer off your face, Sam. A good few of us have done this sort of favour before. And a parcel arrives at the messenger's office.

BRODIE: It will this time.

DELANEY: A case of Scotch is nice but money's better.

BRODIE: I'll talk to Garsfeld.

DELANEY: I'd be surprised if you hadn't already. What's in this for you?

BRODIE: Nothing. Just the job I was elected to do.

DELANEY: No consultancy fee? No small retainer? Garsfeld can afford to part with some of the profit.

BRODIE: I can't afford to take it.

DELANEY: For how much longer?

BRODIE: As long as I can. I don't want to join the amateurs. All the brief-cases, all the office phone calls, all the part-timers who make more outside in a month than we spend in a year. All the excuses for not going on committees, all the phantom directorships. Not me, Joe. I'm a full-time MP.

DELANEY: And a mug. We both are. I had a bloody

great rates bill in this morning. The coloured one: 'Dear Sir, Unless.' You think about it, Sam. And if anything gets offered, you grab it.

Brodie shakes his head and then grins.

BRODIE: Onward with the movement. Patches and pride. Get the banners out.

DELANEY: Just remember *this* idealist has his price. But I'll round up the loyal trade union brothers for you. Whatever happens.

Delaney gets up and starts to leave.

BRODIE: Thanks, Joe.

Killane and Janie are still standing at the bar.

KILLANE: In the end, Annie Mackinnon had to tell the association chairman about it. And he rang his solicitor to ask what the penalty was for using the scout hut for improper purposes. And that's how Andersley Young Conservatives lost two of its jumble-sale committee.

JANIE: I think it's a shame. Hanky-panky beats all those tedious knots and how to identify lichens.

The Minister is seen entering the Strangers' Bar, looking for someone Brodie waves to attract Killane's attention.

Killane turns, sees the Minister, hurries away.

KILLANE: Excuse me.

As Killane moves towards the Minister, Brodie gets up and goes across to Janie Killane.

MINISTER: You were looking for me, Killane.

KILLANE: Yes, Minister. I gave your PPS the details.

MINISTER: If it's to attract industry, I'll be delighted to attend any reception you care to lay on. Just let me know in time. But a trip to Andersley on the matter is quite out of the question.

KILLANE: I know you're busy, Minister, but it's important. And the local association would appreciate it very much.

MINISTER: Quite out of the question, Mr Killane. I'm sorry. (*Takes the edge off his firm refusal.*) Don't look so downcast. People exaggerate my importance. Remember the quotation: 'Ministers are only necessary to tell civil servants what the public will not stand.'

Killane nods as the Minister leaves smartly before any other members can accost him.

Janie Killane is talking to Sam Brodie.

JANIE: You're both taking an awful lot of trouble just to butter up these two foreign gentlemen.

BRODIE: Sixteen hundred jobs, Mrs Killane. It's worth a lot of trouble.

Killane comes back to them, speaks to Brodie.

KILLANE: Reception, yes. Andersley trip, no.

BRODIE: That's it, then.

Brodie looks disappointed but Killane is not willing to give up.

KILLANE: No, it isn't. He'll be there. Pendleton can lean on him.

Brodie nods, the disappointment fading.

4

Interior. Andersley Conservative Club. Night.

Sir George Pendleton, Sir Joseph Conran and Cliff Lambert are talking quietly, taking decisions and planning.

265

PENDLETON: I'm extremely glad you thought fit to change your mind, Sir Joseph.

CONRAN: Don't get too pleased, George. There's some self-interest. If I don't join, I don't find out what these high-powered businessmen are up to. They might be competitors.

PENDLETON (*Who knows Conran's approach well*): They might also be customers.

CONRAN: Or customers. I've thought of that as well.

Lambert is showing signs of impatience, juggling the folder of papers in his hand.

LAMBERT: As a simple unbusinesslike Labour agent, what do you want me to do? Shall I call a meeting, Sir Joseph?

CONRAN: You do that. Get round the council and lay it on. Tell them it's the big stuff. You know all the chairmen. Tell them to push it across. Tell them why and where. Tell them I said so and tell them I want their manners showing.

LAMBERT: I might have to 'ask' a few of them.

CONRAN: If you do, I want to know the names.

LAMBERT: I'll start now. I've got to see Sam Brodie's wife first.

CONRAN (*Smiling*): Oh, yes, I heard about that.

Lambert leaves quickly and with some relief.

PENDLETON: Drink, Joseph?

CONRAN: As soon as you like.

PENDLETON: I thought so. They told me about your meeting. How are you getting along with the new union agreements?

CONRAN: It would take all night to tell you. I'm spending more time calling people 'brother' and sorting out the small print than I am running the job.

PENDLETON: I've given up. It's a job for specialists so I've appointed one. Not like the old days.

CONRAN: Nothing ever was, George. One thing that doesn't change is you get older. I'm looking forward to seeing what these two mysterious foreign money-bags are like.

5

Interior. London hotel room. Night.

Garsfeld is replacing a telephone receiver and paces the room as he talks to Killane and Brodie who are sitting with an attitude of some expectancy in the low chairs.

GARSFELD: They're on their way up now. You've seen the dossiers on them. Froebel's old man ran up a couple of sheds in the mid-west to the third largest industry of its kind in the States. Froebel kept it there and then spread to Europe. A quiet, gentle sort of guy. Don't let it fool you. Vandergraf's the heavy. What he's got, he built himself. He owns it and says so. And it's big. They both take their own decisions and take them fast.

KILLANE: I've never seen you nervous before, Joe.

GARSFELD: Money always makes me nervous. Especially when it's mine and I stand to lose some.

There is a tap on the door and the head porter, tipped in advance, ushers in two men, gives a small salute and shuts the door quietly.

One of the men is Bill Froebel. He is about forty-five, well-tailored, quiet, soft-spoken, the best type of cultured successful American with the steel of ambition only showing through occasionally.

The other man is Eddy Vandergraf. He is about fifty,

a big solid Dutchman who has cultivated the steam-roller characteristics he was born with and prides himself on not wasting words, movement or money.

There is a quietness stemming from ability in both men and with this comes a polite, hard confidence.

Both men carry neat folders which contain details of the itinerary which Garsfeld has planned for them.

Garsfeld moves towards them as Killane and Brodie rise. The introductions go on over a flurry of hand-shakes which include a barely perceptible stiff bow to individuals from Vandergraf.

GARSFELD: Welcome, gentlemen. Settled in comfortably, good flight?

He gives both men time to say 'yes, thank you' and 'yes' before he moves into introductions. Garsfeld is now very relaxed and completely cool.

GARSFELD: I'm very glad to be able to introduce Mr Sam Brodie and Mr John Killane. They're the two Members of Parliament for Andersley. Mr Froebel, Mr Vandergraf.

FROEBEL: Glad to know you, gentlemen. Appreciate you giving up the time. (*To Garsfeld*) This is a very interesting programme you've mapped out for us, Mr Garsfeld.

GARSFELD: I'm glad you like it.

VANDERGRAF: We shall need a morning with figures first.

GARSFELD: Obviously.

FROEBEL (*To Killane*): I've been to your House of Commons but never the House of Lords. I'm looking forward to that. Pugin was the architect?

KILLANE: In his best Victorian romantic style. I like it very much.

268

VANDERGRAF (*To Brodie*): And there in your House of Lords we meet also trade union leaders. Strange.

BRODIE (*Laconic*): They like to keep an eye on the opposition.

Vandergraf laughs.

BRODIE: You'll be asked a lot of questions.

VANDERGRAF (*Liking this*): Good. I also will ask.

During this Garsfeld has moved to the small bar.

GARSFELD: I thought we'd have a drink, some dinner, get to know each other before we start the real business.

VANDERGRAF: Genevers, if you have it.

GARSFELD: With a visiting Dutchman, I'd be pretty sloppy if I didn't.

He takes the characteristic stone bottle of Dutch gin, fills a schnapps glass.

FROEBEL: Scotch for me. Malt if it's there.

The bottle of Glenfiddich is used on a highball glass. No ice or water is added. Garsfeld takes it for granted that if someone asks for malt whisky they will drink it in the manner of most malt-whisky addicts.

There is a small quietness in the room. This is a gathering at which social small talk will be kept to its minimum and that minimum has been reached.

Froebel talks as he walks to collect his drink.

FROEBEL: Like to settle one point. Mr Vandergraf and I are both what I suppose you'd call fairly large operators. Separately, of course. If we make a deal, I hope you've enough space for both of us. Mr Vandergraf and I had a very long and interesting discussion about it on the plane.

VANDERGRAF: There's a lot of factory space elsewhere

in this country. So Mr Froebel and I are not prepared to haggle with each other. (*Lifts his glass.*) Your health.

Brodie and Killane look at each other.

6

Interior. Sam Brodie's living room. Night.

Set as previous plays.

Cliff Lambert is standing, balancing a cup of tea. Elizabeth Brodie is sitting very straight in the armchair.

Curled in one corner of the sofa is Brodie's older son, Andrew. Andrew is just sixteen, a stocky boy with an intelligent face and a quiet manner, in his fifth year at grammar school. His hair is not long by London standards but is long enough to be the subject of some reproof by his father. He is wearing jeans and a rollneck sweater—both from Marks and Spencers. He is fresh-complexioned and the main impressions of him are of cleanliness and intentness.

Lambert grins at Andrew, talks to Elizabeth Brodie.

LAMBERT: I shouldn't worry too much, Mrs Brodie. Andrew's only sixteen.

ELIZABETH: Old enough to know better.

LAMBERT: And Mrs Harris was full of her own importance long before they made her Chairman of Labour Women. They reckon she washes her curtains twice a week just so she can tell the neighbours about it.

ELIZABETH: He was very, very rude.

LAMBERT: And he apologised. So they tell me.

ELIZABETH: She won't leave it at that.

LAMBERT: Sam's due up on Friday. He'll fix it.

ELIZABETH: I hope so (*To Andrew*) He'll certainly have a deal to say to you.

ANDREW: I'm sure he will. He usually does.

LAMBERT: None of my business, Andrew, but I'd keep my head down for a bit if I were you.

Andrew looks at him for a moment.

ANDREW: Yes. You would, wouldn't you?

There is absolutely no insolence in this remark. It is an accurate analytical appraisal of what Lambert's reaction would be if the circumstances were reversed.

7

Interior. London hotel room. Night.

Despite Garsfeld's plans for a social evening, business has already started.

Vandergraf and Killane have spread maps and charts on one of the low tables and Vandergraf is writing in a small notebook.

Near them, Froebel and Brodie have their heads together.

BRODIE: I can give you chapter and verse on most of the industrial disputes in the area and the causes. Certainly since the war. I was in on most of them. A sort of one-man fire brigade.

Garsfeld looks at his watch.

GARSFELD: Hate to break it up, gentlemen, but the table's booked for 8.30.

There is a general move and then a tap on the door as a lesser porter ushers Peter Chapman in. Chapman is carrying two reports, spiral-bound with white covers.

271

KILLANE (*Surprised*): Hello, Peter. What is it?

GARSFELD: Gentlemen, this a business associate of Mr Killane's.

Vandergraf speaks to Chapman directly, increasing Killane's surprise.

VANDERGRAF: You have the research? (*Chapman hands over the documents.*) Good. A day early.

CHAPMAN: You're paying a lot of money for the hurry, Mr Vandergraf.

VANDERGRAF: Knowledge is never cheap.

FROEBEL: I didn't know you were a market research man, Mr Killane.

GARSFELD (*Smoothly*): Oh, yes. One of the best. I introduced these two. (*He indicates Vandergraf and Chapman.*)

FROEBEL: You must tell me about it.

CHAPMAN: Be delighted. Any time.

During this Brodie has gone to lean on the small bar and Killane walks over to put a glass down.

BRODIE (*His voice soft but edged*): I'd forgotten the old Tory motto: 'Look after the individual.' And look after him twice as hard when he's yourself.

KILLANE (*The anger starting to show*): I didn't know anything about it. I'm telling you.

Brodie pulls a face of disbelief and moves away from the bar.

Vandergraf has been looking at the research reports while Garsfeld and Froebel gather together the maps and charts on the table.

GARSFELD: So how about some dinner?

There is a move towards the door but Killane stays where he is.

KILLANE: I'll join you in a minute. If that's all right.

GARSFELD: Fine, Johnnie. Fine.

KILLANE: Peter.

Chapman turns and waits until the room is cleared.

KILLANE: Why didn't somebody tell me we were working for Vandergraf?

CHAPMAN: Somebody tried. There's a pile of pink slips at the House of Commons. 'Mr Killane, ring your office.'

KILLANE: I've been busy.

CHAPMAN: So have we.

Chapman rubs his eyes, a lot of tiredness showing now.

KILLANE: Did Garsfeld give you the names?

CHAPMAN: We didn't pick them out of a hat.

KILLANE: We don't use any more of them, Peter.

CHAPMAN: Not much we don't. The Dutchman was a two-week panic job. Some of it farmed out and a four-thousand quid fee. I'll take as many of those as I can get.

KILLANE: And how do you think that's going to look in Andersley? I'm the MP there.

CHAPMAN: And how I know it. I'm the boy that chases up there most weekends just to grab an hour of your time. I know and love Andersley. I love the corrugated-iron hotel beds. I love the sparrow's eggs for breakfast. I love being treated like a man from Mars because I've got a southern accent.

KILLANE: Stick to the point, Peter. No more work for us out of the Garsfeld project. It isn't on.

CHAPMAN: Why? Just tell me. Ethics?

KILLANE: Some of it. Look, it may sound pompous

but I don't want anybody ever to be able to point and say I'm milking the job I've got as an MP. That I use it to tout for business.

CHAPMAN: You're not doing. I am.

During this, and realising that no invitation is forthcoming, Chapman has gone to the bar and poured drinks, one for himself, one for Killane.

KILLANE: So you stop. This is too important. Take Froebel and Vandergraf. They could mean sixteen hundred jobs for Andersley.

Chapman walks from the bar, puts a glass in Killane's hand, takes a deep breath, nerves himself for what he is about to say.

CHAPMAN: John, it's got to be said. And now's the time. The hell with Andersley. What about the dozen or so jobs here? Up the road in the agency we built. Nut-cases who've worked for us for twelve years, grafted for peanuts when the going was rough. If you're talking about jobs, what about them?

KILLANE: I know. Just let me fix Garsfeld first. Then I'll put more time in.

CHAPMAN: Oh no, you won't. Not the time where we need it. Getting business. You'll be running scared, looking over your shoulder, worried about misuse of your precious bloody position as an MP.

KILLANE: I'll sound pompous again. It's a question of honesty. Responsibility.

Chapman hesitates for a moment and Killane finishes his drink. Chapman takes the glass from his hand.

CHAPMAN: This bit isn't going to be easy either. Last week, two thousand quid was paid into your account. The consultancy fee agreed with your partners in the agency we all slog for. Nothing in writing. Just the cheque. And for the last three months you haven't lifted a finger to earn it. So please don't give me the honesty and responsibility chat. (*He puts both glasses on the bar and leaves.*)

Killane watches him go. There has been no anger in Chapman's voice, only the expression of a dilemma and the honesty of long friendship. On Killane's face is the knowledge of this.

END OF ACT ONE

ACT TWO

8

Film sequence.

The House of Commons is seen from Westminster Bridge, moving from the Lords' end up to Big Ben and then back again until the angle changes, taking in the river and then Lambeth Palace and finally showing the river and Lambeth Palace only.

This last viewpoint, featuring the river, is the introduction for the first line of dialogue for the next scene.

9

Interior. Tented reception area. House of Lords. Day.

This interior is that of a marquee in red and white stripes erected to abut the House of Lords.

These lean-to marquees are quite often used for political, diplomatic or commercial receptions and in good weather the guests will move from here to the terrace. They are not, however, usually allowed on to the terrace belonging to the House of Commons.

The interior of the marquee—on this occasion and because Garsfeld is prepared to spend money—may have been carpeted.

Certainly the small tables, gilt chairs, white linen, attentive waiters who have put on their weekly clean shirt, will bespeak an avoidance of false economy.

The scene opens with only Garsfeld, Froebel, Vander-graf, Brodie and Killane—all waiting with a degree of anxiety—among catering staff, one of whom is starting to prepare a tray of champagne glasses. During the dialogue, he will open champagne bottles and start to put glasses on the tray.

Froebel turns from the marquee exit to the terrace, commenting on the film sequence seen earlier.

FROEBEL: 'Sweet Thames run softly'. That view is really something. And isn't it quiet here?

KILLANE: Sometimes. One of the few privileges of being an MP. At least they provide you with a small oasis while the rest of the world goes by.

VANDERGRAF: I, too, am impressed. But where are the people?

During this Brodie has been reading a newspaper, not for pleasure but for professional reasons, scanning quickly through the political reports in The Times. *He looks up from this, the only one there who is an old hand at these receptions.*

BRODIE: It's always like this. All these parties are.

GARSFELD (*The host's nervousness showing*): This is not a party, Mr Brodie. It's a little more than that.

BRODIE: To us, yes. To the others? (*He shrugs and by now he and Garsfeld have moved away from Killane and the two businessmen.*) Word of advice, Mr Garsfeld. Act as if it's a party. Don't hustle. Or if you do, don't let it show.

Garsfeld nods, willing to accept the advice.

10

Exterior. St Stephen's entrance to the House of Commons. Day.

A policeman watches as a chauffeur-driven limousine draws to a halt. The chauffeur gets out, opens the door for Sir Joseph Conran—whose car it is—and Sir George Pendleton.

Pendleton moves towards the House while Conran gives instructions to the chauffeur.

CONRAN: This shindig should be over by about six. You can get back here then and tell the policeman who you're waiting for.

11

Interior. Tented reception area. House of Lords. Day.

Almost half the invited guests have now arrived and waiters are circulating with trays of champagne. The guests form a cross-section of the influence which Garsfeld hopes will impress Vandergraf and Froebel. There are members of the House of Lords in formal suits and tweeds, there are trade unionists, bulky men tending to emphasise conversational points with jabbing rostrum gestures. There are quiet civil servants, narrow document cases clamped under their arms as they manipulate glasses and cigarettes.

Throughout the scene, Killane, Brodie, Froebel, Vandergraf and Garsfeld will circulate. They will move from group to group collectively or separately and introductions, handshakes, smiles will always be in evidence as Froebel and Vandergraf are made aware of the people they are meeting. Occasionally, small leather cases will flash and business cards be exchanged, largely from Froebel and Vandergraf.

Killane moves away from the group he is attached to when he sees Chapman enter the reception.

KILLANE: Somebody should have told me you'd been sleeping on the camp bed at the office. Like old times.

CHAPMAN: And the old result. It still makes me filthy-tempered and talkative. But if Vandergraf's paying panic money, he's entitled to my insomnia.

KILLANE: We'll organise something. I'll work on it.

CHAPMAN: Sure. But not now. Go and mingle. (*Softly, no gesture.*) Heil Ted.

Killane grins at him and moves away. Chapman turns to see Janie Killane enter with two oddly assorted elderly gentlemen. One is an unmistakable aristocrat with the bland and piercing gaze and the mandatory unnoticed sprinkling of dandruff. This is Janie's Uncle Charles. The other is an elderly Labour life peer, attired in the good blue serge suit he bought fifteen years ago in Bradford and unconscious of its shine.

Janie reaches up to kiss Uncle Charles quickly on the cheek, almost has to reach down to pat the head of the Labour life peer and then moves towards Chapman.

JANIE: Peter, darling.

CHAPMAN: Hello, Janie. (*Nods towards the two peers.*) Love your new admirers.

JANIE: They are sweet, aren't they? Uncle Charles and his new Labour friend. They've just discovered they use the same nursing home. And they both have the most sinister designs on the night sister. Couldn't wait to get rid of me to talk about it.

CHAPMAN: Talking won't give them heart attacks. I hope. (*Looks round.*) Where's the booze?

Janie hardly needs to crook an elegant finger. There will always be waiters hovering when Janie Killane is in any room.

279

Chapman takes a glass of champagne from the proffered tray and Janie reaches across to take a glass from the far side. She sees Chapman's startled look.

JANIE: Ginger ale, Peter. By arrangement.

Chapman takes a cigarette from the silver container also on the tray and looks at it before he reaches for a lighter.

CHAPMAN: House of Lords' cigarettes. It says. That's a new brand on me.

JANIE: Give you that authentic aristocratic cough.

As Chapman lights his cigarette, he sees Sir George Pendleton enter and moves very quickly.

CHAPMAN (*To Janie*): Excuse me.

Chapman takes Sir George's arm and turns him the two or three paces necessary to introduce him to Eddy Vandergraf. Chapman moves in smoothly with a quick 'excuse me' to the people to whom Vandergraf has been talking.

CHAPMAN: Mr Vandergraf, may I introduce Sir George Pendleton?

VANDERGRAF: Ah yes. (*The handshake and stiff small bow.*) I'm delighted, Sir George. I've heard a great deal about your firm.

PENDLETON: Yes, we're doing very well with exports to Holland now.

VANDERGRAF: If one can accept the long delivery times.

PENDLETON: We have to look after the home market first.

VANDERGRAF: Then you should expand.

PENDLETON: I'm getting a little old for that sort of empire-building ambition, Mr Vandergraf. We do quite comfortably, thank you. I understand we'll have the pleasure of seeing you in Andersley quite soon.

VANDERGRAF: Tomorrow or the day after. Tell me, Sir George. This new range of sub-assemblies you have now. What's the capacity on that?

PENDLETON (*A little taken aback by the directness*): My dear Mr Vandergraf, we must spend an hour or two together in Andersley. I'll be delighted to show you. (*To Chapman*) Is the Minister coming?

CHAPMAN: So they tell me.

As this group breaks into small talk, Chapman fascinated with his new brand of cigarettes, Brodie, Bill Froebel and Delaney are seen. Their discussion is interesting and animated, men who know their jobs working at it.

DELANEY: Of course, there's union influence on the Party. You can add it up. In '69—the year before the election—Labour Party income was about £360,000. The Unions chipped in £270,000 of that.

FROEBEL: I'd checked on the figures. It's the influence I'd like to ask you about. Not the congress resolutions, the real strings.

Delaney looks at Brodie.

BRODIE: I could tell you but it would take time. Main thing to remember is that the trade union movement as a whole—the TUC—doesn't have any real power. Full stop. It can advise, arbitrate, make a noise. The dog-fights are still between individual unions, individual managements and about individual cases. But if there's a fight, it helps to know the referee.

FROEBEL: You mean they change.

DELANEY: All the time. Depends who's acceptable.

FROEBEL: And you still don't have binding contracts with unions here. So anybody investing a pile of real money is taking—in my ill-informed and humble opinion—a hell of a risk.

281

DELANEY: Unless he knows the ropes. Like Sam. Or even me, come to that.

BRODIE (*To Delaney*): Don't be modest, Joe. When they open the door of the smoke-filled room, often as not you're the only one on his feet.

Another group is seen consisting of Sir Joseph Conran, Chapman and Killane.

CONRAN (*To Killane*): You've managed a good turn-out. Is the Minister here yet?

CHAPMAN: Everybody keeps asking *me* that.

KILLANE: He'll be along shortly. Thank you for coming down, Sir Joseph.

CONRAN: Never hurts to see what you lot get up to. (*Looks round the area.*) Looks like a mixture of both party conferences in here. (*Waves to someone in another group, then sees Sam Brodie, still talking to Froebel.*) I see Sam Brodie's giving somebody the gospel.

KILLANE: That's Bill Froebel, one of the men we're trying to impress. Let's move in.

As they move across to join this group, the Minister with his Parliamentary Private Secretary in attendance enters and there is a certain amount of head-turning. The Minister advances on Sir George Pendleton, who is obviously an old friend.

MINISTER: Hello, George. How nice to see you. Must be important if they can drag you away from Andersley.

PENDLETON: And for you to be here, too. How's life as a Minister?

MINISTER: It goes on. The pegs outside the Cabinet Office carry the label of what you do rather than who you are. So that twice a week you're reminded that some day somebody will succeed you.

PENDLETON: Still the objective viewpoint.

MINISTER: Oh, yes.

PENDLETON: What about coming to Andersley? We could get in some shooting.

MINISTER (*Smiling*): Do you know, that's the first real inducement that's been offered to me.

Delaney is seen talking to Vandergraf as Brodie moves Froebel across to meet the Minister.

DELANEY: Read the newspapers. New firms, new industry. *And* new brooms. They sweep clean. You take a firm that's been in a town for fifty years, people know where they are. They like that. They like the neighbours to know who they're working for.

VANDERGRAF: Which could be wrong. A labour force should be mobile.

DELANEY: It depends what you want. Where I come from—and Andersley as well for that matter—you'll get more work done if a man's settled.

VANDERGRAF: I still do not understand the mistrust of movement. The mistrust of new firms—especially foreign ones.

DELANEY: Nor do I. But I don't understand the weather either. It's just a fact of life.

Killane comes across.

KILLANE (*To Delaney*): Excuse me. Mr Vandergraf, perhaps you would like to meet the Minister.

VANDERGRAF (*To Delaney*): Thank you. That was most instructive.

As he moves away, Delaney is able to speak softly to Killane.

DELANEY: That's two cases of Scotch you owe me.

Conran is seen talking to Brodie.

CONRAN: You've really laid it on, Sam. All that's missing is the choir from Westminster Abbey.

BRODIE: They're still practising. They'll be along later.

CONRAN: What train are you catching?

BRODIE: The seven o'clock—if I'm lucky.

CONRAN: I'll drive you up if you like.

BRODIE: No, thanks, Sir Joseph. I usually work on the train anyway.

CONRAN: I'll catch it with you. All right?

BRODIE (*Puzzled but nodding*): All right by me. Thanks for coming down today.

CONRAN: It's in the usual good cause. Mine. I had some people to see down here anyway. (*He catches Brodie as he turns to mingle again.*) They reckon your Andrew's playing up a bit.

BRODIE (*Poker-faced, hiding the worry*): Yes, Elizabeth phoned. I'll sort him out.

Killane is seen talking to Joe Garsfeld.

KILLANE: We've made the rounds Joe. Now let's just leave them to it. They're both too old for nursemaids.

GARSFELD: The last guys I heard them talking to were doing everything but singing the Red Flag.

KILLANE: Good. So now they know. Besides, it'll make them appreciate Sam Brodie.

The Minister is talking quietly to Sir George Pendleton.

MINISTER: All right, George. As a personal favour to you, I'll come to Andersley.

PENDLETON: I hate asking, Robert, but it's important. We'll keep the official side as short as we can and then you and I can get some fresh air and chat. Put our feet up.

MINISTER: Count on it.

Janie Killane and Chapman are seen standing a little apart and people are starting to leave.

JANIE: 'The tumult and the shouting dies—The captains and the kings depart.'

CHAPMAN: If you think our ancient sacrifice is Garsfeld's humble and contrite heart, somebody's going to have to re-write Kipling.

JANIE: What a little Golden Treasury of Verse you are.

CHAPMAN: Oh, I'm that, baby doll. Among other things.

JANIE: I know. John rang me. He's very worried.

The crowd has now thinned enough for small private conversations to be possible and Bill Froebel is talking quietly to Sam Brodie.

FROEBEL: I'm not making any firm decisions yet, Mr Brodie. But if I move an expensive factory into Andersley, I'll need a lot of management help. And the first place I'll need it is in labour relations. Now, I've listened to people talk about you and they say you're the expert. So I'd like you to think about coming to work for me.

BRODIE: I've already got a job. I'm an MP.

FROEBEL: That wouldn't change. I mean on a consultancy basis. Just think about it. I'll need a top man and I'll pay top rates.

BRODIE: I don't really need to think, Mr Froebel. Thanks for the offer all the same.

FROEBEL: Leave it open.

He hands Brodie a heavily embossed business card.

The Minister comes across for a farewell handshake and Killane brings Vandergraf over.

12

Exterior. St Stephen's Entrance. House of Commons. Day.

Four or five cars are drawn up with their drivers waiting. Among them is Sir Joseph Conran's driver.

One by one the doors of the cars are opened and they drive away quite quickly. Other guests leave the reception on foot. The policeman salutes four or five he knows, watches impassive. He has seen all this before.

13

Interior. London hotel room. Night.

A post-reception inquest is taking place between Garsfeld, Froebel and Vandergraf.

FROEBEL: That was a remarkable piece of organisation, Mr Garsfeld. It certainly answered a lot of questions for me.

VANDERGRAF: At the top. Where the questions get answered.

GARSFELD: I'm glad you thought it was worthwhile, gentlemen. I've prepared a list of the people you talked to and I have a couple of secretaries typing up letters. The usual sort of thank-you routine that goes on in this country.

VANDERGRAF: And gives people your office address and telephone number in case they're needed.

GARSFELD: I've arranged for us to fly up to Andersley tomorrow. Killane and Brodie are on their way up there now. You'll be able to meet the people who run City Hall. See what you're buying. The people you're buying it from.

VANDERGRAF: I've made arrangements to travel by train tomorrow, Mr Garsfeld. I shall meet you in Andersley.

Garsfeld looks surprised but Froebel smiles. Garsfeld should know better because this is the way Eddy Vandergraf operates. He will be organised only as far as it suits him.

14

Interior. Dining car. Night.

Conran and Brodie are easing themselves into seats at a table for four. There is a hovering steward to whom Conran gives a pound note and a reserved sign appears immediately on the table.

Brodie leans back and watches this.

BRODIE: The most expensive thing in the world— privacy. That's why these Greek fellows have to buy their own islands.

CONRAN: You get what you pay for.

BRODIE: Or you buy what you can afford. Why the sudden desire for my company, Sir Joseph?

CONRAN: Thought I'd buy you a meal. You got me kicked out of the chairmanship . . .

BRODIE: You were voted out of it. Mainly by Ernest Dewhurst.

CONRAN: And you.

BRODIE: And me.

CONRAN: But that's all finished. We've had rows before. (*With meaning.*) *And* we'll have them again.

BRODIE: That sounds better. How is Ernest anyway?

CONRAN: Still in hospital but he's all right. George Pendleton sent him some grapes and he wanted to send them back because they weren't peeled. Said he knew as much about gracious living as any bloody Conservative.

Brodie laughs at this as Killane and Janie pass their table. Both he and Conran nod at them but Killane and Janie make no move to stop.

CONRAN (*Looking after Killane*): I thought he was brighter than that. You don't win many political medals carting an ex-wife around. Especially one like that.

BRODIE: That's his business. (*His dislike of personal gossip shows.*)

CONRAN: You never gossip, do you, Sam?

BRODIE: Only when I'm hanging out the washing. What do you want, Sir Joseph?

CONRAN: I want you to come and work for me. New Bill, new union agreements, I can't cope any more. Not can't—don't bloody want to. You know more about it than I do and people trust you.

BRODIE: Which one of those are you buying?

CONRAN: Both. Fifteen hundred a year, use of company car, reasonable expenses.

BRODIE: About what you'd pay a junior salesman.

CONRAN: You'd only be part-time. All right, two thousand.

BRODIE: No, thanks. I don't want a part-time job and if I did, I could do better than that.

CONRAN: You're a mug, Sam.

BRODIE: Sure. I'm an MP.

15

Interior. Another section of the same dining car. Night.

Killane and Janie are seated and a passing steward smiles and nods at Killane.

JANIE (*Noticing this*): Quite a celebrity, aren't we?

KILLANE: Just a regular customer. On my free pass.

JANIE: Mr Garsfeld offered to buy my ticket. He's under the illusion that my finishing-school accent adds what he calls a touch of class to his organised junkets.

KILLANE (*Grinning*): Depends who you use it on. And to say what.

JANIE: I shall restrict myself to comments on the outrageous price of black pudding, my views on clog-dancing and the occasional 'Ee by gum'. (*The last three words are still in faultless crystal English.*) Besides, I'm really up here to help you.

KILLANE: You've talked to Peter?

JANIE: Oh, yes. Who's fond of you and worries about you.

KILLANE: And thinks I've taken a small leave of absence from the human race.

JANIE: Which is a subject I know about.

KILLANE: Stop blaming yourself for that. You're all right now.

JANIE: Am I? I hope so. When a man's a drunk, it can be comic. When a woman's a drunk, it's pathetic.

KILLANE: You've read the books. Booze isn't the disease, it's the symptom.

JANIE: And the disease is a sick mind.

KILLANE: Which can be cured.

JANIE: Oh, yes. It still doesn't stop the strange rooms being squalid or the strange men animals from another jungle where you've forgotten how to scream. And the private clinics without mirrors and you think: 'How kind, I don't want to see what I look like.' It isn't kindness. It's to stop you breaking the mirrors and slashing your wrists with the pieces.

KILLANE: I know a little about it so don't go on. I watched it for four years. I hung on as long as I could.

JANIE: And you didn't give me any sonatas about it being for the good of the children.

KILLANE: Don't whitewash me too much. I threw you out in the end.

JANIE: You had reason. Drunks are always frightening. It's the unpredictability.

KILLANE: Yes, I was frightened a lot of the time. For you, the children. For me even. I had to survive.

JANIE: But you were frightened for me. You're perhaps the only person in my adult life with the courage —which seems an odd word—to be steadfastly kind to me.

KILLANE (*Lightly*): That's what it said in the contract.

JANIE: Stop sounding like Joe Garsfeld. Politics has some of the unpredictability of drunkenness. And people—who love you—are now getting frightened for you.

KILLANE: I happen to think it's worth it. It's what I want.

JANIE: But look at the price. If you aren't careful, you'll throw away twelve years you spent building an agency you believed in. And I, my dear, am an expert in throwing away years—and counting regrets afterwards. So I shall be around to remind you of the waste and tell myself that I'm repaying a small part of past help.

Killane nods and then smiles at her. He is aware of concern on the part of both Janie and Chapman.

16

Interior. Sam Brodie's living room. Night.

Cliff Lambert is on his feet about to leave and Elizabeth is sitting in the armchair. Andrew is on the sofa, sprawling slightly.

ELIZABETH: Are the wives invited?

LAMBERT: The presentable ones. (*Grins.*) You. for instance. Tycoons' corner. 5.30 sharp.

Brodie comes in, carrying his hold-all.

LAMBERT: Hello, Sam.

Brodie kisses Elizabeth who rises, obviously very pleased to see him.

BRODIE: Hello, Cliff.

Brodie looks at Andrew who sits up a little straighter.

LAMBERT: I've just been passing the word. Reception at the Club tomorrow. *The* Club, the high-class one. Pendleton and Conran's bipartisan three-line whip.

BRODIE: I'll wear a clean shirt.

ELIZABETH (*Indignant*): You always do.

BRODIE: Joke.

LAMBERT: Sort out a nice blue one. Churchill lives. Good night.

BRODIE: See you, Cliff. Thanks.

Brodie moves to the desk, looking at Andrew as he does so and starts to take papers out of his hold-all.

ANDREW (*Again without any insolence*): Can we get it over with, please? I'd like to go upstairs and read.

BRODIE (*Not hard, just firm*): You'll move when you're told. (*To Elizabeth*) Tell me about it.

ELIZABETH: (*Despite herself, instinctively defending her elder son*): It wasn't all Andrew's fault.

ANDREW (*Soft, ironic*): To be fair.

BRODIE (*Harder now*): And you'll speak when you're spoken to.

ANDREW: Yes, Dad.

ELIZABETH: Mrs Harris was on about the Common Market and a lot of foreigners running the country. And Andrew told her she was talking a load of unmitigated out-of-date tripe.

BRODIE (*To Andrew*): Did you?

Andrew nods.

BRODIE: Go on.

ELIZABETH: And she said: 'It's Labour Party policy and your father says the same thing.' And he said: 'I'm sorry about that. But he's not my responsibility. And it doesn't alter the dubious morality of his Party doing an about-face. And you're still talking pernicious rubbish.'

BRODIE (*To Andrew*): Nice choice of words. If you forget about respect for your elders.

ANDREW: Dad, I don't mean to be cheeky. Not then. Not now. But I read a lot worse every week in Hansard. From so-called grown ups.

BRODIE: Thank you for the 'so-called'. Anything else?

ANDREW: Can I say what I believe?

BRODIE: That's what you've been taught.

ANDREW: I take O levels this year. All my life—that sounds funny doesn't it?—I've heard politics. Mostly one side. Now, I've got to read the history books and the newspapers, really read them. I've got other people I can ask questions.

BRODIE: The news isn't facts. Sometimes facts aren't the truth. And all three don't necessarily add up to knowledge.

ANDREW: I'm not talking about knowledge, Dad. I'm talking about politics. I know you work hard. I've seen you. But what does politics solve?

BRODIE: I don't know. I do know it's a bit fashionable to be anti-politics.

ANDREW: Not if you're who I am. An MP's son. (*Frowns, tries to think.*) Look, for instance, I want a badminton racquet. I can't ask for one. You'd say 'Get out and earn it'. I'd like to. But can you imagine the Mrs Harrises. 'Brodie's lad's got a paper-round.'

BRODIE: You could have asked. It's your birthday soon.

ANDREW: No, Dad. (*Factual.*) I'm here all week. I see mother worrying about the money. I see you work. Then I look at us and this. (*Glances round the room.*) And the other kids at grammar school and what they've got and their parents have got and I honestly don't think politics is worth it. I'm not being cheeky, Dad. It's what I think.

BRODIE: All right, Andrew. Go upstairs and read.

ANDREW: Sorry, Dad.

Elizabeth waits for Andrew to leave, then looks at Brodie and sits down, her face showing pain as Brodie conceals his own hurt at his son's honesty.

293

Brodie puts a hand on her hair, takes Froebel's heavily-embossed business card from his pocket, places it carefully against the jug on the mantelpiece.

END OF ACT TWO

ACT THREE

17

Interior. Dining car. Night.

Eddy Vandergraf, Sir George Pendleton and Peter Chapman are seated at the table.

VANDERGRAF: Is it far to Andersley?

PENDLETON: Nearly three hours.

VANDERGRAF: Good. Then we can start now.

Vandergraf nods to Chapman who gives Pendleton a copy of the research document commissioned by him.

CHAPMAN (*In explanation*): That's why I'm here. You and Vandergraf's make a roughly similar range of products. These are figures on the present market, suggested new markets, and potential for growth.

PENDLETON: I've seen market research before, Mr Chapman.

CHAPMAN: Yes, Sir George. But perhaps not as detailed as this.

VANDERGRAF: For five years—maybe—there'll be room in Andersley and this country for Pendleton's and myself. After that (*Draws a finger across his throat.*) for one of us. Not me.

PENDLETON: We've faced outside competition before— and survived it.

CHAPMAN: I've also heard you talk to John Killane about retirement.

295

PENDLETON: An old song. Usually round my birthday.

VANDERGRAF: Why not retire? You have politics, farms. Get on with your fox shooting.

PENDLETON: Hunting.

VANDERGRAF: What's the difference. The fox is still dead. (*To Chapman*) Excuse me. (*Passes a small folded slip of paper to Pendleton.*) That's the price per share I'm prepared to offer for your family's seventy per cent holding in Pendleton Limited.

PENDLETON (*Reading the figure on the slip*): This is a very fair price.

VANDERGRAF: Fair for both of us. Business *can* be fair. It depends who's doing it.

PENDLETON: But if you could squeeze me out in five years, why bother to buy me now?

VANDERGRAF: Now? I can buy reputation, the Pendleton name. A name for workmanship, honesty, a tradition as a going concern. Cheaper in the long term than establishing my own.

PENDLETON: That seems a good reason for me not to sell.

VANDERGRAF: I'm also purchasing a reputation for rather slow delivery, indifferent after-sales service and cautious research and development.

PENDLETON: If I sell—and I say if—what about my workpeople?

VANDERGRAF: Would remain. A steady work force is perhaps your biggest asset. This I learned yesterday.

PENDLETON: And management?

VANDERGRAF: Too many golf players. I'd honour existing contracts but no more.

PENDLETON: And my own position? I'd like to keep some interest.

VANDERGRAF: Then remain as chairman. But advice only. Contact only. No control. (*Quite gently for him.*) That may be the most difficult part.

PENDLETON: I'm not so sure. It was always a question of duty rather than ambition.

VANDERGRAF: So?

PENDLETON: I'd prefer to sleep on it.

Vandergraf touches the somewhat dubious antimacassars which are a feature of British Rail.

VANDERGRAF: Take a nap.

CHAPMAN (*Grinning*): I think Sir George means he'll give you an answer tomorrow.

The explanation is unnecessary and brings a pitying glance from Vandergraf. He means simply that he is in a hurry.

18

Interior. Killane's hotel room. Andersley. Night.

Set as previous plays.

Janie Killane is wandering around the room while John Killane is looking at papers on the dressing table.

JANIE: I've got a different room but they've given me the same bed as before. The upholstered trampoline. Every time I turn over heavily, it throws me at the wash-basin.

KILLANE: I'll change rooms if you like.

JANIE: Oh, no. The staff sound confused enough as it is. Or perhaps I need an interpreter. The porter asked me how I was. And I said 'gradely' and he said he hoped I'd be better soon. I'll never trust J. B. Priestley's dialogue again.

As she talks, Janie has been pouring a drink—just one—from the tray. She walks across to give it to Killane.

KILLANE: Just keep practising. Thanks, Janie.

There is a tap on the door and Pendleton comes in, carrying the research document given to him by Chapman.

PENDLETON: Oh, I do beg your pardon, John.

JANIE: Just leaving, Sir George.

KILLANE: Come in, come in.

There is a languid wave from Janie but her disappearance is swift and efficient.

PENDLETON: She worked very hard at the Lords' reception. I meant to thank her. However . . .

KILLANE: Yes, I know. It may not be wise for her to come up here. People talk.

PENDLETON: Unfortunately.

Killane nods, the distaste for this attitude showing.

PENDLETON: I travelled up with Vandergraf. He wants to take over Pendleton's. Based on this. (*He offers Killane the research document.*) He also—surprisingly, I thought—advised me to talk to you. May I?

The last question is in reference to the drinks tray, and, for the first time, Killane takes in the older man's concern and worry.

KILLANE: Of course, Sir George. I'm sorry. (*He moves quickly to the drinks tray, pours whisky, knows the other man's habits well enough to add two fingers of water.*)

PENDLETON: Mr Killane, I don't know what to do. And the decision is entirely mine. Vandergraf's price is fair—more than fair. But if I accept his offer, I may deprive Andersley of the four or five hundred new jobs he'd provide if he set up his own factories here.

KILLANE: If.

PENDLETON: I realise that. But the 'if' doesn't change the morality of the decision. My family has been well-served by this town. We have a duty to it—however old-fashioned that may sound.

KILLANE: I don't think duty and morality are old-fashioned, Sir George. I think you have to add them to the one hard commercial fact. These figures. And figures are my business. There's only room for two of you in the market for about four years.

PENDLETON: Vandergraf said five.

KILLANE: Pessimism. Then one of you will fold.

PENDLETON: You think it'll be Pendleton's.

KILLANE: I'm sure it will. Nothing personal, Sir George. The figures again. The record.

PENDLETON: If I sell, then at least I ensure continuity of employment for people who've been with me for a long time. Who *are* Pendleton's.

KILLANE: That's it. Loyalty to the whole town or just a section of its people. (*Ironic, remembering the dozen people who work for his own agency.*) It's a fairly common problem.

PENDLETON: What would you do, Mr Killane?

KILLANE: I'd sell. (*He picks up the research document from the bed, flicks it with his finger.*) I'd have to.

PENDLETON: Thank you. I'm much obliged.

Neither man likes the decision especially in view of the previous hopes entertained that Vandergraf would bring new jobs in instead of taking over existing ones.

19

Interior. Sam Brodie's living room. Day.

It is the following day.

Brodie is dark-suited, pulling down his waistcoat, fiddling with the knot of his tie. Elizabeth is neatly and simply dressed—also in her best.

They are continuing the discussion following Andrew's views of the previous evening.

ELIZABETH: I could manage when the boys were younger. I don't know enough now. They're both too bright, that's the trouble. (*Smiles.*) Take after you.

BRODIE: Not the road I'm going.

ELIZABETH: You're happy with it.

BRODIE: At somebody else's expense.

Elizabeth finally straightens his tie for him.

BRODIE: You remember when I was in government and you came down and I was having tea with an old lady on the terrace?

ELIZABETH: I wondered who she was. She seemed to know everybody. I meant to ask you.

BRODIE: And I wouldn't have told you. She was married to an old boy from the north-east, a good MP. Kids grown up, saved all his life to buy a bungalow. Bought it, moved in. Then his wife was too lonely. Every week she'd come down with him on a Monday. Sit on the terrace or in the Central Lobby. There wasn't anywhere else for her. Some of us would stop and chat and buy her a cup of tea. And she'd be grateful. My Christ, grateful. And she did it for eight years. And then he died and she went back home on her own.

ELIZABETH: Come on. Let's get off to this reception. See if we can sell Andersley to the big world outside.

Brodie touches her arm to turn her, kisses her lightly on the cheek. She looks up at him with a shade of surprise. He is not a demonstrative man.

ELIZABETH: Just don't get selling Sam Brodie. You don't have to.

20

Interior. Conservative Club. Andersley. Day.

A reception is being held here which is almost a reprise of the previous reception seen at the House of Lords. These dignitaries, however, are at the local level—sober-suited councillors of both political persuasions, some of them with their ladies. The same sense of businesslike circulation is present with Vandergraf, Garsfeld and Killane forming a group as Janie Killane, Chapman, Sam Brodie and Elizabeth Brodie move round, nodding, chatting, shaking hands.

All the club stewards have been pressed into service, white-coated and not as smooth and professional as the House of Lords waiters and the trays they carry contain assorted drinks.

Garsfeld is doing his best to conceal his disappointment as he talks to Pendleton and Vandergraf.

GARSFELD: I hope you're not being too hasty about this decision, gentlemen.

VANDERGRAF: It's our money, Mr Garsfeld. Therefore our privilege to be hasty. I should like to thank you. We shall do business again.

There are handshakes to Garsfeld and Killane.

PENDLETON: I'll see you to the door, Mr Vandergraf. My car's waiting to take you to the airport.

VANDERGRAF: And we meet in Rotterdam in two days.

301

This is said as Vandergraf and Pendleton leave and Garsfeld's bitterness is able to show as he turns on Killane.

GARSFELD: There went one pigeon. On the wing. Wide and free.

KILLANE: You've still got Bill Froebel.

GARSFELD: No thanks to you. And that's not settled yet. Pendleton said he'd sold out on your advice.

KILLANE: Not my advice. The figures.

GARSFELD: Is there a difference? My old buddy, Judas Killane.

KILLANE: Let's save the punch-ups till later.

He has seen Froebel approaching.

KILLANE (*To Froebel*): What do you think of the estate, Mr Froebel?

FROEBEL: Nothing but good. Access, fabric, communications.

KILLANE: You'll be coming here then?

FROEBEL: With this degree of support, very probably. (*Looks at Garsfeld, smiles slightly.*) It will depend, of course, on the sort of terms I can pin Mr Garsfeld down to. That's going to be a lot easier with Eddy Vandergraf out of the running.

GARSFELD: Don't count on it.

KILLANE: I'll leave you two to barter.

Janie Killane and Chapman are at one side of the room, watching the reception in progress.

CHAPMAN: Andersley on show. And not a flat hat or a whippet in sight.

JANIE: Hate whippets. Always remind me I should go on a diet. And where's John's agent, the dutiful Miss Mackinnon?

302

CHAPMAN: In Austria. Ostensibly ski-ing. Probably locked in a frenzied tango with some muscular instructor.

JANIE: I'll take six to four on Miss Mackinnon. I thought you had ambitions there.

CHAPMAN: I'm the lethargic type. I'll wait till the excess energy's been worked off first.

There is a flurry of activity and people turning as the Minister enters, PPS by his side, and Sir George Pendleton moving to welcome him.

Cliff Lambert is talking to Sir Joseph Conran.

LAMBERT: Here we come. The Minister. The top brick on the chimney. Even our lot are bowing and scraping.

CONRAN: There's a good turn-out. You did well.

LAMBERT: So did Pendleton.

CONRAN: And they've all met our two new Andersley industrialists?

LAMBERT: Oh, yes. The birthright's been produced and everybody's sniffed the mess of pottage they're swopping it for. The tradesmen on our respected council have been getting their bids in for business. The others are about to produce daughters of marriageable age for offer to the new managerial classes. The biggest self-interested jug-up this place has ever seen. And for what? A Dutchman and a Yank.

CONRAN: Britain for the British. I didn't think you'd be a little Englander, Cliff.

LAMBERT (*Rueful*): Nor did I. But then I've never seen it happen in the flesh before. I think I'll have a drink. I may have several.

Janie Killane has moved across to talk to Elizabeth Brodie.

JANIE: You're Mrs Brodie. What a lovely frock. I

wish I knew about home dressmaking. Oh dear, that was tactless. I didn't mean . . .

ELIZABETH: You're nervous. That's all.

JANIE: How did you know?

ELIZABETH: Because I am. It's part of the job. And you say the first thing that comes into your head. I once told a lady mayoress about Woolworth's corsets.

JANIE: In that case, we'd better stick together and talk to each other. Who's the strange lady over there who looks as if she cuts her own hair? With a tin-opener.

ELIZABETH: Mrs Harris. Chairman of Labour Women.

JANIE: Oh, dear. Again.

ELIZABETH: And I've got to go and talk to her. Wish me luck.

JANIE: Fervently.

Conran has walked up to Killane.

CONRAN: They reckon you told Pendleton to sell up.

Killane shrugs.

CONRAN: Your lot don't change, do they? In it for them.

KILLANE: They also reckon you'll be supplying Froebel with components if he moves in. At least for two years.

CONRAN: What's wrong with that? It means jobs.

KILLANE: And profit. Or do you call it something else when you're wearing your Labour Party hat?

They are both looking across at Froebel who is talking very quietly to Sam Brodie.

FROEBEL: About that job, Mr Brodie. The labour relations one.

BRODIE: I'll let you know.

FROEBEL: I'll need somebody. Too many American firms think England's an extension of the States. It isn't and it costs them three years of expensive strikes to find out. I don't want that.

BRODIE: Nor do I.

FROEBEL: If not you, you'll help me find somebody?

Brodie nods and Froebel puts out a hand. To both Brodie and Froebel, the handshake is binding.

BRODIE: My pleasure.

FROEBEL: It's very important.

BRODIE: I know. To me, too.

The Minister has made his rounds and is surveying the scene affably, Sir George Pendleton at his side.

PENDLETON: Good of you to come, Robert. I'm grateful.

MINISTER: Don't be. It's reassuring to be reminded that this is where it all really happens. And how easy it all looks from here.

PENDLETON: It isn't. Not really.

MINISTER: I know. It's just that you lose sight of constituency affairs when the summons from the PM arrives. You go in a door halfway down Whitehall, about a mile of corridors, all very secret. Then No. 10. And then wait while your colleagues come out. Asking them what they've got. Hoping the Ministry you want hasn't been dished out to somebody else—especially someone you dislike. Joining the elect. And it's rather like a school prize-giving.

Peter Chapman and Elizabeth Brodie approach Sam Brodie at almost the same moment, Chapman reaching expertly for a glass from a tray en route.

CHAPMAN: Do you know what a head-hunter is, Mr Brodie?

305

BRODIE: I read the business sections. A firm that specialises in looking for top executives.

CHAPMAN: Conran was talking to one when he was in London. Labour relations. The job specification fitted you. (*He takes in Brodie's surprise.*) So you aren't the only one in the running and the salary quoted was three and a half grand.

BRODIE: How do you know?

CHAPMAN: Use the right pubs.

BRODIE: Why should you do me any favours?

CHAPMAN: God knows. I don't like you very much and I don't like this town very much. But I'm not a politician and I just have this weird non-political belief that everybody should get a fair crack of the whip.

He turns and Elizabeth Brodie puts a hand on his arm.

ELIZABETH: Thank you, Mr Chapman.

CHAPMAN (*Indicating Brodie and smiling*): I'd divorce *him* and buy a good canary.

Garsfeld is seen hurrying across to catch Killane.

GARSFELD: Froebel wants to fly back to London now. He needs lawyers.

KILLANE: Is it on?

GARSFELD: As good as. He's a handshake man who means it. But I'm still left with fifteen per cent of a factory estate to peddle.

KILLANE: Better than I'd thought.

GARSFELD (*Peremptory*): I want to see you at the hotel tomorrow.

KILLANE: Demand or request, Joe? Take your time.

GARSFELD: OK, request.

KILLANE: Then I'll be there.

306

Froebel comes up to them together with Pendleton and Conran and there are farewell handshakes.

This is watched by Chapman and Janie and the reception is starting to clear.

CHAPMAN: Here we are again. Full ashtrays and empty glasses.

JANIE: Any news on what portions of our native heath have been exchanged for trade goods?

CHAPMAN: Garsfeld was smiling. That has to be cash in the bank.

The Minister has also been making his farewell rounds and pauses to take Killane on one side.

MINISTER: A word, Mr Killane. You seem to have got what you want for Andersley but you've made a great nuisance of yourself in so doing. It may not improve your chances of political preferment. More so now that Sir George Pendleton will be less active.

KILLANE: You mean now his firm's contribution to party funds will stop. As well as the nuisance.

MINISTER: A little of each. Only fair to remind you.

KILLANE (*Ironic*): I'm very grateful, Minister.

The irony is not full and Killane's face changes as he realises that there is a lesson to be learned here. There is some disappointment too. He had expected kudos and not blame but the Minister's warning is quite fair and a useful reminder.

21

Interior. Sam Brodie's living room. Night.

Sir Joseph Conran is sitting comfortably on the sofa with a cup of tea. Elizabeth is in one of the armchairs and Sam Brodie is leaning on the mantelpiece.

BRODIE: About that job, Sir Joseph. I'll take it.

Conran glances at Elizabeth.

ELIZABETH: We've talked about it.

BRODIE: I'll join the part-timers. I've done my share of the rest.

CONRAN: I think you're being sensible.

BRODIE: For once. (*He takes Froebel's card from the mantelpiece.*) By the way, Froebel offered me the same job.

CONRAN: Take it then. He'll pay twice as much as I will.

BRODIE: And expect a lot of influence I'm not prepared to deliver. At least you know the system. Who I am, what I believe in. What I'll do, what I won't do. All about whatever principles I've got. They won't change.

CONRAN: I don't expect them to.

BRODIE: But we'll put them in the service contract. Just in case.

CONRAN: That's a bit sharp, isn't it?

BRODIE: Or businesslike. Did your executive search people find anybody?

CONRAN (*Quickly understanding*): Oh. (*Grins.*) Nobody as good as you.

BRODIE: So the principles cost extra. The money can stay the same. (*To Elizabeth*) If my bag's ready, love, I'll catch the early train.

22

Interior. Killane's hotel room. Night.

Peter Chapman is lying on the bed, drink in hand. He is watching Killane put papers away in a document case.

CHAPMAN: Well, you made it. The caravan's resting here for good and the dogs can stop barking. Froebel's in.

KILLANE: That's not sure. Yet.

CHAPMAN: Oh, but it is. He asked me to handle all the attitude and product development research. Worth fourteen grand.

Chapman looks puzzled. Killane is not really listening to him, absorbed in another problem.

KILLANE: There's still a big chunk of factory space to fill. (*A thought occurs to him.*) Wait a minute. Peter, give me that report on Vandergraf.

Chapman gets up wearily, passes the report to Killane.

CHAPMAN: You should be golden boy. Political hero now. Next week Prime Minister.

KILLANE (*Not looking up from the document*): That's what I thought. But that isn't the way it works. I won a factory and lost a party subscriber.

CHAPMAN: That makes two idiots. We should wear badges.

KILLANE (*Looking up now*): How come?

CHAPMAN: I turned Froebel down. Told him I'd have to ask you and the answer was sure to be no.

KILLANE: So tell him we've changed our minds. There's a telephone over there. Use it. Tell Froebel we want the job. Tell him we've already started.

309

CHAPMAN (*Moving quickly*): Yes, bwana. And whoopee.

Killane is still absorbed in the Vandergraf figures.

23

Exterior. Westminster Bridge. Day.

Film sequence.

Brodie is leaning on the parapet on the opposite side of the street to that once occupied by Wordsworth. He looks at the Thames, the Houses of Parliament, picks up his hold-all, walks towards Big Ben.

24

Interior. London hotel room. Day.

Garsfeld is pacing the room while Killane and Chapman sit easily in the conference area.

GARSFELD: Yes, it's all signed. So Froebel's in. I still took a loss.

KILLANE: Not a loss. Just a slight cut in the profit. You panicked just a little, Joe. You got greedy.

CHAPMAN: And how far would you have got at all without him and Brodie?

GARSFELD: I've still got space to fill.

KILLANE: Fifteen per cent. Vandergraf will take that.

GARSFELD: Forget it. He's flown.

KILLANE: He'll fly back. On Peter's figures, he'll need every square foot you've got for expansion space when he takes over Pendleton's. It'll start out as storage, container packing but he'll take it now. While you're still wailing and think he's gone for ever.

CHAPMAN: Small bet?

GARSFELD: I never bet. Except in one-horse races. Can I see those figures.

KILLANE: Not a chance. Somebody else paid for them. Just take my word for it.

The telephone rings and Killane moves very quickly to pick it up from the small table at the conference area.

OPERATOR'S VOICE: A Mr Vandergraf is calling Mr Garsfeld from Rotterdam.

KILLANE: Mr Garsfeld's not here.

GARSFELD: Give me that phone.

KILLANE: He's not expected today. I'll ask him to call Mr Vandergraf but I can't promise when. (*He puts the telephone down and turns to Garsfeld.*) You'd make a lousy spider, Joe. You don't know how to sit and wait. (*On his feet now, moving towards the door.*) I'll see you in ten minutes, Peter. I'll soften Froebel up first.

GARSFELD: Why the hell anybody tries to do business in England, I'll never know.

KILLANE (*At the door*): We have great entertainment value and strange traditions.

He leaves and Garsfeld turns to Chapman.

CHAPMAN (*Resigned*): I'm with you. I don't know why anybody bothers either.

GARSFELD (*Crossing to bar to get a drink for Chapman*): It's beginning to sink in. Tell me, Peter. What figures could you find quickly on property feasibilities for the north east of Andersley? Classy residential.

Planning status. That sort of thing. Just a small deal, walk-around money.

CHAPMAN (*Accepting the drink*): Depends on the fee. And of course, John's approval of the job.

Chapman raises his glass and Garsfeld shakes his head, still baffled.

25

Exterior. Westminster Bridge. Day.

Film sequence.

Killane is seen leaning in a similar position to that of Sam Brodie. He looks out over the Thames towards the Houses of Parliament and then Lambeth Palace, remains there for a moment and walks towards the House.

[*Credits*]

Play Six

WHAT ABOUT ENGLAND?

Cast

SAM BRODIE	*Colin Blakely*
JOHN KILLANE	*Michael Gambon*
PETER CHAPMAN	*William Gaunt*
ANNIE MACKINNON	*Joanna Van Gyseghem*
ELIZABETH BRODIE	*Margaret John*
JANIE KILLANE	*Hilary Dwyer*
SIR JOSEPH CONRAN	*Bill Owen*
SIMON HASELTON	*Gerald Flood*
SIR ROBERT WENSLEY	*Colin Gordon*
CLIFF LAMBERT	*Richard Hampton*
GEORGE TAYLOR	*Charles Taylor*
ELIZABETH BRODIE (daughter)	*Joanna Cookson*

Interiors

1. Conservative Committee Rooms, Andersley
2. Sam Brodie's living room
3. Conservative Club, Andersley
4. Killane's hotel room
5. British Rail dining car
6. Whips Office, House of Commons
7. Hall and gun-room alcove at Haselton's manor house
8. London taxi interior

Exterior

1. Killane entering the House of Commons

ACT ONE

Titles

1

Interior. Conservative Committee Rooms. Day.

Set as previous plays.

Annie Mackinnon is working busily behind the desk and the postal tray is high with incoming mail.

Peter Chapman is helping Annie sort some of this while Janie Killane leans elegantly against the wall.

A postman comes into the room carrying two large bundles of letters tied round with string.

Janie talks as Chapman cuts the string on the bundles and he and Annie start to open letters.

JANIE: What a lot of post. Anyone would think it was John's birthday.

ANNIE: Here's a typical greeting. 'I must protest in the strongest possible terms . . .'

CHAPMAN (*Opening a large envelope*): And here's another petition. From teachers and parents at the Gilborough Primary School.

ANNIE: They're nearest.

JANIE: Is this a private language or can anyone use it?

Annie, still busy, hands a newspaper to Janie Killane.

CHAPMAN: Read all about it.

ANNIE: They want to tear down the almshouses at Gilborough and put up an open prison.

JANIE: Much less peaceful. (*Reads.*) 'Why should more than a hundred of Andersley's old people be

317

evicted to make room for thieves and layabouts from all over the country.' Why indeed? (*Reads.*) 'And will our children be safe if men with records of violence are roaming our streets?' (*She shudders, despite herself.*) It frightens me.

CHAPMAN: Tidings of comfort and joy. You're a great help.

ANNIE (*To Chapman, sharply*): And *you* don't live here.

There is a tap on the door and a man comes into the room. This is George Taylor, a resident of the Gilborough almshouses. He is straight-backed, neatly dressed, a man of about seventy with a great deal of quiet natural dignity. For most of his life, he worked for the local council as a carpenter on building maintenance and there is a craftsman's pride and neatness about him.

ANNIE: I'm sorry, Mr Taylor, Mr Killane's not back yet.

Taylor holds up the petition on a clipboard he is carrying.

TAYLOR: I wanted to give him this. We've all signed it.

ANNIE: I'll see that he gets it.

TAYLOR (*Respectful but obstinate*): I'd rather give it him myself.

CHAPMAN: He's probably still at the Club. I'll give you a lift up there, if you like.

TAYLOR: If it's no bother. Thank you very much.

Taylor starts to leave with Chapman and turns, almost in appeal, to Annie.

TAYLOR: It's wrong, isn't it? They can't chuck us out for a load of criminals. What harm have we ever done?

318

2

Interior. Sam Brodie's living room. Day.

Set as previous plays.

Sir Joseph Conran and Sam Brodie are sitting in armchairs.

At the other side of the room, Sam Brodie's daughter, Elizabeth, is sitting on the floor playing with building bricks. Crouched near her and occasionally helping is Cliff Lambert—who is obviously fond of the child.

Brodie is shaking his head and Conran emphasises a point with a jabbing forefinger.

CONRAN: You can be as progressive as you like, Sam. But we've got council elections coming up. And if we let good almshouses get knocked down for a bloody open prison, we're in trouble.

LAMBERT: And what the hell is an 'open prison'? It's either a prison or it isn't.

BRODIE: It works in Scandinavia.

CONRAN: So do reindeer. But this is Andersley.

BRODIE: The inspector showed me the other three sites. This is the safest. These people have got to be put somewhere. (*Quietly, with some of the pain showing, indicating his daughter.*) Like she has to be.

Lambert moves quickly across away from the child, defends her instinctively.

LAMBERT: That's a lot different, Sam, and you know it.

BRODIE: Not in principle. You and I call it an establishment for the educationally sub-normal. The people living round there call it 'the daft kids' school'.

LAMBERT: Unfair argument. It's not the same. Not at all. It just shows how you feel. And why.

319

CONRAN: And you're forgetting the council elections. Now let's go and see what Haselton's got to say about it.

Conran rises and Brodie reaches for a coat.

BRODIE: I know what he'll say. And I know Haselton.

LAMBERT (*Grinning*): Just keep your hands to yourself. I'll wait with the girl until Elizabeth gets back.

Lambert moves back to the young Elizabeth and her building bricks as Conran and Brodie leave.

3

Interior. Conservative Club. Day.

Set as previous plays.

John Killane and another man are standing under an eighteenth-century map of Andersley near the fireplace.

The other man is Simon Haselton, Conservative MP for the constituency adjoining Killane's. Haselton is about forty, tall, good-looking, arrogant. He is a considerable landowner and extremely efficient farmer, a ruthless modern-day squire who has not quite shed the methods of free-booting ancestors. He is High Tory by birth, breeding and conviction, holding down a safe seat almost by right, as a family perquisite. Despite the arrogance, however, there is a deep conviction about the man. It is possible to disagree violently with him but any dislike will always be tinged with respect.

HASELTON: Naturally, I'm very interested. (*Indicates the map.*) Gilborough's where our two constituencies meet. On the river bend.

KILLANE: And you own all the land.

HASELTON: Most of it. Some of it leased or given to the council by my more stupid or public-spirited forebears.

Killane smiles at Haselton's disdain for this form of public spirit.

HASELTON: Not a laughing matter, Killane. Haseltons have held river land and hills round it since the first Charles gave the valley to one of my ancestor's bastards in return for two hundred fighting men.

KILLANE: He still lost.

HASELTON: Yes, of course, you're one of the new Tories. The computer breed.

KILLANE: Certainly not the squirearchy.

HASELTON: Which you despise.

KILLANE: Oh, no. Just High Tory versus Low. I still respect the tradition.

HASELTON: But did nothing to earn it.

KILLANE: So I can be factual about it. The fighting men are romantic but the almshouses we're talking about were built by another of your ancestors. It was a late attack of piety and he hoped the gesture would help to cure the syphilis he caught at sixty-three.

HASELTON: Nothing like a grasp of local history to impress the constituents. With your tuppenny majority, I suppose it's necessary. The seat I hold's been safe for fifty years. You have to go down to Westminster and talk. I don't. I go when I please. So that I can stay up here and *do*.

KILLANE: Well, now's your chance. Unless you want an open prison next to the family domain.

HASELTON: I don't want one so we shan't get one.

KILLANE: There's a small thing called the democratic process.

321

HASELTON: Lip-service paid by the persuasive to the gullible. It doesn't take decisions.

Killane laughs again, shaking his head.

KILLANE: On the statistics, I suppose you're just about possible. Among 320-odd Conservative MPs there has to be at least one throwback to the Middle Ages.

HASELTON (*Accepting Killane's good humour*): More than one, Killane. And everybody always knows where we stand.

KILLANE: They should do. You've been standing there for a long time.

Haselton looks beyond Killane to see Conran and Brodie come into the room.

HASELTON: Here are two of the comrades. They seem to be looking for us. So now you can be as egalitarian as you like. I have a strong stomach.

Haselton goes straight into discussion with Conran and Brodie without any polite formalities.

HASELTON: Afternoon, Conran. I take it this is what you require.

Haselton produces a neatly typed and folded letter from his pocket which Conran reads briefly.

CONRAN: Formal opposition to the prison scheme.

HASELTON: I've sent a copy to the Minister with a personal note.

Killane in his turn produces a letter and gives it to Conran.

KILLANE: And this is mine. I've listed letters and petitions.

CONRAN: Good. I'll put these with the official council protest.

HASELTON: What about you, Brodie?

BRODIE: I think we're all tearing into this too quickly. I don't think we're being realistic. You know as well as I do that if the Army or the Home Office or any public body wants land badly enough they get it. With the sort of methods that make compulsory purchase look like a gentle request.

HASELTON: Realism or your well-known concern for the underdog?

BRODIE: Somebody's got to look after underdogs. Too many people like you have a habit of kicking them. (*Turns to Conran and Killane.*) If we co-operate on this prison scheme at the beginning, we can put in our own safeguards. Fight it and we'll have no say at all.

CONRAN: Not on, Sam. Forget it. I'm against. So's the Council.

KILLANE: I'm with you, Sir Joseph. We've got to fight it. If we make any claim at all to represent constituents. A lot of letters, a lot of them very frightened.

BRODIE: Of what? Something they don't know about.

CONRAN: And they don't want to wait till there's a prison next door before they find out.

HASELTON: Quite obviously, I disagree with Brodie.

BRODIE: The day you agree with me is the day I go out and buy some spare parts for my head.

HASELTON (*Directly to Brodie*): We did manage to agree once. We both voted against entry into the Common Market. You, because your masters turned coat and you scurried after them. Myself, because I've no intention of farming good land at a profit to subsidise a rabble of scruffy, inefficient peasants on the other side of the Channel. Good-day to you.

Haselton moves away as George Taylor comes into the club with Chapman and approaches the group.

HASELTON: Hello, Taylor.

TAYLOR (*Traditional respect showing now*): Good afternoon, sir. (*Holds up the petition.*) We've all signed this. Like you told us.

HASELTON: Good. Give it to our friends, will you?

Taylor moves across to Conran, Brodie and Killane.

BRODIE: Hello, George. How's it going?

TAYLOR: Nicely, Mr Brodie, thank you. Bit worrying now though. (*To Killane*) Your friend gave me a lift up.

Killane looks across the room and Chapman lifts a drink in salute. This is also seen by Conran.

CONRAN: He's not a member here.

KILLANE: Anywhere they serve strong drink, he's a member.

BRODIE (*To Taylor*): Will you have something, George?

TAYLOR: No, thank you, Mr Brodie. Not here. (*A brief old-fashioned flash of someone who knows his place shows in this.*) Everybody at the almshouses has signed it, Mr Killane. (*He hands the petition to Killane, wants to leave, slightly uncomfortable.*) Tell your friend thank you for the lift. I can get the bus back.

Taylor leaves, not hurrying, looking round him once curiously, still retaining dignity.

CONRAN (*Indicating Taylor*): What do you want, Sam? A roof over his head or a little modern cubicle for some half-barmy kid who thumps old shopkeepers.

BRODIE: I want both. They've both got a right to live.

KILLANE: But perhaps one of them's earned a little more right than the other.

BRODIE: Earned. Profit and loss. The Tory theme tune. Like Haselton.

KILLANE: He stands for what he believes in. As I do. (*Some edge in the voice now*). But I can see why you'd dislike him.

BRODIE (*Quite softly*): Oh no, Mr Killane. I like Simon Haselton. I like him very much. I should carry a photograph of him in my wallet. Just in case I ever forget that everything he stands for, I'm against. Just in case I ever waste energy that I should be using to wipe him and people like him off the face of the earth. You and him are on the same side. And sometimes I forget about you, too. (*To Conran*) See you later, Sir Joseph.

Brodie stalks out and Conran looks impassively at Killane.

4

Interior. Sam Brodie's living room. Day.

Cliff Lambert is putting a tea-cup down on the table just before leaving. Sam Brodie's wife, Elizabeth, is talking to him.

ELIZABETH: Thank you very much, Cliff.

LAMBERT: For what? Sitting in the warm and playing with building bricks. I could get used to it. Beats working.

ELIZABETH: Will Sam be long?

LAMBERT: I shouldn't think so. Unless he goes over to Conran's in his new company car and does a couple of hours in his new office at his new labour relations job.

ELIZABETH: It's not stopping his MP's work. You see that.

LAMBERT: The other way, if anything. He works twice as hard just so people can't complain about him having two jobs.

325

ELIZABETH: It's making him irritable enough. What's wrong, Cliff?

LAMBERT: I don't know. Principle, first. But that's just me. Sam's entitled to his choice and I know the money's useful.

ELIZABETH: Conran? Is that bothering you?

LAMBERT: A bit.

ELIZABETH: The two of them have had arguments before.

LAMBERT: It's different now. Sam's on the payroll.

5

Interior. Conservative Club. Day.

Chapman has joined Killane and Conran and is giving Conran a thin spiral-bound document.

CONRAN: This doesn't look much.

KILLANE: If Andersley had to pay for it, that's about two hundred-quidsworth of land useage research.

CONRAN: You're taking plenty of work out of this town. You can afford to make a small donation in return.

KILLANE: It's already been donated, Sir Joseph. Put your collecting box away. I don't want this prison any more than you do but we'll need reasons and evidence.

CHAPMAN: Then that's not going to be much use to you.

CONRAN: Why?

CHAPMAN: It's just not very hopeful. The authorities are always leery of giving details of prisons in case some bright lad uses them to organise break-outs. But if you take comparable towns and existing prisons, there are quite a few with the same land-use pattern as Gilborough. Agricultural land with a wedge of residential and schools. You can't use that research as evidence against.

During this speech, Cliff Lambert has come into the Club and hurried across to try to interrupt Conran. Conran gestures at him and Lambert waits and listens.

CONRAN (*To Chapman*): What would you do?

CHAPMAN: Buy a set of brass knuckles and go to bed as soon as it's dark.

LAMBERT: You would. But then you don't live here.

CHAPMAN: Hello, Taff. Heard from Karl Marx lately?

LAMBERT: He's dead.

CHAPMAN: Don't you believe it. Just grow a beard.

LAMBERT (*Ignoring Chapman*): Sir Joseph, there's been a planning committee meeting called for Friday.

CONRAN: Who asked for that?

LAMBERT: The deputy planning officer. The new one. Ernest Dewhurst wants you there if you can make it.

KILLANE: It's a waste of time. They can meet till they're blue in the face about this prison. They can't do anything about it.

LAMBERT: Then why the meeting?

CONRAN: We'll have to wait till Friday and find out.

6

Interior. Conservative Committee Rooms. Day.

Janie Killane is rather desultorily helping Annie Mackinnon to open letters. She reads them and places most of them on the large pile which consists of complaints about the prison.

ANNIE: Don't bother with that, Mrs Killane.

JANIE: Oh, I'm quite happy. Part of the small satellite system—you, Peter, me, those earnest ladies in the hats—which revolves round John. And, besides, previously I've always been on the *receiving* end of any welfare work. (*Opens an envelope.*) Goodness, there's a letter here in Arabic.

ANNIE: That's Mrs Thomson. And it's not Arabic, it's just her handwriting. (*She looks at the letter.*) Another complaint about the prison. Why here? Why us?

JANIE: How do you feel about it?

ANNIE: I think John's right. There's a clear mandate from constituents and he's taking it.

JANIE: Not them, you.

ANNIE: I've picked the coward's way out. Following orders. As an ex-social worker, I know some of the problems. I should be in favour of the prison.

JANIE: But as a lady who's out and about—mostly at night—all over Andersley, you're frightened. I would be.

ANNIE: I shouldn't be frightened. It's even part of my job not to be. Analyse it coldly, check with party policy, see how it affects my MP. So I wonder why I read all these terrified letters and there's a voice in my head shouting : 'Yes, we've got to stop it.'

As Annie speaks, Janie is looking curiously at a fairly large envelope with crude printing as the address.

Annie sees this, moves very quickly to take it from Janie, tears the unopened envelope in four and throws it in the waste-paper basket.

ANNIE: Don't read that one. I know what's in it.

JANIE: What, dear?

ANNIE: The usual ugliness. Telling me what he'd like to do to me. He's a regular. One of our local nut-cases.

JANIE: And soon he'll have a lot of little friends to play with. (*Sincere, again the small shudder.*) I'm glad I don't have to make the choice.

7

Interior. Hall and gun-room alcove of Simon Haselton's manor house. Night.

The manor house is largely Queen Anne with some late-Georgian additions but parts of the building pre-date this. It cannot be classified architecturally but has grown almost organically into a comfortable profusion of warm and weathered brick.

The hall stems from the older part of the building with a tall stone fireplace, flagged floors, dark panelled walls below some exposed beams and brickwork.

There are good valuable carpets on the stone and the interior is genuine country gentleman, a mixture of simple expensive antiques—all functional—and purpose-made farm furniture.

The hall is large but some degree of intimacy is provided by an alcove in which a big desk stands against a wall where guns and fishing rods hang. On the corner of the desk is a silver drinks tray, the Waterford decanters not quite matching but all the glassware authentic. Riding crops and an otter's head, neat filing cabinets of farm documents, sporting prints all add to the air of casual comfort and individual taste but under the comfort is a great deal of money.

Haselton uses this area of the house to receive bailiffs or tenant farmers or minor gentry calling on him.

There are sufficient amenities for the social functions to be observed but these functions will be limited.

Haselton is a private man and this part of the house is the public space in which he prefers to operate. Only family and close friends are received elsewhere in the house.

Simon Haselton, dressed in roll-neck sweater, good casual trousers and short riding boots, is moving across to the decanters.

Standing near him, wearing a sheepskin driving coat over a very formal blue suit and in the process of removing string driving gloves is Sir Robert Wensley —the Conservative Whip seen in Play Four.

WENSLEY: I'll take a glass of Madeira, Simon.

In Haselton's lexicon, Madeira is reserved for elderly aunts and his face shows it.

HASELTON: Madeira?

WENSLEY: With a biscuit, if you please.

HASELTON: If you insist. (*Pours Madeira from a decanter, takes the silver top from a polished teak biscuit barrel.*) You haven't driven a detour of eighty miles just to scrounge a glass of sticky wine.

WENSLEY: No, it's parliamentary business.

HAMILTON: So I gather. Killane telephoned and said you wanted to see him here as well. Must say you've a damn nerve using my house as an extension of the Whips' Office.

WENSLEY: Don't bluster, Simon. You know why I'm here.

HASELTON: Bluster? At you? You flatter yourself. Being a Whip's given you delusions of grandeur.

WENSLEY: No. Only the power to protect reasonable Party men from your type of arrogant irresponsibility. First, your attendance record at the House is abysmal. (*The next phrase is an order.*) It will improve.

330

HASELTON: I'm invariably paired. (*Smiles slightly.*) Or make other arrangements.

WENSLEY: Such as having two or three Opposition Members on tap who are prepared to jump through hoops in return for a weekend's shooting. The Opposition Whips have been told of this, given the names, and your support there has ended.

HASELTON (*Unmoved*): I doubt that very much. But we'll see.

WENSLEY: Second, you'll stop your constant rabble-rousing at agricultural functions.

HASELTON (*Mocking him*): Whatever happened to freedom of speech?

WENSLEY: Freedom—not licence. Though I'm sure your bucolic friends find it amusing when you claim that Mr Heath has joined the Common Market mainly to get free French lessons.

HASELTON: They seem to.

WENSLEY: A taste for schoolboy humour. Usually after too much port. Perhaps forgivable. What is completely unforgivable is your savage and public intention to fight each and every step on the Market—against the decision taken by your own Party, now in Government, and carrying out the manifesto on which they were elected—because of your own personal, narrow and parochial viewpoint. (*Again the order.*) It will stop.

HASELTON: I don't think so.

WENSLEY: On your family crest, Simon, there's the word loyalty.

HASELTON: In which I believe. But I reserve the right —now and always—to define in my own terms to whom that loyalty is properly owed.

WENSLEY: Then resign.

HASELTON: No. You govern the rest of the country. I'll spend time and money looking after my particular piece of it.

WENSLEY: I'm now warning you formally. Persist in your present brand of selfish and misguided individualism and I shall take steps—personally—to enforce the consequences on you.

HASELTON (*Quite unmoved*): Have another glass of sticky wine.

He turns and pours as a butler ushers John Killane into the alcove area.

WENSLEY: Good evening, Mr Killane.

KILLANE: Good evening, Sir Robert.

WENSLEY: You're spending a good deal of time in Andersley these days.

KILLANE: On fairly important local issues. It's justified. The Garsfeld factory estate, now this proposal for an open prison.

WENSLEY: Which you're opposing.

KILLANE: Yes. Violently.

WENSLEY: You've studied party policy on prison reform?

KILLANE: Yes. I disagree with most of it. It's based —in my opinion—on inconclusive figures and an element of unproven and biased psychology.

Wensley takes a small notebook from his waistcoat pocket, scribbles in it.

WENSLEY: In that case, I'll see you're on the next committee for it. You can attempt to put your theories into practice. It may be salutary. If you can spare the time.

KILLANE: I'll try.

WENSLEY: I hope you'll do better than that. Between business trips for your own research agency and important local issues, your attendance at the House lately seems to have fallen away from its previous high standard. This is a reminder, no more. You know the difficult times the Government's facing and I'm looking to all Members for the fullest possible support. Which includes both of you. Good night, Gentlemen.

Wensley leaves and Killane looks suitably reprimanded.

KILLANE: I see why they call the Whips' Office the *real* police station at the Palace of Westminster.

HASELTON (*Unimpressed by it all*): Do they?

8

Interior. Sam Brodie's living room. Night.

Elizabeth Brodie, Cliff Lambert and George Taylor are seated as Sam Brodie paces up and down.

BRODIE: That Council Meeting's taking its time.

ELIZABETH: Sir Joseph said he'd ring.

LAMBERT: If he's got anything to say. Which I doubt.

TAYLOR: What do you think, Mr Brodie?

BRODIE: I don't know. I don't think the prison can be stopped.

ELIZABETH (*To Taylor*): They'll find you somewhere else to live.

TAYLOR: I don't mind that. It's what they're doing it for. Makes no sense. And nobody can stop it.

LAMBERT: Not for want of trying.

TAYLOR: I've always known the almshouses at Gilborough. Used to walk the river there when I was courting. You could see kingfishers. All blue and quick. I never minded being pensioned off there.

Brodie sits on the arm of the chair, looks at his watch.

BRODIE: He won't ring now.

TAYLOR (*Rising*): And I've bothered you enough.

ELIZABETH: No bother at all. Nice to see you.

TAYLOR: I'd better be going anyway.

LAMBERT: I'll run you back.

Lambert and Taylor are shown to the door by Elizabeth.

ELIZABETH: Good night, Mr Taylor. Come and see us again. (*She closes the door and turns to Brodie.*)

ELIZABETH: It isn't fair, is it?

BRODIE: Fair? Nothing much in the world is, love. Including being born and dying. Winners and losers. And if society's got to have prisons—and it has—somebody's got to live next to them.

ELIZABETH: You're opposing it though.

BRODIE: Oh, yes. No choice. Too much fear, too much prejudice. None of it rational. So neither is my opposition. And things like this are never rational. If I were God and had to say yes or no, I'd still not be sure of coming up with the right answer.

The telephone rings and Brodie moves quickly to pick it up.

BRODIE (*Into telephone*): Yes. Hello, Sir Joseph. What? Yes, you're right. I'd better get over there. If Killane's talking about corruption.

He puts the telephone down, turns to Elizabeth, his face showing puzzlement and worry.

END OF ACT ONE.

ACT TWO

9

Interior. Conservative Club. Night.

Killane and Brodie are listening to Sir Joseph Conran who is exuding good humour.

CONRAN: This new deputy planner—Lawson—was doing most of the chat. When he wasn't using a pointer on his coloured charts. Like being back at bloody school.

A steward arrives, puts a tray of drinks on the small table.

BRODIE: What's this for?

CONRAN: Celebration. There's not going to be any prison.

Brodie looks at Killane who nods.

KILLANE: And it stinks.

CONRAN: Don't be so sensitive, lad. We all got what we wanted.

KILLANE: Tell him how.

CONRAN: This was the coloured diagram bit.

KILLANE: Somebody had drawn the wrong line on the development plan and they were four years finding out.

CONRAN: Not their fault. You remember the '68 floods, Sam. Town Hall basement full of water. We lost a lot of papers and stuff.

KILLANE: And Councillors Briggs and Williams seem to have very long and accurate memories.

335

BRODIE (*Picking up Killane's bitterness*): What are you getting so aggravated about? You don't want the prison.

KILLANE: I know I don't. But I like opposition to be legal. And I don't like being conned.

BRODIE: Who by?

KILLANE: Simon Haselton.

CONRAN: There's a nasty suspicious Tory mind for you. Doesn't even trust his own people.

Killane's attitude is doing nothing to puncture Conran's euphoria.

BRODIE: How?

KILLANE: The Council's suddenly discovered that Gilborough and the almshouses aren't designated as agricultural and recreational land after all. Oh, no. They're industrial. Part of an infill development with some housing. A mistake. A nice conveniently flooded mistake.

BRODIE: Which multiplies the price of the land by fifty. And the compensation you need to fork out if anybody wants to put a prison on it.

KILLANE: So no prison. They've priced it out of the market.

BRODIE: Very neat. Who pushed it through?

CONRAN: Lawson, Briggs and Williams. All good lads.

KILLANE: The next bit's even neater. Unanimous approval for a planning application for the almshouse site and four thousand feet of river frontage. Put in by Simon Haselton for a company called AOF.

CONRAN (*Starting to lose his good humour*): On very fair terms. That's Haselton land leased to the Council. And the Council participate in development profit.

336

BRODIE (*Softly*): If you wanted to buy anything—like a planning committee—there's a lot of money in that sort of kitty to buy it with.

CONRAN: Hold on a minute. Not as much as you'd think. It's agricultural industry. Food packaging and processing.

KILLANE: True. He could have made a lot more with something else.

BRODIE: But still a pile of money.

KILLANE: And people were still bought. And that's why it stinks.

CONRAN: Money's not always nasty. Provided it's used properly.

BRODIE: Tell us about 'properly'.

CONRAN: In a minute. (*To Killane*) Lawson was quoting yards of figures, Mr Killane. Sounded just like you. Do you know anything about this AOF?

Killane takes a cheque book from his pocket, starts to write.

KILLANE: Yes. We did a survey for them. Transport and access.

CONRAN: Handsome. Must have been worth a few bob.

KILLANE: Two thousand pounds. I didn't know it was Haselton.

CONRAN (*Ironic*): I believe you. Thousands wouldn't.

BRODIE: I believe him.

Killane removes the cheque and offers it to Conran.

KILLANE: Do you want to send the cheque back or shall I?

Conran takes the cheque and tears it up.

CONRAN: Don't be such a bloody fool. You did the work for it. (*The good humour eroded now, the hard*

337

local politician showing.) And now let's cut out the theory and the chatter and look at the facts. The main one is no open prison for Andersley. Right?

Killane and Brodie nod.

BRODIE: At a price.

CONRAN: Second, financial benefit for the town as well as Haselton. They're the two things to remember. So let's keep quiet.

Conran rubs his face before continuing and a lot of this man's sincere concern for the town shows as he overcomes his own hardness and attempts to persuade rather than bully.

CONRAN: I'm not pushing, I'm just stating a case. (*To Brodie*) Kick up a fuss and we've got two Labour Councillors on charges—only charges, mind, not convictions—of corruption. That'll cost us the next council election. You want that, Sam? Hand the Town Hall to the Tories on a plate?

BRODIE: That's a soft question. You know I don't.

KILLANE: And if I don't keep quiet, I discredit another Tory MP with some very influential connections.

CONRAN: That's it. And why? What for? Because he managed to get a prison cancelled when we couldn't. He did our job for us.

BRODIE: Nobody's arguing with you. It's just the method. The principle.

CONRAN: I'd rather have results. I don't think we can all afford to have consciences as tender as you two. I had a lot of letters about the prison as well. Another thing, gentlemen. We've got surmise and theory by the bucket. We don't have a tadpole's drink of proof.

10

Interior. Killane's hotel room. Night.

Set as previous plays.

Annie Mackinnon is working at the dressing table, Chapman is lying on the bed, drink in hand and Janie Killane is wandering up and down the room.

CHAPMAN: If John leaves it much longer, all the throbbing night life of Andersley on Fridays will have ended. The revellers crept into the dawn. The orchids wilted. The champagne bottles empty. The orgy over.

ANNIE: He means the fish and chip shop will be closed.

CHAPMAN: That's a rough translation.

JANIE: Don't say that. I'm starving. What about our restaurant?

ANNIE: The Linden will hold the table. We're always late.

CHAPMAN: I've sometimes had bacon and eggs for dessert because it's too late to get up for breakfast. It's a hard life being a politician's partner.

ANNIE: Try being his agent with welfare cases on the phone at seven in the morning.

JANIE: You're a volunteer though, dear. Peter's a reluctant conscript.

CHAPMAN: I *was* nearly in the army once. Had a flat overlooking Chelsea Barracks.

JANIE: How patriotic.

Killane hurries into the room.

KILLANE: Sorry. You should have gone on for dinner.

ANNIE: What did Conran say?

KILLANE: Nothing good. Look, you go on. I'll have a sandwich here.

339

ANNIE: You'll be lucky.

CHAPMAN: He's gone on hunger strike again.

Chapman moves, takes Annie's arm.

CHAPMAN: Come on.

JANIE: Make it sandwiches for two.

Chapman is very quick to notice Killane's worry and Janie's perception of it.

CHAPMAN: Oh. See you tomorrow then.

Chapman breezes Annie out of the room.

Janie crosses to the drinks tray, lifts a glass in enquiry.

Killane shakes his head.

KILLANE: Do you know Simon Haselton?

JANIE: Oh, yes. DSO, MC and Bar. The last of the freebooting landowners. A very dangerous man.

KILLANE: I think I'm going to have to try and chop him.

Janie, worried before, is even more worried by this.

11

Interior. Sam Brodie's living room. Night.

Sam Brodie is sitting in an armchair, balancing a teacup. Elizabeth is listening intently to him.

BRODIE: Conran made sense. He wasn't dictating for once. Just putting the facts.

ELIZABETH: It all sounds reasonable to me. And you've got no proof. Leave it be.

BRODIE: We can't. I can't. Not with two councillors and a planning officer on the fiddle. Where will they start to operate next?

ELIZABETH: But how do you prove it?

BRODIE: I don't know.

ELIZABETH: Then why try? Think how pleased old George Taylor'll be.

BRODIE: And a lot of other people.

ELIZABETH: Wait till next weekend. Think about it. A week won't make any difference.

Brodie nods.

12

Exterior. House of Commons. Day.

Film sequence.

John Killane is seen hurrying into the House of Commons.

13

Interior. Whips' Office. Day.

This room is quite small—desk, filing cabinets, piles of order papers, utilitarian furniture. A feature of the desk is a photograph of Wensley's family and two or three bottles of pills flanking it.

Wensley is facing Killane.

WENSLEY: I understand that Andersley is no longer to have a prison. Though I'm delighted to see you're still showing an interest.

KILLANE: I heard it was one of your subjects.

WENSLEY: Before they made me a prefect.

KILLANE: How's the site for a new prison chosen?

341

WENSLEY: There haven't been many. Not enough in my view. But it's a mixture of need—national and regional—and availability. And cost, of course.

KILLANE: The need? Within a radius of—what?—thirty miles?

WENSLEY: Depending on population density.

KILLANE: And usually it's easiest to approach another government department for the land. Ministry of Defence. The Forestry Commission. Those two have got about three million acres between them.

WENSLEY: That's the usual way. But there are others.

KILLANE: But that's usual?

WENSLEY: Yes.

KILLANE: Then Gilborough makes even less sense. There's enough Ministry land within thirty miles to build a dozen prisons. Unless we've got a public-spirited landowner.

WENSLEY: That could have been Haselton. In fact, I know it was Haselton. He rang me up to find out whom he should talk to about prisons just over a year ago. Thought it odd at the time.

KILLANE: So he could have offered the land in the first place, told officials there'd be no trouble, then changed his mind.

WENSLEY: Second thoughts, more important things to think about. Don't waste your time trying to work out—ever—what Simon Haselton is up to.

KILLANE: Pressure of public opinion?

WENSLEY: Oh, no. Haselton's never listened to anything like that in his life. Which doesn't make my job any easier.

KILLANE: Thank you, Sir Robert.

342

14

Interior. Dining car. Night.

Set as previous plays.

The train is starting to lurch into motion and whistles are heard.

Janie Killane and Peter Chapman are just sitting down at a table for four.

Chapman is shaking his head.

CHAPMAN: If John thinks he's going to take on Haselton and that mob of uppercrust cut-throats behind AOF, we'd better ring Brussels and hire a band of mercenaries.

JANIE: That's what I tried to tell him.

CHAPMAN (*Looking at his watch*): I hope he's caught the train.

JANIE: One day he'll have to travel up in the guard's van. Crouched among the racing pigeons and mail-bags.

CHAPMAN: The way he's minding his own business these days, that's probably where he is now. Happy opening the mailbags and reading the letters.

JANIE: Happy?

CHAPMAN: I was using the word loosely. Occupied.

JANIE (*Persisting*): Busy, not happy.

CHAPMAN: Yes. (*Starts to read a menu he already knows by heart, wants to change the subject.*)

JANIE: Why?

CHAPMAN: If you don't know the answer to that, you don't really want to know.

JANIE: I know the answer. I want to hear you say it.

CHAPMAN: Being busy, occupied, whatever you call it was the only thing that kept John sane in the four years before he divorced you and the year after it. It's now habit. It isn't happiness but he tried that once.

JANIE: And it didn't work.

CHAPMAN: So he settled for less. How little would you settle for, Janie?

JANIE: As much or as little as I'm given. And accept either with gratitude.

CHAPMAN: You aren't just passing the time? Idle weekends in Andersley? You always used to get bored easily.

JANIE: Not now. There were too many long days in rooms with no handle on the inside of the door. I managed to learn to be concerned about other people.

CHAPMAN: Good. That makes two of us.

Killane comes up to the table with the dishevelled breathlessness of anyone who has caught a train at the very last minute.

Chapman looks up at him.

CHAPMAN: We've just formed a new club. It's called 'Don't vote for John Killane—just worry about him.'

Killane smiles and sits down.

15

Interior. Sam Brodie's living room. Night.

Lambert, seated, is talking as Brodie walks up and down the room.

Elizabeth is sitting on the sofa. She is sewing and looks up from time to time, listening carefully but not joining in the conversation.

LAMBERT: I've only had a week, Sam. Bits here and there but not much. Nothing you can call proof. (*Angrily now.*) I don't see it's our job to find proof. Give it to somebody who will.

BRODIE: You mean blow it. Turn it over to the police or the Town Clerk or whatever.

LAMBERT: That's what it'll come to, eventually.

BRODIE: Have you told Conran that?

LAMBERT: No need. I know what I'm going to do.

BRODIE: I'll try and stop you.

LAMBERT: You can't. I don't think you want to.

BRODIE: And you're right.

Lambert gets up and goes across to the telephone, stands near it.

LAMBERT: So let's get on with it.

BRODIE: No, Cliff.

LAMBERT: What about principle? What we believe in?

BRODIE: What Conran calls the tender consciences. How much good do we do, Cliff? Locally, I mean. Re-housing, welfare, industrial compensation. The whole ragbag of constituents with problems.

LAMBERT: We do what we can.

BRODIE: How do we do it?

LAMBERT: Quietly, most of the time. Bypass the red tape and the forms. Ring the Town Hall, the Labour Exchange, the Infirmary. Know the right name in the right office. Put a word in, drop a hint. See the right councillor in the right pub. Lean on him if we have to.

BRODIE (*Wearily*): So whose throats are we cutting if we get the council—our council, our party—slung

345

out at next month's election because of this Haselton fiddle. Not ourselves. Just the people we're supposed to be able to help. We've got to keep it private for a bit.

Lambert nods, pushes the telephone away.

BRODIE : But that doesn't stop me making visits.

16

Interior. Conservative Committee Rooms. Night.

Sir Joseph Conran is talking to Annie Mackinnon.

CONRAN : I wasn't a councillor in 1953. That's when the development plan was passed.

ANNIE : And it's been amended three times since. There have got to be some minutes somewhere.

CONRAN : Councillors Briggs and Williams. They reckon they took notes.

ANNIE : Produced miraculously after the flood.

CONRAN : Leave it alone, my girl. Tell Killane he's got better things to do.

The telephone rings and Annie picks it up.

ANNIE : Yes? Yes, Mr Brodie. He should be here any minute now. No, there's nothing else important on. Yes, I'll tell him. (*She puts the telephone down and turns to Conran.*) Sam Brodie wants John to meet him in half an hour. They're going to see Simon Haselton.

17

Interior. Hall and gun room alcove of Simon Haselton's manor house. Night.

346

Haselton is facing Brodie and Killane who have not been asked to sit down or offered a drink although Haselton has a glass in his hand.

HASELTON: Conjecture. No more. And impertinent conjecture at that.

BRODIE: Still worth talking about.

HASELTON: Unless I choose to turn the dogs on you as common trespassers.

BRODIE (*Smiling, slightly, meaning it*): I'd probably reach you first.

HASELTON: Yes, you would. You have the mentality. Some hundred and thirty years ago there was a minor uprising in this area. Labourers led by people like you. There weren't enough jobs. So they hanged a few landlords and then there weren't any jobs at all. Rather like present-day strikers. The attitudes haven't changed.

BRODIE: And the landlords are still much better organised.

HASELTON: Of course. (*To Killane*) You're keeping strange company, Killane.

KILLANE: Put your feudal airs and graces away, please. I have a list of directors of AOF. They represent a lot of money and a lot of influence. And they have a high reputation for lots of discretion. I don't think they know how or why you acquired the Gilborough site for a processing plant.

HASELTON: Then you're wrong. They know both how and why.

KILLANE: Good. So we can ask them.

HASELTON: Ask away. It's common knowledge. And if you didn't spend so much time cooped up in offices, you'd know it too. This country has the most efficient farming industry—industry, mark you—in Europe. And free trade. And the cheapest food.

BRODIE: Subsidised by the Government at three hundred million pounds a year.

HASELTON: Bread for the masses, Brodie. With football pools and television providing the circuses. Surely, you don't disagree with that.

KILLANE: We've all done our agricultural sums lately. We've had to.

HASELTON: Then you should have arrived at the result. When this country enters the Common Market, the money you mention will go into a special agricultural fund. Spread all over Europe. And all food imported from an efficient Commonwealth will be taxed to bring it up to agreed Common Market prices. The cost of a potato will be set by an Italian peasant with an ox-cart and the profit from all our knowledge and all our expensive machinery will be used to support thousands like him. By law. This offends me. There will be a completely new system. I intend to beat that system. And men who farm hundreds and thousands of acres will help me. You don't want a prison for Andersley. I don't want a prison for England.

END OF ACT TWO

ACT THREE

18

Interior. Conservative Club. Day.

Conran and Lambert are sitting on the sofa with a tray of coffee in front of them.

CONRAN: Is that it? All of it?

LAMBERT: Yes.

CONRAN: I don't call that proof of anything.

LAMBERT: It's the best I could do. And I'm going to have to tell Sam Brodie.

CONRAN: He'll tell you the same. You need a lot more. And for God's sake, tell Sam to talk to me before he goes rushing round doing anything.

LAMBERT: I'll try. Killane wants to see you as well.

CONRAN: What's he found out? (*Sighs deeply.*) Why can't people mind their own business? Why is it nobody can leave things in peace?

19

Interior. Killane's hotel room. Day.

Peter Chapman is sitting at the dressing table, a clipboard in one hand and a drink in the other.

Killane is sitting on the bed with a document file on his knee.

Chapman takes a drink and shakes his head in appreciation.

349

CHAPMAN: I need this after two day's walking up and down Tooley Street. The food-trade jungle. I'll never be able to go into a grocer's shop again without seeing all those hard-faced men snarling f.o.b. and c.i.f. down telephones and buying grub by the warehouseful.

KILLANE: Can Haselton beat the system?

CHAPMAN: It's possible. They were all very cagey.

KILLANE (*Glancing down at the document he is holding*): And AOF isn't popular in the food trade. They're already doing a lot of direct selling and the middlemen and brokers are getting squeezed.

CHAPMAN: It'll depend on two things. Food doesn't have to carry its country of origin on the label any more. And nobody can ask a tin of strawberries where it came from. Or a pound of butter if it speaks English. There's a nice 'Once upon a time' story there. A few years ago shiploads of tallow were going to Belgium from the States. It got processed there and ended up here as English refined lard. So anything's possible if that story's true. What have you got?

KILLANE: Bits. AOF are punting around for refrigerated ships. Panama flag. I did a breakdown on Customs and food inspectorate at docks. It isn't detailed but it looks ludicrous. Not enough men, not paid enough, not trained enough. And when the legislation changes it'll get worse. Too many forms, not enough people. Oh, and AOF has just bought a print firm. Name the label, they'll print it.

CHAPMAN: I like it. I'd rather fiddle bills of lading and use my wits than sit on a tractor in the pouring rain.

KILLANE: Haselton's also booked a lot of deep-freeze capacity—until he can build his own at Gilborough. He's retained specialist lawyers and accountants and he's negotiating with buying agents—mostly behind the Iron Curtain. He's already got the Commonwealth contacts.

CHAPMAN: He's taking a lot of trouble. What's it for?

KILLANE: I think he's going to try to work a small free-trade area of his own. He's going to drag in food from a lot of England and the rest of the world. And when it comes out of Gilborough, it could be from anywhere. And he'll take the lawsuits as they come.

CHAPMAN: He'll still have to sell at Common Market prices and contribute to this agricultural fund he's against.

KILLANE: Not really. He's got storage, freezing, processing. He can sell it or hold it. He can offer bulk discounts, free delivery. He can sew it up.

CHAPMAN: And make a lot of money.

KILLANE: Yes. But I honestly think that's incidental. He can also keep food prices down if he wants. There's a weird distribution of profit clause in the AOF articles. As I read it, Haselton is also going to be in a position to run his own private system of subsidies to British agriculture.

CHAPMAN: He can't do it.

KILLANE: I think he can. And look at that list of people behind him. It's worked out. The system is only just being set up and that's the best time to beat it.

CHAPMAN: Why should he?

KILLANE: Pride mainly. Some justification of what he believes in. The rest of the country can go in if it's stupid enough. Haselton isn't going to join. Besides he's a farmer. It's about the most personal aspect of going into Europe there is. Even if you've got only half a dozen fields, it's these you're giving up. It's land. It's tangible. It's not a car assembly line or a semi-detached. It's a field you walk in the evening to look at the crops you've planted and sweated over.

CHAPMAN (*Baffled by it all*): And you're another country boy. Thank God I was born in Hackney.

20

Interior. Sam Brodie's living room. Day.

LAMBERT: I'm dead sure it's Councillor Briggs and Councillor Williams. Forget the Planning Officer. He's just a bright lad with a coloured pencil who thinks he's Christopher Wren. Give him a drawing board and pat him on the head and he's yours for life.

BRODIE: I can believe it about Briggs. He's Labour but he's still a bit of a snob. A few drinks and a day's shooting and he'd do anything Haselton told him. Touching his cap.

LAMBERT: He's also got a nice new car. Well, not new. 500 miles on the clock. You don't buy a car that size on what Briggs earns. It's all his and there aren't any hire-purchase payments.

BRODIE: Who bought the car in the first place?

LAMBERT: Haselton's bailiff.

BRODIE: Nothing to stop somebody giving a motor car away if he wants to. How long's Briggs had the car?

LAMBERT: Just over a week. (*Disgust showing.*) It's a cheap old price for a sell-out, isn't it?

BRODIE: What about Williams?

LAMBERT: Business. As usual. He's just put a down payment on four new transporters for this ready-mix business of his.

BRODIE: And they'll need a lot of concrete when building starts at Gilborough.

LAMBERT: It's supposed to go out to tender.

BRODIE: Not if Haselton's organising the contract. And paying the bills.

LAMBERT: Have we got enough?

BRODIE: I'd like more. I'd like reasons.

LAMBERT: Perhaps Killane's got those.

BRODIE (*Touch of bitterness*): Must be nice to have a whole agency you can turn loose when you want to find something out.

LAMBERT (*Mildly*): You've just joined commerce yourself. You can't knock it any more.

At that moment Elizabeth Brodie comes in accompanied by George Taylor.

ELIZABETH: I met Mr Taylor in the street. He's got a message for you. So I asked him in to tell you in person.

BRODIE: What is it, George?

TAYLOR: It's from everybody at the almshouses. I know all the trouble you took, Mr Brodie, and they wanted me to come and see you to say thank you.

Brodie looks at Lambert. There is nothing he can say.

21

Interior. Hall and gun room alcove of Haselton's Manor House. Night.

Haselton is sitting on the desk swinging his legs.

Wensley is standing facing him.

HASELTON: Certainly. I admit it. The initial offer was made in good faith to the prison people. I withdrew it as soon as I found out about the amount of prejudice and fear it was likely to cause.

WENSLEY: Was certain to cause. Inevitably. And the prospect of an open prison at Gilborough made any other scheme massively acceptable.

HASELTON (*Smiling slightly*): I conformed merely with public opinion.

WENSLEY: Somewhat of a departure for you.

HASELTON: 'For one lamb that strayeth etc. . . .' As Party High Priest, you should be thankful.

WENSLEY: If I believed it.

HASELTON (*Arrogant*): Believe what you like.

WENSLEY (*Producing a piece of paper*): Here's next week's Order Paper. It contains two three-line whips on your favourite subject. I want you at Westminster and I want you in the aye lobby.

HASELTON: I shall be there. But not in the lobby you choose. Remember what Edmund Burke said: 'My God, my country and my party.' In that order.

WENSLEY: People always quote that. They forget what happened afterwards. He lost his next election.

HASELTON: It will serve as an epitaph. I'd prefer to be remembered for my principles and my actions rather than crosses marked on voting papers by a brain-washed mob.

22

Interior. Conservative Committee Rooms. Night.

Annie Mackinnon is at the desk, stapling together a sheaf of newly-typed pages as Killane and Chapman come into the room. Killane is carrying an overnight bag and a briefcase.

354

ANNIE: Hello, John. I managed to reach Wensley. He's over at the Club with Brodie and Conran. They're waiting for you.

KILLANE: I'll get over there. Did you finish the typing on this Haselton business?

Annie gives him the typed pages.

ANNIE: Yes.

KILLANE: No comment?

ANNIE: I'm just the agent.

CHAPMAN: And disillusion is setting in.

ANNIE: Only with myself. John, I'm resigning.

CHAPMAN: Hey, now, wait a minute. Martyrs are old-fashioned.

KILLANE: Is it Haselton? This business?

ANNIE: Nothing as extravagant as that. It's just me.

KILLANE: And politics?

ANNIE: If you like. I'm doing nothing. Politics is starting to get a bit too slow. Too impersonal.

KILLANE: Sometimes too devious?

ANNIE: Perhaps. I tried but it's not really my line of effort. I should have stuck to social work and the simple things and the simple results. Like seeing kids in one slum family get cured of scabies. Like stopping an old lady in a tenement from dying of pneumonia. Not organising jumble sales.

KILLANE: I think it *is* Haselton. So what should I do?

ANNIE: What you'll always do. The best you can. Only the weak sisters like me pack up. They're waiting for you at the Club. Can we keep in touch?

KILLANE: I'd like that. Thanks, Annie.

Killane leaves quickly and Chapman turns.

355

CHAPMAN: And what will I do at weekends now? I'll have to find another interpreter, another trusty native guide.

ANNIE: You might even have to do some work.

CHAPMAN: If I end up as a victim of the white-slave trade in Andersley, it'll be your fault.

Chapman is doing his best to cheer up Annie Mackinnon and has not quite realised the extent to which her decision to resign has upset her.

ANNIE: Don't, Peter. I couldn't stay.

Chapman realises the upset, walks across to put his hands lightly on her shoulders.

CHAPMAN: Sorry. (*Hesitantly, the voice concerned.*) Buy you a big drink?

Annie nods.

23

Interior. Conservative Club. Night.

Conran, Brodie, Wensley and Killane are sitting in a private corner.

WENSLEY: I've heard what you all have to say and I'm inclined to agree with you. But we've still nothing tangible to go on. Except that Haselton is capable of it.

BRODIE: Capable of getting away with it, more like. (*Nastily.*) Or is it that what you want? Hush it all up.

KILLANE (*Snapping*): He's here at everybody's invitation. Take your Party hat off.

WENSLEY: Mr Killane's demonstrated very ably the theory of what Haselton plans to do. But it's yet to be put into effect.

BRODIE: He'll do it. I know him.

WENSLEY: You, Mr Brodie, have two Labour Councillors involved. One with a car, one with a building contract. Both responsible for the planning committee decision.

CONRAN: Which we've yet to prove was a fiddle.

BRODIE: Then why wasn't there a planning file at the Ministry? Like there always is.

CONRAN: I've told you. After the flood, they wrote and asked the Ministry to send the file back for copying. It never arrived.

WENSLEY: Possible. Unlikely but possible.

BRODIE: So he'll get away with it.

CONRAN: A mistake. They happen.

KILLANE: Where do you stand, Sir Joseph?

CONRAN (*Hard*): Where I've always stood. Watching people. If two of my councillors are on the violin, I want to know.

Killane reaches into his briefcase and takes out a copy of a magazine.

KILLANE: So try this. Before environment became fashionable, there was a good magazine called *Interbuild*. Architecture, sociology, building technique. With very enlightened publishers. Its editor was a bit of a cowboy but, in 1961, it published a solid ten-page feature on Andersley including a reproduction of the development plan and all amendments. (*He opens a magazine at its centre which is covered by a development plan. The magazine passes from hand to hand.*) It shows very clearly that Gilborough was never zoned as industrial.

BRODIE: I'll accept that as proof.

WENSLEY: And so will I. So probably would a Court of Law. If it's necessary to go that far.

357

BRODIE: It's necessary.

CONRAN: No, Sam.

WENSLEY: I'd prefer to do it quietly.

KILLANE: I wouldn't. And we're not going to.

WENSLEY (*The authority showing*): Mr Killane, this is a Party matter. You may have to take instructions on it.

CONRAN: That goes for you as well, Sam. I'm not losing council elections.

KILLANE: Not good enough. I want something doing.

WENSLEY: Then let's do it quietly. I'll personally guarantee—in writing, if necessary—that Haselton is not adopted for the next election and, if possible, forced to resign before then. Both Government and his local association will see to it.

BRODIE: All the nice quiet backroom pressures.

WENSLEY: They're effective, Mr Brodie. You know that.

CONRAN: And I'll make sure that Briggs and Williams never get anywhere near a council chamber again. By God, I'll make sure.

KILLANE: That still leaves Haselton with his private free-trade scheme.

WENSLEY: I disagree. Nationally and locally, certain steps can be taken. I can have a word with the Ministry of Agriculture, the DTI, Customs and Excise. Still quietly. Theories, no more. The Attorney General, perhaps.

CONRAN: And I'll talk to the Borough Surveyor. I'll clout Haselton with more building bye-laws than he knows exist. I'll make him put up his bloody processing plant with a micrometer. It'll take him years.

KILLANE (*The bitterness starting to show*): All slow, all furtive. It'll work but what a way to do it.

BRODIE: I think I'd like to go outside for a minute. Get some fresh air.

CONRAN: I think you'll both do as you're told.

WENSLEY (*Hard again*): I don't like this business either but it's a fact and it's one aspect of politics. And you're both politicians. By choice.

CONRAN: If you don't like the heat, stay out of the kitchen.

WENSLEY: Remember one thing. Scandal benefits nobody. The headlines over one corrupt politician bring us all into disrepute. They forget the men of integrity, and this makes a mockery of the work these men do. Mockery of the work you do, gentlemen.

CONRAN: Take our word for it.

KILLANE (*To Brodie*): We have to, don't we?

BRODIE: Yes. We do. But we don't have to like it.

Killane picks up his overnight bag and leaves.

24

Interior. Sam Brodie's living room. Night.

Elizabeth Brodie, in dressing-gown, is wandering worriedly round the room. She looks at the clock on the mantelpiece which shows 12.30. She hesitates, then switches out the main light, leaving one table lamp burning on Brodie's desk and goes to bed.

25

Interior. London taxi. Night.

Janie Killane is seen as she pulls down the window and shouts:

JANIE: John! Over here.

Killane appears at the window, opens the cab door, drops his hold-all on the floor, gets in. He is both surprised and pleased to see her.

KILLANE: How did you know which train I'd be on?

JANIE: I've met them all since eight o'clock. The driver thinks I've adopted him.

KILLANE: Why?

JANIE: Peter said you were brooding. I know how introspective you get on trains.

The taxi starts to move off.

KILLANE: Where have you told him to go?

JANIE: Highgate. That's where you live, isn't it?

KILLANE: Yes. What about you?

JANIE: Don't worry about me.

KILLANE: Somebody's got to.

JANIE: Not you. You've done your share. If you like, you could come and have a drink at Chesham Place. Oh yes, I keep drink in the house. Just to remind myself I mustn't touch it.

KILLANE: I wouldn't be very good company at the moment.

JANIE: Who cares? And forget about Simon Haselton. The world's too large and we're too small—at least on our own—to ever alter it.

KILLANE: That shouldn't stop anybody trying.

JANIE: You've forgotten to use the figures.

KILLANE: I suppose I have. Fine, I'm a statistician. I can take a sample of any 630 people. Politicians, street-singers, bus-conductors, anything. In that sample, there has to be a proportion of liars, thieves and cheats.

JANIE: And saints and idealists.

KILLANE: For once the figures don't help. There's no double rule at the bottom of this page. Just a bloody helplessness and that's the system. I don't think I've got enough patience. And I know that's what I need.

JANIE: And comfort. But there's nowhere you can turn for comfort. Not for this. It would give me some small purpose in life to look after you. I said once I wanted you to take me back and didn't know how. Less selfishly, I should take you back. Or offer what there is to offer. No strings. There can't be. I may or may not be a reformed character. A risk you can't take—dare not take—on any permanent basis. So take it on a temporary one and when the need exists, we can help each other. (*Slightly self-mocking.*) A minor form of politics.

Killane smiles ruefully, leans forward to tap on the glass partition separating them from the driver.

KILLANE (*To driver*): Would you take us to Chesham Place, please. Not Highgate.

26

Interior. Sam Brodie's living room. Night.

Sam Brodie, wearing an overcoat, is sitting in one of the armchairs.

On the table next to it is a bottle of whisky and Brodie is sipping reflectively at a generously charged glass.

The clock on the mantelpiece shows 3.45.

Elizabeth Brodie comes into the room.

ELIZABETH: What are you doing up at this hour?

BRODIE: I went for a walk. And now I'm drinking the Christmas whisky. In case it doesn't keep until next

Christmas. And I'm surveying a political spectrum which seems to have all the primary colours missing. One of the colours is courage.

ELIZABETH: You've got that.

BRODIE: I wish I could be so sure. I've also got a good job with Conran. Nothing like a full wallet to make you move that bit more slowly.

ELIZABETH: It's about time somebody told you how tired you were as well.

BRODIE: So fight the good fight without me.

ELIZABETH: You've done your share. What more do you want?

Brodie takes a drink. He is not drunk but there is enough whisky in the system to slow his words very slightly and for the words to be chosen with care. There is no pomposity, no self-pity.

BRODIE: The future of everybody is going to depend on honest men. But Haselton's honest in his way. So's Killane. Perhaps. I try to be honest. It's the only label worth having. Not Labour, not Conservative, not the Pope. Sometimes you have to postpone the honesty. A compromise now for a triumph later. But it will all depend on the honest men. Always. Now and forever.

ELIZABETH: Come to bed, Sam.

Brodie nods, rises, glass still in hand, walks to the desk where the table lamp is shining on a copy of Hansard *which is next to a pile of past copies.*

He look down at them for a moment before moving away but leaves the light still shining on them.

[*Credits*]

362

Member of Parliament

by THE RT HON ROY MASON, MP

The Rt Hon Roy Mason was born in Yorkshire and began work at fourteen as a miner at the coal face. He became branch secretary of the National Union of Mineworkers and entered Parliament at the age of twenty-eight—in 1952—as Labour MP for Barnsley. He has held the posts of Minister of Power, President of the Board of Trade and Postmaster-General.

'Bye, Dad, see you on Friday'. 'Ta-ra love, try hard in your exams.' 'Bye sweetheart . . .' The hurried good-byes to wife and kids as the Northern MP prepares to go to London for a week on the Westminster treadmill. Goodbyes every Monday . . . Hellos every Friday. Parted for work and for a week—every week the House is in session. A constant trial for families, a strain on family life, a burden of responsibility thrust upon a mother to head the household every week. This parting is important. It must be sweet. Irritants can smoulder to angry fires within a Parliamentary week. The MP cannot afford rows with his family—together their time is too short.

To the treadmill? Yes—to the MP who is devoting his life to politics it CAN be a sort of treadmill grind. And to most MPs—the hard core of the main political parties—it is. And it is damned hard work. Long hours, bad working conditions, non-stop pressures on party and the man. No factory inspectorate would happily pass the conditions in which Members work.

Work? MPs work! It's only talking and cocktail partying. Nonsense! Well, is it? The Northern Member from the Andersleys of Britain will leave his bed and breakfast hotel in London straight after breakfast, arrive at the House at 9–9.30, ring his wife—ask if all is well—collect his mail (usually a bundle of it—12,000 to 15,000 letters per day arrive for MP's consumption), hurriedly glance through his mail, snatch a coffee at

363

10 a.m. and then prepare to enter Committee. These are mini-Parliaments with many of them sitting every morning from 10.30 until 1 p.m. Two hundred and fifty MPs could be locked up in these sessions— vetting and amending the proposed legislation. The Housing Finance (Fair Rents) Bill sat in Committee for nearly 300 hours and one sitting lasted from 10.30 a.m. one morning until 1 p.m. the following day—a twenty-seven-and-a-half hour shift with one break for a meal.

The Committees normally adjourn at 1 p.m., giving time for lunch before Parliament proper begins its daily task. Parliamentary questions begin at 2.35 p.m. after allowing five minutes for Prayers. Meanwhile, there may well be visitors eager to go in the Strangers' Gallery. Little do they realise the scramble and cadging that will have gone on to obtain their tickets—a Member is allocated two tickets every nine Parliamentary days. Hence the 'runaround' if visitors come on the wrong day.

The debate of the day commences at 3.30. MPs try to listen to the 'Openers' but the many calls upon their time often preclude this. Group meetings are taking place during the afternoon—Foreign Affairs, Shipping, Aviation, Trade, the Miners, the Engineers and so on. Keeping abreast of all an MP's special subjects takes time. Time, too, must be found for dictation with his secretary, speech preparation, preparing Private Questions, receiving constituents.

During the afternoon, the pressures build up. Members inwardly worry about their performance, inner tensions start gripping the guts. They do tend to compare their activities alongside other colleagues—their speeches and publicity creating in their turn envy and jealousy. On top of all this, consultants, public relations officers, firms, local authorities and their own political party demand time to listen to their presentations. Yes—I think it *is* a treadmill but once you get accustomed to the pace it is hard to get off.

Of course, the Andersleys of Britain give the Member a very special headache—the mono-economy of an

364

old Northern town for too long dependent upon one major labour-intensive industry, now running down. Unemployment rising, few job prospects, school leavers frustrated. So the Member becomes embroiled in a particularly difficult struggle—the survival of his town (and possibly his job)—to convince a minister and the government that his town's prospects are bleak and the need for urgency in granting Industrial Development Certificates (IDCs). But his is only one town amongst many and consequently in this fight for movable industry, for jobs, for hope, colleagues are pitted against each other—MP against MP, region against region—each in turn parading their mayors, town clerks and planners before ministers in their fight for their Andersley's survival.

Monday to Friday is therefore concentrated political activity. Then Friday, in the morning, if possible, he sets off home. MPs are expected to work at all times and almost every day. Friday however is crucial. This is the only time he can meet the town clerk, the housing manager, contact personally the managers of social services and the Ministry of Employment. They are all on a five-day week—lucky blighters. Fridays are spent straightening out local heart-burns. Friday night, too, is always one that is diaried months ahead. The House has risen, the Member is home, the demands pile up. Party meetings, lectures.

Home? Well, yes—but not in it.

Saturday morning is the Town Hall surgery—the necessary leveller. Bump, right down to earth, the real lessons one learns about life—unemployment, pensions, housing, broken families—often a mass of unhappiness. Often the Member will emerge, weary, despondent, indeed near to tears, yet more keenly resolved to 'right wrongs', 'seek justice', 'to help'. After all, that's what *they* came for, that's what *he* is there for—and *he* said he could do it.

Sunday, the blessed day, with the family—the only time one can guarantee having a meal together—talk over family problems, think about a holiday perhaps, squeezing it in between the House rising in August and the kids going back to school in September. As July wears on, Members begin to ache for a recess. Hot weather and they become more irritable penned in the Pit of Parliament, anger shows itself in the House and the home. The hours of work are mad but the timing of the sessions is ludicrously outdated.

What then is the attraction? The lure of lucre? Not exactly. In 1964, the British MP belonged to the most pauperised Parliament in the world outside Pakistan. Even today at £4,500 minus many expenses, he still is one of the lowest-paid and hardest-worked Parliamentarians in the world. His Canadian counterpart gets £7,407, and Belgium £5,050 and in Italy £7,550. Strange, isn't it? Aspirants queue to be short-listed, flit from seat to seat and even those who lose their seats yearn to get back to Westminster.

What is it, then? Glamour, fascination, MP behind the name? Or is it really a desire to serve, a commendable public spirit, an urge to further his party's aims—or possibly the attraction of power? Well, I think it is a combination, depending upon the make-up of the man. After all, Parliament is a microcosm of the cross-section of British people—weak and strong, good and bad—but fortunately in our democracy and because of its selection system, the substantial block of our representatives are honourable men; honest and substantial characters who toil full time on your behalf.

The Andersleys of Britain should be grateful—they really are being faithfully served.

Trust the People

by SIR DONALD KABERRY, BT, MP.

Sir Donald Kaberry has been Conservative MP for North-West Leeds since 1950 and has held the posts of Assistant Whip and Under Secretary. He trained as a solicitor and has, over a long period, been a member of the Council of the Law Society. On Leeds Council for twenty years, he is now an honorary alderman, and is prominent in public works, including the governorships of schools and hospitals.

At the present time, there are 630 Members of the British House of Commons. Like racehorses, they run in all shapes and sizes and, even more so, in all ages and conditions. So far as constituencies are concerned, it is certainly 'horses for courses' and when some people ask, 'How did he—or she—get there' they are perhaps reflecting upon the broad cross-section of our British people which the House of Commons presents.

The Members live in something akin to a goldfish bowl in the House of Commons at Westminster. All their actions are noted in differing ways and receive so many varied interpretations that it seems the wish is often father to the thought.

I know that Edmund Ward went to enormous trouble in his research for the series of episodes of *The Challengers* and he certainly managed to reproduce the atmosphere in which so many of the controversial scenes in political life in a constituency take place.

Work in the House of Commons calls for physical fitness as well as mental capacity. Much of it is un-advertised and is routine office work. It is connected with the personal cases of constituents seeking redress against ministerial departments and it is for the Member to pursue the minister and his department to the absolute limits to ensure that any semblance of a wrong is corrected.

Perhaps from this side of the Member's activities arise the phrases 'a good Party man' or 'a good constituency Member' or 'a good House of Commons man'. Though all have their separate meanings they all add up to the fact that a Member of Parliament doing his duty, caring for his constituents' interests as well as the general welfare of the country, has to have utter devotion to the work he is called upon to do.

In the House of Commons the strength and weaknesses of Members soon become known amongst each other. Contacts daily and often hourly in the lobbies, in committee meetings, in refreshment rooms and even other places soon reveal one's strength of character—or perhaps lack of it.

There are, of course, many duties carried out in the House which receive no medals or praise in constituency life. The tramping through the division lobbies throughout a night's sitting brings no reward at home in the constituency and the only comment is likely to be 'you look tired' or 'what stupid hours you keep to discuss such important matters'.

So against all this background how do the characters created by Edmund Ward live up to reality? Well, have a look in the mirror and decide whether *you* look like any of the characters. Or imagine you do. For Edmund Ward has sought to present through his characters in *The Challengers* some of the facets of Parliamentary life and the problems an MP has to meet in his constituency. They are not comprehensive and they can be more fully extended in a further series. He has brought out, however, the reliance of even the best Member of Parliament upon his divisional party organisation and more especially upon close and efficient contact with his constituents. There is nothing new in the phrase 'the grass roots in politics'. For generations past politicians have used the phrase 'Trust the People' and have always sought as relief from frustration in the House of Commons a new mandate from the people. Today more and more organisations and societies are being created to preserve or protect the special interests of one section or another of our community whether those interests be personal liberty or preservation of amenities or more minor matters. Though all serve a useful purpose, it is, at the end of the argument, the people as a whole—all sections, not just members of smaller societies—who must be counted. They are the people who are to be trusted. The Member is merely the representative of the constituency electors and having arrived at Westminster he must exercise his knowledge and discretion as best he can until the next time he stands before them for a fresh mandate.

I think Edmund Ward has shown that it is wise to 'Trust the People'.

Creative Reality

by CHRIS DUNKLEY

Chris Dunkley was born in Yorkshire and joined a local
paper when he left school. He joined *The Times* in 1968
and is now its specialist in mass media and one of its
television critics.

The attitude of the British public towards the press
has traditionally been dichotomous: the cliché 'You
can't believe what you read in the papers' has been
fairly evenly balanced by 'Of course it's true—it says
so here in black and white'. Perhaps because of a
widespread and persistent (though clearly mistaken)
belief that the camera cannot lie, the attitude towards
television is by no means so equivocal. On the whole
people do believe what they see on the screen with
their own eyes, and frequently they 'believe' even when
they know that they are watching fiction.

But most viewers sooner or later—and with television critics, probably sooner—are likely to have this
faith at least temporarily undermined by a programme
on a subject in which they have specialised knowledge:
seeing what he judges to be a travesty of his profession
in a serious television programme, an architect (for
instance) may start wondering whether all other programmes on subjects of which he is ignorant are perhaps equally undependable.

So, as a former reporter on a local weekly newspaper where I was in very close contact with the town's
party politics, it was with some apprehension that I
watched the first of Edmund Ward's new series, *The
Challengers*. But I was delighted to discover that, as I
wrote in *The Times* the next day, 'Mr Ward showed an
admirable familiarity with his subject', and indeed his
description of the personalities, the physical surroundings, and the mixture of inanity and profundity in
debate which characterise local party politics could
easily have been based on the town where I worked.

371

But why such anxieties, anyway, about a series which was clearly fictional and designed to entertain, rather than documentary and designed to inform? Because the line which most people believe they can detect clearly dividing fact from fiction is actually imaginary: no such division exists. Rather there is a wide middle ground between the two extremes where it is often impossible to disentangle one from the other.

Fictional programmes, particularly of the drama/documentary variety, are frequently capable of portraying reality more accurately than strictly 'factual' productions—*The Challengers* being a prime example. Reviewing a novel by Maurice Edelman, Richard Crossman recently said: 'The sources of this period of Disraeli's life, though suppressed until recently, are surprisingly extensive. Having mastered them completely Mr Edelman wisely put them aside and created a work of pure imaginative fiction which rings far truer than any piece of historical reportage.'

Far from being a paradox, that is an important truth which is ignored far too often by television personnel, many of whom work on the reverse assumption: that only through 'objectivity' will the truth emerge on screen. But even a piece of unadulterated news film can only be—at best—one rendering of reality as sieved through the senses of the cameraman and sound technician. Move the vantage point and reality shows a different facet, as the most truthful groups of court witnesses continually prove with seemingly contradictory evidence. But when a dramatist such as Edmund Ward renders his version of the facts (albeit via the medium of 'fiction') no such hit-or-miss chances are necessary.

Calling on a cumulative backlog of experience, he can select and portray events with a degree of control forever denied the maker of pure documentaries who may run out of film—or sneeze—and miss for all time a crucial sequence. The dramatist simply reloads and reshoots. Edmund Ward and his team are expert in this art of conveying creative reality.

Lobby Correspondent

by IAN AITKEN

Ian Aitken is Political Correspondent of the *Guardian*. Following university and military service, he worked for *Tribune* and then the *Daily Express* as both Foreign and Political Correspondent.

It is more than ten years since I made my first arrival at the Palace of Westminster clutching a ticket to the Commons press gallery and an editor's letter to the Sergeant at Arms asking for my inclusion on the Parliamentary 'lobby list'. Strictly speaking, the two documents entitled me to no more than an uncomfortable backless seat in the gallery and the right of admission to the members' lobby. It quickly turned out that they had changed my whole way of life.

I walked in by way of New Palace Yard a normal, healthy reporter with a normal, healthy family life besides my professional existence. By the time the doors of the press gallery lift had closed behind me, I had become a kind of bacchanalian prisoner-monk at the start of a voluntary life sentence. Family and friends had been left behind for a new universe composed of miles of carpeted corridors and stone-flagged courtyards, with a new language and mysterious customs.

I found that many of my new colleagues had been serving at the altar of political journalism for up to forty years, referring lightly to legendary national figures as 'Harold', 'Hugh', 'Alec' and 'Quintin'. They knew the feet of clay as well as the noble brows, and could translate a simple cliché into a front page splash in a matter of moments.

But I was offered only one piece of useful advice by my elders and betters. 'First establish where the lavatories are,' I was told. 'Then find out where the bars are. When you have mastered both, you will have all the equipment you need for the job.'

It was good advice, but not as easy to follow as it sounded. There are seven bars in the House of Commons alone, and I am still discovering lavatories I did not know existed. One of the bars, the holy Members' Smoke Room, is impenetrable to reporters, and at least one other in the recesses of Guy Fawkes's cellars is still unknown to many of my less dedicated colleagues.

But all have uses to a lobby correspondent which go far beyond the needs of comfort and conviviality. They are places where conversation can take place, and conversation is the essence of the political journalists' trade. Politics is talk, and scarcely a fraction of it takes place in the debating chamber or the upstairs committee rooms. Much of the real talking takes place in the bars, the corridors, the lobbies—and sometimes even the lavatories.

Some of it is entertaining beyond the wildest dreams of television chat-programme directors. A great deal of it is plain boring. But some of it is news, and the job of the lobby correspondent is to listen, analyse and remember it (even through a haze of Federation bitter) so as to share it with the paying readers next morning. It is a delicate business, subject to the over-riding rule that the source of sensitive information must never be revealed except with express permission. Hence the magic incantations: 'Senior ministers insist...', 'Opposition leaders claim...', 'Left-wing MPs believe...', and 'Whitehall sources argue...'

It is a ludicrous language, which has laid lobby correspondents open to the charge of being gullible hacks who swallow whole the propagandist output of government and party machines. But it is a poor reporter who cannot weigh the motives of his informant or judge the reliability of his information. Experience counts, and many an MP has found that one misleading leak has severed his links with 'the media' for ever.

It works in a rough and ready way because politicians need the press no less than the press needs politicians. And by no means all of it is simple publicity-seeking. MPs and even ministers may seek to shape events by the judicious leak, sometimes aiming to wreck government plans by exposing them prematurely, sometimes to soften-up public opinion in advance of action, and sometimes to blacken a rival or opponent. It is up to the reporter to pick his way through conflicting versions of events and motives and make his own allowances for bias.

A visitor to Westminster lucky enough to secure a ticket to one of the special galleries can see the whole process at work as he crosses the stone cavern of the members' lobby. The seekers after truth pace the granite floor or lounge against the walls, awaiting the arrival of a well-informed source or an MP in revolt. A despairing reporter, pinioned by a notorious back-bench bore, watches helplessly as the minister he has been hunting for up to an hour strides from the chamber and out towards the members' exit. In a corner, behind the letter-board, a noted muckraking MP hands a photocopy of an anonymous letter to a nervous young lobby man. A left-wing propagandist touts for signatures to his latest Early Day Motion, and distributes copies to any reporter within reach. 'We'll have a hundred signatures by tonight', he says over and over again. Suddenly the amiable policeman in the corner appears to go berserk, throws his head back to bellow 'Deee-vision', and the whole scene jerks into movement. The seekers after truth scuttle for the doors to make way for a snap vote, and MPs begin to pour in towards the division lobbies from doorways all round the hall.

The despairing reporter cheers up as he intercepts his Minister darting back for the unexpected division. The nervous young man with the anonymous letter hurries to a telephone to tell his news desk what he has found—and to warn them to check it for libel with the office lawyer. The policeman returns to placidity, pegging back the swing doors to let the flood of chattering Labour and Tory MPs pass through. 'Ten bob to a pint of Fed you don't know what this division's about,' says the man from the *Guardian* to an MP hurrying down Ways and Means Corridor to cast his vote for the millennium on the motion 'clause 2 stand part'. He doesn't.